THE EXOTIC

SUNY Series, The Margins of Literature
Mihai I. Spariosu, editor

THE EXOTIC

A Decadent Quest

Dorothy M. Figueira

State University of New York Press

Published by
State University of New York Press, Albany

Printed in the United States of America

For information, address State University of New York
Press, State University Plaza, Albany, N.Y., 12246

Production by Dana Foote
Marketing by Bernadette LaManna

Library of Congress Cataloging-in-Publication Data

Figueira, Dorothy Matilda, 1955–
The exotic : a decadent quest / Dorothy M. Figueira.
p. cm. — (SUNY series, the margins of literature)
Includes bibliographical references and index.
ISBN 0-7914-1629-1. — ISBN 0-7914-1630-5 (pbk.)
1. Exoticism in literature. 2. India in literature.
3. Literature, Comparative—European and Indic. 4. Literature,
Comparative—Indic and European. I. Title II. Series.
PN871.F62 1994
809′.91—dc20 94-1591
CIP

10 9 8 7 6 5 4 3 2 1

CONTENTS

ACKNOWLEDGMENTS

The chapters of this book have evolved gradually toward their present form, and I have benefited from comments and criticisms of colleagues at several institutions. The prehistory of each piece prior to its final revision in this volume follows:

Chapter 1 was delivered at the Mosaics Contexts Conference (1987), the Modern Language Association annual meeting (1988), and the American Comparative Literature Association annual meeting (1989). A version of this chapter appeared in *Comparative Literature Studies* 26, no. 4 (1989).

Various versions of chapter 2 were presented at the Southeastern Nineteenth Century Studies Association conference (1988), the Religion Department of Barnard College (1988), and the Department of German at Indiana University at Bloomington (1989). A partial version of it will appear as "Die Flambierte Frau: Satī in European Culture," in *Satī, the Blessing and the Curse: The Burning of Wives in India,* edited by J. S. Hawley (Oxford University Press, 1994).

Chapter 3 was presented at the International Society for the Comparative Study of Civilizations conference, Champaign-Urbana, (1990). An earlier version was published in *Monatshefte* 81, no. 4 (1990).

Versions of chapter 4 were presented at the Religion Department Colloquium, SUNY at Stony Brook (1990), and the American Academy of Religion, mid-Atlantic regional meeting (1990).

Subsections of chapter 5 were presented at the Fifth MacMaster Colloquium on German Literature (1987) and the American Academy of Religion annual meeting (1987). The Wagner section is the fruit of a NEH faculty seminar on Wagner held in the summer of 1990 at New York University. This piece was presented both at that seminar and at the Modern Language Association annual meeting (1990).

Parts of chapter 6 were presented at invited lectures in the French Departments of Stanford University (1988) and the University of South Carolina at Greensboro (1989).

Parts of chapter 7 were presented at two separate panels at the Modern Language Association annual meeting (1991).

I wish to record my gratitude to colleagues who have taken the trouble to help me in various ways. I owe a personal and intellectual debt to John S. Hawley of Barnard College, who has offered encouragement as well an numerous opportunities to present my work to a varied audience. I wish to thank Paul Courtright of Emory University for providing me with a forum in the early stages of this project. My friend and colleague Louise O. Vasvari has been invaluable in making suggestions that have improved various chapters. My colleague Thomas Kerth has elucidated a number of points in my translations. I would also like to thank Professor Ulrich Weisstein of Indiana University at Bloomington for sharing with me his insights into Wagner's exoticism. The Wagner chapter as a whole benefited from an NEH Seminar in musicology under the direction of Professor Robert Bailey of New York University. Financial support for various parts of this enterprise came from the Mellon Foundation. My editor, Carola Sautter, guided me judiciously in bringing this volume to fruition. I thank Wanda Mocarski for her computer wizardry, Donna Sammis for her skills as a librarian, and my dear friend Loretta Celitan, who has provided much insight into the lure of exoticism. Throughout this endeavor, my brothers, mother, and mother-in-law have offered moral support. Above all, I wish to thank my husband, John, who has indefatigably read, reread, and critiqued these pages.

Introduction

Do you know, O beautiful of the beautiful,
My bayadera with eyes of jade,
If they could lend me their wings,
Say, do you know where I would go?

Without taking a single kiss from the roses
Across valleys and forests,
I would go to your half-closed lips,
O flower of my soul, and there I would die.[1]
—Théophile Gautier, "The Butterflies"

In this poem, Gautier evokes the fragility and beauty of man's desire for escape. The longing to go somewhere strange and unusual conditions this flight. Pleasure is even delayed in anticipation of the fulfillment of one wish, extinction in the moment of apprehension. Gautier addresses his words to a bayadera, an exotic prostitute who dances in Hindu temples. Does he invoke her inherent poetic potential, or does she serve some other purpose in the poem? For that matter, why does the poet address his poem to a quintessentially exotic figure?

A dictionary definition of the term *exotic* offers an initial signification of "foreignness." Invariably, it will also suggest that the exotic exerts a special force, that it can be strangely or unfamiliarly beautiful and enticing. This physical and (meta)physical identification at the heart of the exotic accounts for the tension often present between extraneity and the erotic.

What purpose does the exotic serve? Beyond its evocative and poetic possibilities, the exotic exists as a mode of self-definition. It does so in two respects. On the initial level, the exotic functions as a mode of escapism. Exoticism exhibits a "philosophical nostalgia" for a "traditional, binding, serenely fatalistic order."[2] H. H. Wilson noted that his translation of the *Viṣṇu Purāṇa*

> will be of service and of interest to the few, who in these times of utilitarian selfishness . . . can find a resting place [*sic*] for their thoughts in the tranquil contemplation of those yet living pictures of the ancient world which are exhibited by the literature and mythology of the Hindus.[3]

The exotic also provides a fertile base for philosophical, religious, and literary speculation and serves as an exemplar justifying preexisting cultural trends. The satirical use of the exotic can provide a shield to protect authors from strict censorship. Fiction with an exotic allure can present in the most piquant and prudent manner conceptions that an author strives to render in an acceptable form. Elements of masquerade also enter into exotic formulations: "We need not become Brahmins or Buddhist or Taosze altogether, but we must for a time . . .[4] Play-acting plays an important role in self-definition and self-realization. The exotic allows one to transform one's own mediocrity.[5] Most importantly, however, exoticism never realizes what it sets out to achieve. Henry H. H. Remak has remarked that the exotic quest does "not terminate with the exploration of a particular culture" but spins off "in search of a different set of cultural elements in order to satisfy psychic and/or physical *Wanderlust*."[6]

The exotic is seen as a function of the "Other," alterity, the "Female," *différence,* and subalterneity. It has recently been suggested that Indological discourse "represents the Other in commentative terms as radically different from the Self. It is a gross distortion of Self or the opposite of Self." Mother India can even represent Melanie Klein's good mother toward which the West responds with the construct of India as the bad mother.[7] Behind the "promise of Orientalist discourse of a unity of human nature," it is suggested that there is really the "disturbing" hidden agenda of consolidating the hegemony of the "Euro-American Man":

> It is necessary for the Other to be the way he/she is because of its environment, its racial composition, or its (inferior) place

> on the evolutionary scale. Once the reader comes to know the natural reason for the other's otherness, the threat of it is neutralized. The Explanation is, thus, one which restores the unity of Mankind, with Western Man as is perfect embodiment.[8]

In short, what we in this study term "the exotic" has entered critical debate in many forms.

Certain critical strategies, such as Edward Said's theory of Orientalism, seek to unsettle idealist quests for meaning, but are undermined by the polarities of intentionality. Orientalism holds to the belief that cultural differences were uniformly repressed in service of a hegemonic agenda. However, Said's presentation of Orientalism as discourse poses several problems from a methodological and conceptual point of view. In terms of methodology, Said's model of Orientalism demands a unified European/Western identity at the origin of history that posits an integral relationship between Ancient Greece and modern Western Europe. In the oldest European textualities, Said discovers an ideology of modern imperialist Eurocentrism already inscribed.[9] In Said's transhistorical formulation, Europe, motivated by a unitary will to inferiorize, created its own identity by establishing the *différence* of the Orient. All European knowledges of non-Europe are thus tainted.[10] Said focuses on the colonizers as repositories of power and the colonial subject as a fixed, passive object of discursive domination.

In Said's analysis, Western textualities about the non-West are viewed in isolation from how these textualities have been received, accepted, modified, challenged, overthrown or reproduced by intelligentsias of colonized countries.[11] The unidirectionality of his approach overlooks the inherent ambivalance of the relationship between the colonizers and the colonized, a relationship that vacillates between the poles of power and subjugation, desire and disavowal, and idealization and rejection. As Aijaz Ahmad has shown, not only does Said presume continuous European literary textuality as immanent in a canon of Great Books, but he subscribes to the "idealist metaphysic" of Great Books (questioning the greatness of some of these great books). In this manner, he duplicates the very tradition he debunks,[12] the tradition of canonical texts from a comparative literature and philological canon and the narrative method for analyzing high canonicity. Modern orientalists are present in all authors who treat the Orient and modern imperialism, an effect of their discourse. Thus, Orientalism "delivered" the Orient to colonialism and colonialism begins to appear as the product of Orientalism.[13]

The Deconstructionist critique of Western Idealism or logocentrism assigns a marginal position of racial/cultural/historical otherness. Committed to the Derridean articulation of *différence* and *signifiance,* this criticism fixes "the place of otherness . . . in the west as a subversion of western metaphysics and is finally appropriated by the west as its limit-text, anti-west."[14] Critics of Western Idealism and colonialism, whatever their stripes, have fully embraced recent critical theory and incorporated it in various guises into their discourse. The Deconstructionist critique of Idealism and logocentrism, which subverts apparent meaning and conceptions of reality, particularly in its "decentering" of traditional focal points of power, has found very sympathetic readers in the Third World.

Gayatri Spivak, a translator of Derrida, seeks to deconstruct colonialist discourse and the position of indigenous peoples, especially women, within this discourse. Regarding Spivak's project, Henry Louis Gates states: Spivak has merely renamed what Derrida calls "writing" with the term *colonial discourse* and added the necessary corollary that "all discourse is colonial discourse."[15] Spivak presents the text as unable to answer back to the epistemic violence of an imperialist project.[16] She restricts the space in which the colonized can be written back into a text. In the words of Benita Parry, the virtual elimination of the colonized in Spivak's theory is particularly ironic given the "interventionist possibilities" that "are exploited through the deconstructive strategies devised by the post-colonial intellectual."[17] The critic's intellectual ability to "plot a story, unravel a narrative and give the subaltern a voice in history" stands in sharp contrast to that same critic's deafness to the utterances of the native voice.[18] To the contention that the Orient has always been silenced, one must ask, by whom? Voices are not silenced. Either the critic's voice drowns them out or they just do not appear in the "archive" which the critic selects.[19] The primacy which the critic assumes for him- or herself is due to their positioning themselves in lieu of the Other as object of discourse. Following the trend set by Said, the critic becomes the "orientalist subject" (with the variants "colonialist subject" and "post-Colonialist subject"). Ahmad has pointed out the hazards of such postures on the part of critics based in Western metropolitan centers who wield the tools of European cultural apparatus.[20]

The Marxist literary critic Fredric Jameson entered into the critical debate through a discussion of modern Third World literature. For Jameson, and to a certain degree, Spivak, Third World literature becomes a counter-canon, a narrative of authenticity, good faith, liberation itself.[21] His comments have been criticized for their totalizing effect.[22] His theory—which hypothesizes all Third World texts as national allegories in which the political and personal (libidinal) are conflated—seems to run aground in its attempt to generalize the staggering diversity within Third World cultural waters. Jameson theoretically juxtaposes the cultural frameworks of the contemporary West, with its "radical split between the public and the private, between the poetic and the political"[23] domains, over against a Third World where public and private are enmeshed. Critics of his approach note that the Third World has never evinced such homogeneity, and that especially urban Third World writers experience the same alienation from their sociocultural context as Western writers do.[24]

A difficulty for Marxist, post-Structuralist, and Deconstructionist theorists with respect to the exotic lies in their inability to confront the ambivalance within Orientalisms and their habit of seeing subjugated peoples as "unproblematized" victims "caught in the hinges of history."[25] It is here that the Subaltern critique intervenes. By focusing on the domain of politics in which the principal actors are subaltern groups and classes, "history from below" exposes the ideological character of traditional historiography, which it terms "elitist." The works of Partha Chatterjee and Ranajit Guha, two of the most challenging writers of the Subaltern school, seek to strip away ideological and critical misrepresentations of the social and political situations within South Asian society. Their arguments stress the complexity of the societies in question and the forces working within them. Elitist historiography of either the colonialist or the nationalist type is criticized[26] and rejected in favor of a framework that stresses the intersection of popular consciousness with new forms of class domination shaped by the politics of the modern state.[27]

Homi K. Bhabha has contributed significantly to the critical discussion by contesting the underlying presupposition of Orientalism that all power and discourse are possessed entirely by the colonizer. He believes that power and knowledge function ambivalently and that a variously positioned colonial object appropriates or mimics the terms of the dominant ideology and uses them to offer resistance. Bhabha's theory has, at face value, double attraction. He liberates the colonized from their "inscription as Europe's shackled other" and, *pace* Spivak, recognizes that the subaltern can, indeed, speak for him- or herself. Most refreshingly, however, Bhabha sets some limits on critical discursive power and problematizes the position of the professional spokesperson for the subaltern.[28]

The work of Franz Fanon has been particularly useful in bringing to light the inherent complexities within the position of colonized peoples. In Bhabha's use of Fanon's work, we see echoed the conflicting impulses that define exoticism: the search for human origin, the origin of art and poetry, and racial purity and cultural priority in order to "normalize" multiple beliefs. The narcissistic and aggressive projections onto the Other to compensate for a perceived "lack" in the European "individual" and context find clear parallels in exotic literature. Particularly useful to this present study are Fanon's perception of the subjugated as simultaneously fetish and phobic object. Bhabha speaks of the metaphorical masking of the fetish as a narcissistic object choice acting in relation to the metonymic trope that functions to figure a lack. Here Bhabha brings together Freud's concept of the fetish, Fanon's experience of the colonial subject as Other, and Lacan's schema of the "Imaginary." Important for both Bhabha and Fanon is Lacan's theory of the way individual subjects are constituted. Gates maintains that "Lacan's discourse exemplarily maps a problematic of subject-formation onto a Self-Other model that seems to lend itself to the Colonial Encounter."[29]

As seen from the preceding summary of the critical discourse an initial irony presents itself: Orientalist, Deconstructionist, and post-Colonialist criticism are clearly bound to contemporary Western critical discourse. Western critical theory alone provides the language and ideological parameters within which this critique is developed. Moreover, Otherness, subalterneity, alterity, and Orientalist and Colonialist discourse are abstractions used to identity complex phenomena. In this present study, therefore, I will avoid this critical nomenclature, as it has been sapped of any connotative force, or, rather, overburdened with polyvalent significations. Instead, I use the traditional literary term *exoticism* to describe the object of my study. I have borrowed this term from the study of European national literatures, which I see to be the domain of my investigation and whose studies of the scholarly, literary, and philosophical emplotment of India I seek to supplement.[30] Moreover, I contend that the more recent critical terms support various ideological consensuses that are not necessarily or universally supported by texts outside what has become an Orientalist canon. The restrictive canonization that has developed in recent critical discussions inevitably involves a re-creation of the past through the invention of "precursors for the present."[31] I am very suspicious of this critical tendency (indeed mandate), which sets out to examine literary texts as expressions of an underlying power relationship where some hierarchy is always imposed. Introduced with respect to language by Benveniste and codified with respect to the study of the apparatus of power within social institutions by Foucault, discussions of hegemony have come to dominate in an all-too-predictable fashion the critical discourse of East-West artistic relations. However, this study does not attempt to supplement critiques based on power relations. It attempts, rather, to problematize the specific narrative that reads Romantic appropriations of India in literature and scholarship solely through the metaphor of colonization.

I would like to suggest that the appropriation of the Other is more complex than Said allows in his restrictions.[32] As elucidating as a vision of Indological discourse in light of Gramsci may be, a reader encounters difficulties when confronting texts that do not support the current critical tendency and that present the East as superior and idealized. I am not denying those instances of East-West reception whose contours express political exploitation, but the present-day desire to subsume everything under a hegemonic agenda ignores the rich history of extra-political motivations.

Nothing much exists beyond Foucault's epistemic power, Derrida's logocentric thought, and Said's Orientalist discourse. All is viewed as repetition with *Différence*. While nihilistic tendencies in deconstruction have been questioned by critics who ask whether there can be any true representation of anything, the Manichaean vision of post-Colonialist criticism has yet to be seriously challenged.[33] By halting the discussion at the concept of power, interweaving, imbricating, and embedding all discussions in multiple reveries concerning the variations of domination/dominated relationships, the critic's fantasies all too often promiscuously displace the consciously fictionalized objects of inquiry. Here, perhaps, lies the "postmodern" hegemonic discourse of criticism that theorists such as Parry and Ahmad have begun to investigate. Indeed, I take as a point of departure Parry's insight that the dissolution of the binary opposition (colonial Self/colonized Other) encoded in post-Colonialist criticism into a dichotomy necessary for domination posits a discourse of liberation and a call to arms.[34] As much as some critics would like us to believe, criticism is not an "act of insurgency."[35] The West not only has produced the colonialist, but also has informed most interpretations of colonialism.[36] Therefore, it may be of some value to begin this investigation with the following question: Which "politics of projects" are involved in the Orientalist and post-Colonialist critical processes? Not only do the motivating forces behind these theoretical positions warrant closer examination in and of themselves, but I suspect that the historical and ethical judgments that have generated recent criticism reflect upon the dynamics of the exotic project in general. In fact, I would go so far as to suggest that exoticism, Orientalist/post-Orientalist criticism, and what might be termed "institutional esotericism" in the form of scholarship often arise from like motivations and fulfill similar desires.

Now, in literary critical circles, it has become a fairly prosaic task to question the presuppositions behind methodological dogmatism, as witnessed by the recent Deconstructionist debacle. Furthermore, recent historical events have challenged the validity of Marxist interpretive models. Students of literary theory look on in apprehension as Deconstructionists and academic Marxists retool themselves as feminists and multiculturalists, their "politics of projects" being all too apparent. However, some disciplines that have borrowed heavily from the jargon and missionary zeal of literary theory have not undergone a similar rigorous scrutiny. In particular, the curious Western academic speciality, need, and pastime of making the Other one's cause have avoided sociological and psychological evaluation. No one questions why the Western humanist's and social scientist's cultural "superiority," power, and influence, rather than the quality of their work, skill, or insight, make their work acceptable to Indians and Westerners alike. Nor does anyone wonder why we are not reading a canon of scholarship and popular commentary on India written by Africans, Latin Americans, or visiting commentators from elsewhere in the Third World.[37]

So the student with an interest in matters pertaining to India experiences an interesting phenomonon when confronted by volume after volume that purports to deconstruct normative texts. How can authors pretend to ferret out hegemonic processes, when their perception of the field consists of a jealously-guarded, limited repertory of acceptable topics and a particularly dogmatic refusal to engage alternative forms of inquiry? How can practitioners in a field that is notoriously homogeneous and conservative (its radical pretensions notwithstanding) deconstruct normative texts while they create their own "dominant fictions"? Having read their Foucault and Lacan, these scholars certainly know that to normalize is naughty. Nevertheless, they do so with impunity. They may call for "libertarian, non-repressive and non-manipulative"[38] studies of other cultures and peoples, they may read texts as a "form of power, a cultural instrument of political power,"[39] but ultimately their understanding presupposes a view of their subject as "simple-hearted victims of colonialism."[40] Their position as Westerners making the East their specialty, with all the commercial and ideological enterprise of self-validation that this posture implies, stands at odds with the ideology of much of their discourse.[41]

How, then, do such politics of scholarly projects relate to the topic at hand? The preceding discussion would seem tangential were it not for the striking similarities between the behavior of the historical seekers after the exotic examined in this volume and that of practitioners of contemporary criticism and scholarship. Although what I am suggesting demands a detailed analysis in itself, for the purposes of my argument a few necessary observations must suffice.

Institutionalized "esoteric" scholarship, the critical theory dealing with Orientalism, and the exotic quest itself all evince a tendency to normalize the discourse that represents their objects of inquiry. This normalization has created a dominant fiction based not on what is included, but on what is excluded. In the case of scholarship, included are those studies that focus on discrete technical problems within language, translation, or reception of philosophical and religious concepts. Equally privileged are studies based on current critical theory. Cross-cultural studies are admissible if they accede to the parameters of the critique of Orientalism. Here the underlying assumption is that of the aggressive, sadistic colonizer over against the oppressed (castrated) colonial Other.

Excluded are studies that call for broadening the scope of linguistic/philological inquiry. Specifically, any opening of the discourse to include the Western subject acting through his or her desire and need to disavow is strongly discouraged. This includes examining the Western artistic/scholarly subject as he or she treats the Eastern Other as an object of consciousness. Equally rejected are studies that "problematize" the East-West encounter in a way that threatens to undo the imperialist/victim binary.

As we shall see in this volume, the East has historically functioned as an object of desire within scholarly and artistic reception. What I would like to emphasize is that little in contemporary scholarship contradicts this ongoing mode of apprehension. Desire is always for something but is engendered by an experience of lack within the subject for which the desired object provides imaginary compensation.[42] As Homi Bhabha shows, the East "figures" this lack for the Western subject and sets in motion a complex, often contradictory process of idealization and rejection, desire and disavowal, on the level of the imaginary. The ego of the Western subject not only is implicated in, but in a real sense is determined by, this process as it binds problematic impulses to a normative structure. In the reception (and study) of the East, this process inevitably leads to the need to normalize the concept of the East within the world. The Western subject's experience of adequacy within the world has always hinged on the mastery of desire and lack; consequently scholarship has always found itself within the ideological apparatus of the dominant fiction.[43]

It is on the level of disillusionment following desire that an aporia exists, exposing an inadequacy within the dominant fiction that opens the possibility of refiguring the reception of the East. In present times, the normative function of this fiction is seen in the way scholarly approaches that challenge dominant assumptions are rejected not merely for mounting the challenge, but often because of the way race and gender are inscribed within this challenge, that is, because the conceptualization of race and gender is polyvalent, refusing strict adherence to either traditional approaches or so-called cutting-edge methodologies.

As the above comments suggest, I view Orientalist/post-Colonialist criticism and some forms of "esoteric" scholarship as functioning as exoticisms in terms of their need to experience adequacy on the level of language. Since the object of my inquiry is to illuminate the process of exoticism, I shall not intentionally enact exoticism in my critical methodology. In other words, this present volume will not adhere to the dominant fiction of Indology or the master narrative of Orientalist criticism. It posits the existence of alternative readings and alternative exotic texts that do not affirm the hegemony of one culture over another. As opposed to imperialist exoticism, whose very presence in a canon of Orientalist and post-Colonialist criticism problematizes the versatility of those critical systems,[44] "exoticizing" exoticism primarily concerns itself with the privileging of other cultures,[45] where the exotic not only is fetishized but also empowers.

This study, therefore, only becomes exotic to certain specialist readers because of its literary methodology, cross-disciplinarity, and comparative perspective. Those who seek (or demand) a study focused on South Asian texts and experience will not find it here. To the institutional spokesman for the subaltern,[46] I must assert the validity of reading European literature in and of itself, even when it addresses a consciously fictionalized "Orient." As Nandy asserts, India is not the non-West, it is India.[47] However, I am not studying India, but rather that "non-West" that was positioned in India, where India becomes a projective text, inviting one "not only to project onto it one's deepest fantasies, but also to reveal, through such self-projection, the interpreter rather than the interpreted."[48] I agree fully with Nandy when he asserts that "all interpretations of India are . . . ultimately autobiographical."[49] I also agree with Naipaul when he writes that India encourages "the Outsider to build a monument to himself."[50] Whether scholarly or artistic, exotic fiction and nonfiction function as reifications of the Self, and the metaphorical India continues to exist as a geographical area one can love and a sociological space where real 'man' can find himself.[51]

As recent investigations of the workings of eighteenth-century anthropology have revealed, the movement to subjugate is not mutually exclusive of quests for understanding. I will focus therefore on the dialectic of self-understanding inscribed in the exotic quest. My model broadens to include a discussion of psychodynamics of appropriation. The Romantics did, indeed, "appropriate" rather than "understand"

India, but their aims were often contestatory rather than conservative, and the appropriation is part of negotiating the polarities of self-consciousness. The European either was genuinely trying to understand rather than repress cultural difference, or, in fact, attempted to do both.

Therefore, this study seeks to delineate the hermeneutical parameters of exoticism rather than adhere to negative critical stances that psychologize modern fantasies of alienation or problematize (and mystify) ideological perspectives. I offer a hermeneutical model partially drawn from Gadamer, which allows me to view the French and German appropriation of India as attempts at self-understanding rather than simple mastery. This perspective permits me to attach a positive value to exoticism by seeing it as embedded in individual rather than collective agendas. However, my investigation is more socially and culturally based than the Gadamerian hermeneutical model allows, as well as more psychologically inflected.

My approach is simple: I shall identify how the Gadamerian concept of prejudice in the form of specific exotic clichés elucidates the dynamics of exoticism. By isolating these clichés, I am, in fact, mapping out the "garden paths" along which artists and thinkers either were led or willed themselves to be led. In choosing this linguistic term, I commit an intentional *double entendre*. In nineteenth-century linguistics, the comparative rather than the historical method prevailed, which often led to error,[52] the "garden paths" along which these thinkers strayed. Ironically, those linguists who neglected history were often inspired by the botanical model.

I have chosen this conceptual framework for an equally simple reason: Beyond the seduction they have in and of themselves, many critical concepts direct the reader no closer to certain texts or our continuing need for an exotic in our lives. Exoticism is not a discursive practice intent on recovering, "elsewhere," values "lost" with the modernization of European society.[53] Although dreams of empire have been eclipsed, the exoticist project is alive and well.[54] For this reason, I have chosen to be guided by the hermeneutical concept of *Bildung*. What is at stake in exoticism is an act of recognition.

> To recognize one's own in the alien, to become at home in it, is the fundamental movement of the spirit, whose being is only return to itself from being otherwise.[55]

The structure of excursion and reunion defines *Bildung,* or what Paul Ricoeur identifies as the movement of hermeneutical understanding.[56] If the circular structure of hermeneutical understanding is complete, the spirit moves to the strange and unfamiliar, finds a home there and makes it its own or recognizes what had previously been perceived as alien to be its genuine home. Hermeneutical understanding consists of a movement of self-estrangement in which one must learn to know the Other in order better to know oneself. In fact, in a reversal peculiar to *Bildung,* the movement of the spirit resembles a true homecoming; its point of departure was essentially a way station. The initial alienness was a mirage produced by self-alienation.[57] In reality, one only confronts aspects of the Self.

Hermeneutics, focusing as it does on the process that leads to a point of understanding, conceptualizes human subjectivity only to the extent necessary to illuminate this process. Therefore, prejudice and the circular movement of hermeneutical understanding are privileged concepts. The subjectivity that surrounds hermeneutical understanding cannot, in any case, be left out of account, as it is the locus of the failed hermeneutical quest. The nature of the failed hermeneutic is a subject to which I will return at various reprises throughout this volume. The striving subject seeks compensation in and through the exotic for experiences of alienation and emptiness that are perceived as a function of Western society and culture. But the view of the East that conditions the quest is a fantasy, which is seldom if ever understood as such. In many ways, it is the nature of illusion that will be explored in the poses that follow.

The hermeneutical model provides a useful conceptualization and is historically grounded in the period I cover. The dialectic of self-reflection is one that Gadamer himself derived from German Romantics. Hegel approaches the phenomenology of Spirit in terms of a movement involving the self-estrangement of the subject in the object, a movement that culminates in the folding back of the objective into the subjective. Here the terms are either epistemological (subject/object) or psychological (Self/Other). Significantly, the Hegelian phenomenology is the source not only of the hermeneutical model, but also of imperialist historiography that colonizes the Other and that is enabled by, and also qualified by, the hermeneutical dialectic. In fact, the hermeneutical approach that I advocate is not exclusive of Foucauldian historicism. German Romanticism is the conflicted origin both of the former and of those colonizations of the Other that have brought the latter (the cultural critique) into existence.[58]

By projecting themselves through the Other, Romantic writers appropriate the Other for their own purposes, but they also rethink the Self through the Other so as to expand their own cultural boundaries and those of their society. At the same time, in trying to understand the Other, they also appropriate it and colonize it, or at least create the conditions for its colonization. The result, as Foucault rightly asserts, is that, power and knowledge become entwined. However, I want to distinguish such a discussion of power from that found in Said and the grand narratives of "gender, race, nation" ideology of current criticism.

Of particular use to my investigation was Homi Bhabha's Lacanian conception of the lack or primordial alienation that always accompanies a subject's attempts to overcome the dichotomy of Self/Other: the individual over against the world. Bhabha holds that Colonialist discourse is disturbed at its source by a doubleness of enunciation. Bhabha asserts that this "doubleness does not articulate the violence of one powerful nation writing out another [but] a mode of contradictory utterance that ambivalently reinscribes both the colonizing and the colonized."[59] Equally useful will be Jameson's insight regarding twentieth-century Third World literature, which I apply to the nineteenth-century context. Jameson asserts that cultural products of the East are misunderstood by the European mainstream as a result of the split between Western subjectivity and the larger sociocultural context. However, the failure of the exotic quest is not due to any short-circuiting of the exoticist project as it is grounded in history.[60] Rather, it is in the nature of exoticism itself, in what I term the "failed hermeneutics of the exotic quest," that the irresolution of that quest is inscribed.

The exotic differs from the general interpretive venture by virtue of the fact that the "alien" aspect of the hermeneutical equation is indeed esoteric. When people who are world-weary or have lost faith seek a new system of belief in the exotic, they travel farther from home than the ordinary seeker for Self or Truth. The exoteric quest, like art, is democratic: It promises salvation to all seekers. The esoteric or exotic, however, derives from a personal experience of mystical consciousness. It is far less egalitarian. It fosters elitism. Quotidian truth does not suffice—one seeks the superordinate to invest one's existence with greater intensity. The divine spark is present in all, but not everyone realizes it and seeks to reunite his or her spark with the Divine. For this reason, esoteric cults often emphasize service, to detract from their elitist tendencies. An interesting question then becomes: To what extent are those engaged in a Promethean flight attracted to the esoteric or exotic precisely because of its elitist potential? A partial answer is suggested by the controversial nexus that often occurs between Western esotericism and extremist politics. Connections can indeed by drawn between brands of the occult or spiritual philosophy and dubious political ideologies. For example, Julius Evola's combination of Hermeticism, with its sweeping notions of race and valor, led to his active collaboration with the Nazis. A more ambiguous case is presented by the biography and work of Mircea Eliade.[61] Some are zealots out of faith, others are mystics out of choice, and still others (who tend to dismiss contemptuously the former two categories) are elitist by discipline. All are equally absolutist, exclusionary, and dogmatic. While this study specifically addresses the first two types, in a larger sense its concerns apply equally to the philologist and area specialist as well.

I attempt to have my analyses weave back and forth between the scholarly/literary and the social text in ways that give my critique more historical specificity than that of hermeneutics. The European writer's quest Eastward in search of aesthetic models fluctuated between contrasting modalities: Indian culture could be an ideal locus for inspiration while simultaneously providing a rationale for pessimistic apprehension in the face of existence. The plethora of early translations attests to the fact that Europeans were interested in Indian thought. Critics urged Western writers to make formal use of Sanskrit literature as an inspiration for their work.[62] However, there were also those who reacted more to its esoteric potential, flirting instead with the darker and perhaps richer prospect of Indian fatalism. The phantom India satisfied specific tendencies inherent in each modality. These contrasting modalities imbricated in the exotic quest serve a rhetorical function similar to Bhabha's discursive doubling or splitting.

Contrary to the supposition that "Indological discourse holds . . . the essence of Indian civilization" to be "irrational,"[63] I maintain that it was the irrational in the West that impelled many thinkers Eastward to seek a grounding for their irrationality. Certain Westerners believe that the West is in a state of decline, spiritually spent, and that the East possesses some spiritual or aesthetic *élan vital,* of which they hope to partake. Hugo von Hofmannsthal expressed this phenomenon in *Das Tagesbuch eines Willenskranken:*

> It is the individuals, who suffer the sufferings of the time and think the thoughts of the time. And books, that speak of such a pain of the time are the most tragic and become very famous, since they are the only ones that we are almost able to completely understand. What in us comes from vague pain, from hidden torture and effaced longing, each stiffled desire for something else and all disharmonies that the will has stiffled for preservation, these wake to an uncertain life

> and flourish in sympathy with *Tat tvam asi*.[64] In suffering, "good Europeanhood," the nationless clarity of tomorrow, is achieved; the path is too rough for the generation of yesterday and today, two generations of the irresolute and the half-resolute. The seduction draws backwards, the nerve conquering nostalgia, the longing for home . . . Back to childhood, to Fatherland, to the ability to believe, to the ability to love, to lost naivete, to the return to the irretrievable.[65]

Repressed longing responds to the lure of some absolute, whether it be esoteric or politically mystical. In the case of Julius Evola, elitist politics grew directly out of esoteric metaphysics. Are there not others like him? This study will address how esoteric spiritual philosophy ends up as a rationale for political struggles that seem to contradict their core concerns. When core values (such as mercy or compassion) are disengaged from experience, fundamental distinctions (such as good and evil, illusion and reality) blur.

Nietzsche held that the most general type of decadence consists in believing that one chooses remedies.[66] This is why I have entitled the exotic a "decadent quest." With the term *decadent* I suggest a metaphysical inquiry that holds no hope of recuperating the artificial object that it contemplates, but probes rhetorically what from the beginning has been rejected.[67] Thus, in being willed or devised, decadence has a literary quality to it.[68] Nevertheless, as Remy de Gourmont noted, decadence implies a purely negative idea, that of absence.[69] The exotic also functions as "a cipher for the essential aporia of every experience."[70]

The process of appropriating Indian wisdom often brought about the miscegenation of specific issues and themes. Voltaire posited India as the land of reason. The Parnassians sought in India both the ideal locus of art for art's sake as well as the gateway to the abyss. In the case of Germany's reception of Indian religious thought, there developed over the years a filiation between Indian metaphysical concerns and those of Romantic Germany. In the interstices between a presumably original India and the pretense of a filial Germany, curious artistic graftings emerged. Goethe placed the poetic possibilities of Oriental thought in the service of his personal views of Christian morality. Schopenhauer reinterpreted Upanishadic theory of illusion as Kantian phenomenalism. An ethical overlap emerged between Stoicism and Buddhism. Nietzsche abusively reconciled India with Plato, and Wagner annexed Buddhism to a medieval mystical cycle. The ontological question concerning the metaphysical status of the neoplatonic One with respect to the notion of *nirvāṇa* problematized German Romantic dilemmas of action in a revolutionary age. European pessimism, invigorated by Schopenhauer's distorted synthesis of Buddhism and Brahmanism, ebbed and flowed through the spiritual landscape of the nineteenth century. Many were those who immersed themselves in its floods. They saw pessimistic renunciation as an attribute of Indian thought and maintained that the human spirit could only realize itself by withdrawal from dynamic reality:

> Today, two things seem to be modern, the analysis of life and the flight from it. One preserves the anatomy of one's own spiritual life, or one dreams. Reflection or fantasy, mirror image or dream image. The Buddha is modern.[71]

Others managed to struggle out of pessimism to an affirmative view of life prevailing over all pain. When confronted with exotic fatalism, European thinkers either openly embraced it or rejected it.

I will examine how Indian exoticism fluctuated between two poles—at times offering a model of inspiration, at others providing an alibi for despair. Occasionally these two agendas collided, with interesting repercussions. Chapters 1, 2 and 3 direct the hermeneutical model to instances of inspirational exotic quests. These chapters investigate how exoticism does not present examples of completed hermeneutical understanding, although the movement of the hermeneutical process—the excursion into the alien—is essential to any examination of the exotic. I will endeavor to show how the breakdown of the hermeneutical process or its absolute rejection, as in chapter 4, is a recurrent feature of the exotic quest. My discussion culminates in the chapters 5–7 with those quests where India is used in apparently decadent and undialectical ways. These chapters chart how, from the early to the late nineteenth century, Indian exoticism changed from an incomplete hermeneutical endeavor to a decadent denial of understanding and an alibi for cultural despair. The use of the Other as an alibi, and the refusal to put one's prejudices at stake either ideologically or artistically, closes off at the outset any attempt at understanding the Other (or understanding oneself through the Other).

Specifically, I will investigate Indian exoticism's relationship to Romantic primitivism in its different strains: chronological (*Urheimat*), geographical (Garden of Eden), psychological ("childhood of humanity") and ontological (nostalgia for the One). In addition to addressing historical and cultural questions, I will seek to show how this encounter worked itself out differently in France and Germany, the possible impact each country had on the other, and which political and cultural circumstances might account for the difference in their emplotment of India.

My treatment of the material involves the restoration of the extralinguistic context, which includes the retrieving of allusions to sociocultural references and an understanding of the literary, scholarly, and artistic traditions in which the activity of the writer and the comprehension of the audience took place. The modern reader's task in restoration of the linguistic and extralinguistic contexts is important, since in both cases the authors are attempting to subvert tradition. It becomes necessary, therefore, to understand the cultural milieu and genre of the work itself, but also those of the conventions being echoed.

This study is based on certain premises. Examining the fictive India as a locus where the fantasies of Europe are enacted is not tantamount to a repetition of the intellectual follies of colonialism. The claim that such a recapitulation is inevitable betrays an ahistorical ideological conflation of past and present. It should be recognized as such and simply be put to rest. The critical inability to accept anything outside a particular ideological perspective and the terminology that supports it is a great failure of too much of contemporary scholarship.

I follow the ever-prescient Schopenhauer, who maintained that, from the beginning, the European understanding of Indian thought was flawed.[72] However, contrary to Said, I do not believe these misprisions were static and uniform. I shall, therefore, chart the development of two specific Orientalisms and focus on the ways in which the French and Germans misunderstood India as part of their own personal, cultural, and philosophical agendas. At no point will I argue that the Romantics (let alone those who came after them) understood India. However, I do question whether the Romantics were indeed the cultural imperialists that New Historicism claims they were. In fact, I suggest that Romantic misprisions of India were not necessarily racist and conservative, but were sites of an imaginary contestation of the symbolic order of existing society. I support a reading of the exotic as a conflicted contestation of the existing order. The subversive character of the exotic reemerges or is written back into that order and destabilizes its boundaries.

Finally, I must also clarify my intentions vis-à-vis the Sanskrit material. Because the exotic clichés evolved from surviving "texts," the primary level of textual retrieval necessary is of the original semantic denotations and connotations. However, I do not include a modern scholarly interpretation of the texts in question, since it was never an issue of these Europeans' understanding of a "real" Sanskrit text. The material with which they worked had already undergone distortion to several degrees in secondary or, most often, tertiary translations. Such "texts" defy the specialists' need for a normative reading. They are "texts" in a broad sense, as literary criticism tends to define that term as a form of discourse. I have drawn these "texts" from a variety of sources, some conventional (travel narrative, poetry, and novel), others less so (opera, philology, university lectures, and political myth). The India examined in these examples is the India consciously inscribed within the French and German literary and religious imagination. By my choice of such texts, I imply, a feminist critique of the master narrative of Orientalism and the normative canon of Indology. The general statements concerning Hinduism and Buddhism that one finds in this volume, as well as the East-West unevenness inherent in the discourse, are not mine but reflect a lack of differentiation on the part of the authors in question. I have not focused upon the narratological and rhetorical devices that account for this imbalance. Given this project's central concern with issues of translation and misreading, I have felt it unwise to insert contemporary norms of gender neutrality into nineteenth-century texts. Oftimes gendered language constitutes a significant aspect of the original and to render it otherwise would be remiss.

PART I

EXOTICISM: MODEL FOR INSPIRATION OR ALIBI FOR DESPAIR?

1

The Dynamics of Exoticism: Herder's Epigram and Günderrode's Epitaph

An ironic and somewhat chilling literary vignette serves to illustrate the tension between inspiration and pessimism that characterized the German reception of India. A particularly beautiful Sanskrit poem by Bhartṛhari, thought to date from the fourth or fifth century A.D.,[1] was among the first published in a European language. Initially translated into Portuguese and then into Dutch, it appeared in Abraham Rogerius's *Open Deure tot het verborgen Heydendom* in 1651 and in the book's German translation of 1663.[2] The German translation of Rogerius's work greatly impressed J. G. Herder, who refashioned this poem and others in the series.[3]

Bhartṛhari's poem[4] soon reappeared in German literature. Before taking her life in 1806, the Romantic poetess Karoline von Günderrode left Herder's rendition of Bhartṛhari's poem as her epitaph. Although presenting another's poetry as an apologia for suicide was an unimaginative final statement, stranger still was the choice of a Sanskrit suicide note. Although Sanskrit literary works were known to German literary circles in the early nineteenth century, they were not so widespread that an educated German suicide would ordinarily leave a Sanskrit epitaph behind. This strange reappearance of Bhartṛhari's poem exemplifies the darker impulses at work in Germany's Indian *Schwärmerei*. The appropriation of the poem, first by Herder to herald the hoped-for riches of Sanskrit literature, and then by Günderrode as an emblem of despair, offers a macabre and fascinating example of the fruits born of the literary meeting of East and West. How could a single poem offer to one writer an ideal of spiritual strength and to another a rationale for death? The answer resides less in Indian thought than in its emplotment by the West and in tendencies inherent in the will of the individual artist. The India discovered by a writer like Günderrode was principally a phantom arising out of a confrontation with the Self.

Herder's approach to Indian literature is equally marked by the triumph of subjective consideration, in the form of theoretical speculation and personal belief, over objectivity. His rewritings of Bhartṛhari's maxims were not, however, without literary worth.[5] In general, his comments on Indian thought and literature were written in the spirit of nascent German Orientalism. In the early work, the *Ideen zur Philosophie der Geschichte der Menschheit* (1784–1791), Herder described the Hindus as "the gentlest race of man."[6] Indians have respect for all that is endowed with life. Their nourishment is sound and their demeanor as graceful as their spirit.[7] They possess supernatural qualities of spirit, body, and mind.[8] In Herder's view, the Orient and the primitive world, the primitive world and nature, and nature and poetry become synonymous and interchangeable.[9] Herder joined the belief in the anteriority of poetry—which was a heritage of the eighteenth century—to his own variation of the *bon sauvage* theme and posited an equivalence of the Orient and poetry.[10]

Although Herder admired Sanskrit poetry,[11] he distrusted Hinduism. He found its religious symbolism "monstrous" and its philosophical speculation tendentious.[12] This contradiction would pose difficulties when he rewrote Bhartṛhari's poems. In the case of the epigram in question, it led to a distortion of the poem's religious message. Herder wrought his rendition from the German translation of Bhartṛhari. In this version, the poem is as follows:

> O Mother, earth!
> O Father, wind!
> O Friend, fire!
> O Relatives, water!
> O Sky, my brother!
> In all friendship I offer you
> All my respect;
> Because I have lived well with you,
> I now achieve bliss,
> I will gladly leave you all, however,
> And go to heaven.[13]

Herder modified Rogerius's rendition in a minor, yet telling, fashion:

Earth, you my mother, and you my
Father, the breeze, and you fire,
My friend, you my relative, the river,
And you my brother, the sky, I wish you
Respectfully all my friendly thanks.
Here on earth I have lived with you
And go now to the other world,
Gladly leaving you;
Farewell, brother, and friend, father
And mother, farewell.[14]

He omitted the significant point that it is the subject's active being-in-the-world, involvement with the elements of the earth, that allows the "birth of uncontaminated wisdom": "Denn weil . . . Erhalte ich nun die Seeligkeit." Rogerius's version of the Sanskrit original affirms a life-in-the-world philosophy, and goodness and wisdom allow the speaker to escape the endless cycle of rebirths (*saṃsāra*). In fact, the poem presents a prayer of thanks to the physical world offered by one who has gained salvation. Knowledge and experience of the physical world; and immersion in it, function as the path to the Absolute. In the Sanskrit original,[15] as well as in Rogerius's translation, the subject achieves union with God only through this very involvement. Implicit in the Indian formulation is the belief that this world is one of illusion (*māyā*), the overcoming of which effects a second birth in the Absolute and frees the soul from future rebirths. *Nirvāṇa,* the final emancipation and *summum bonum* of philosophical Brahmanism, is conceived as the loss of separate identity by absorption into the supreme and only really existing Being. The images of relation and birth, evoked by anthropomorphized nature in Bhartṛhari's poem, dramatize the theme of deliverance. Herder's version omits entirely the issue of the soul's escape from reincarnation and, in the process, overlooks the optimistic message of the original. Instead, it emphasizes the subject's resignation to death.

The Indian belief in the existence of morphological connections in nature denoting the transference of life fascinated Herder. He wrote several articles on the subject of palingenesis,[16] eventually distinguishing an ascending and a descending type. The latter, which he termed "of the Indian brahmins," was the least useful in the context of his description of cultural progress. The former, however, was of great significance to his thought. Through this type of palingenesis, seen as an historical phenomenon projected into the past and the future, Herder sought to explain the recurrence of cultural events through time and space.[17]

Given Herder's interest in the theme of metempsychosis, the distortion of Bhartṛhari's poem arose neither from ignorance nor from indifference to the subtleties of Indian religious thought.[18] Rather, it was due to the fact that the Indian brand of palingenesis portrayed in this poem stood in opposition to Herder's ideology of progress.[19] The soul's extinction in Brahma would preclude his belief that individual forms can exist again in present and future history.[20] Therefore, in order to align the poem's message with his own theories, Herder suppressed what was—from the devout Hindu standpoint—its soteriological message, namely, that the cycle of *saṃsāra* could be broken and the individual soul spared the pain of subsequent rebirths. In his version, the soul merely goes to another world. Whereas in the German source the soul attained salvation from active living in this world, for Herder it has garnered no benefit from its earthly existence and is happy to leave the world behind. Thus, through his subtle emendation of Bhartṛhari's poem, Herder inadvertantly set the stage for Günderrode's destructive appropriation of the poem.

In the several critical works devoted to Günderrode's poetry, little mention is made of her most "poetic" act, suicide. Born in 1780, Karoline Friederika Louise Maximiliane von Günderrode's life was one of tragedy. From an early age, she was surrounded by death.[21] A pattern of unfortunate loves would teach this intelligent, impoverished, and (by all accounts) beautiful woman the pain of rejection. Poems dating from her early period speak of the deceptions of love and its transitoriness.[22] These poems were inspired by her affection for Carl von Savigny. Savigny's subsequent engagement and marriage to Cunegonde Brentano and Karoline's friendship with the couple introduced Karoline into the intellectual and artistic circle of the Brentano family and, notably, to Clemens, with whom she shared another ill-fated relationship.[23]

In 1803, Karoline met the noteworthy Heidelberg philologist Friedrich Creuzer.[24] Although he was "an ugly man,"[25] Karoline fell in love with him. Their relationship, which lasted two years, was delicate because Creuzer was married.[26] Its cruel denouement was the immediate cause of Karoline's suicide.[27]

Combined with Günderrode's personal experiences of mounting despair was a literary climate characterized by the general interest in death that was prevalent in post-Enlightenment Germany.[28] In this respect, one has only to consider the overwhelming reception of *Werther.* An equally sinister aspect of Romantic love found expression in Günderrode's poetry. In 1805, Karoline began to describe death in metaphysical terms as an alternative to an unhappy love.[29] Toward this end, Günderrode found spiritual grounding in a distorted understanding of Indian philosophy. Creuzer exerted a tremendous influence in this regard. Not only did his selfishness in their relationship ultimately drive Karoline to her death, but he unwittingly supplied the intellectual rationale for despair by introducing her to Indian philosophy.[30] Under Creuzer's guidance, Günderrode's work incorporated counterfeited themes from Hindu metaphysical thought ("Musa," "Die Erscheinung," "Die Manen"), as well as a vague longing for the Absolute. An examination of the work inspired by Günderrode's study of "Hinduism" clearly indicates a troubling metaphysical vagueness concerning the ontology of the Absolute.[31] Did she consider it to be something that exists? Or, rather, did she perceive it as nonexistence? It did not resemble the neoplatonic Absolute, which was in vogue among the Romantics, nor, if we can interpret Creuzer to this effect,[32] did it adequately reflect Indian philosophy.

"Ein apokaliptisches Fragment"[33] describes the religious experience of losing oneself in "the All."[34] In particular, the theme of the soul's movement toward perfection by its rejection of the world animates this prose work as well as several of her poems.[35] The narrator gains deliverance from the strict limits of being "by living in the All."[36]

However, the vision of the soul's perfection through rejection of worldly involvement receives its clearest articulation in the "Geschichte eines Brahminen" (1805). In this work, Günderrode presents exile from the world (*Weltflucht*) as the only viable path to fulfillment. The hero's antidote for the trials of this world consists of a rejection of earthly fetters. His devotion to solitude reflects his transition into death.[37]

The hero, Almar, passes through crisis after crisis, initiation after initiation, from an egotistical existence toward virtue. His ultimate aim resides in the Hindu religious life of an ascetic, whose exile from the world becomes a figurative suicide. In a brahmin hut, Almar learns the unity of, and his own identity with, all beings through the strength of the *Weltgeist* or *Urleben*.[38] The initiate's goal, arrived at through his internal sense (*inneren Sinn* of "Die Manen"), is attained without the aid of human reason. Thus, in the character of Almar, Günderrode projects an idealized type upon whom the world impinges and who is able to renounce it for his own salvation. The brahmin did not dream of the world's redemption, believed in neither humanity nor life, and sought refuge in internal solitude after having repudiated action. Peace, however, as Günderrode presents it in the *Geschichte,* is still a living death. Almar, unlike his creator, accepted the possibility of peace within the bounds of life.

Attachment to existence, as a literary theme and existential possibility, subsequently deteriorated in Günderrode's poetry. Her longing for the Absolute came to express itself through a more intense interest in death, which took several forms. In "Ein apokaliptisches Fragment" and in the "Geschichte eines Brahminen," death is seen as the surrender to the Elemental Spirit.[39] The "Geschichte" specifically represents death as the source of true harmony with nature and with humanity.[40] Successive deaths and rebirths effect a gradual movement toward fulfillment and union with the Absolute (*Urkraft, Eins*). This Absolute is Hindu in the sense that it unites the individual Self (*Ātman*) with the All-Soul (*Brahman*).[41] In the "Geschichte," Günderrode explains this process of awakening in singularly passive terms. The souls wait until, in a mysterious manner, they happen to unite with the *Urkraft* from which they emanated. While they become one with the Divine, they remain themselves; individuality and universality are thus joined.[42]

Günderrode's speculations on death and the afterlife find their ultimate expression in the "Briefe zweier Freunde." The protagonist in this narrative is named Eusebio, a nickname Günderrode had given to Creuzer. The "Briefe" are clearly autobiographical and suggest an erosion of the barriers between narrative and personal history. Eusebio/Creuzer offers his dialoguer/Günderrode an alternative to the seductions of death through Hindu religious books, which she accepts. Günderrode presents the Indian system of thought as a concrete and reasonable theory of immortality: Souls are reborn in new and stronger forms. Particulars, developing through death and rebirth,[43] thus become immortal in the All:

> Everything which is now sun and moon, flower and precious stone, ether and sea is One, a holy thing that rests without cessation in its depths, blessed in itself, eternally embracing itself without desire for the deeds and sufferings of duality which bestir its surface.[44]

Eusebio's interlocutor has come to believe that death and engagement with the All are one. The pantheistic imagery of the "Briefe" calls to mind Karoline's epitaph, as does its call to inaction. The actions of this life are of little value. Rebirth does not depend on the fruits of action. Instead, death is sought, as is rebirth, only with a view toward attaining unmerited ultimate perfection: "What tasks await me, or, what better knowledge can I possibly attain on Earth that I should remain here longer?"[45]

It is not my intention to suggest that Günderrode's fatalistic worldview ensued from Creuzer's sadistic behavior. Nor do I suggest that Günderrode's "Indian" corpus and suicide note were directly inspired by some specific manipulation on her part, or someone else's, of a specific

Sanskrit text. Rather, I suggest that Günderrode's life experiences, a succession of *crises de coeur,* and tendencies inherent in her personality found meaning in a longing for the Absolute conditioned by a flight into nothingness that is structured on a conscious level by concepts culled from Indian philosophy. Herder's distorted version of Bhartṛhari's poem was the final "garden path" along which she strayed. Along what other garden paths might her curiosity have led her? The Indian source material that could validate Günderrode's pessimistic interpretation of Indian philosophy was limited. It involves a simple piece of detective work to discover that the only philosophical text available in translation at the time of her compositions was Wilkins's translation of the *Bhagavad Gītā*.[46] The only additional clue suggesting possible sources of inspiration appears in a letter[47] from Lisette Nees von Esenbeck dating from 2, July 1804, referring to Karoline's extensive reading of Schelling.[48]

In *Vom Ich als Principe der Philosophie* (1795),[49] Schelling presents the Self as the Absolute Self. The goal of existence is the fusion of the individual "I" with the Absolute through the overcoming of *māyā* (illusion), which makes us believe in plurality. These concepts are pure Śaṅkara[50] and pure Advaita Vedānta.[51] The *Upanishads,* a source of this philosophy, were not yet translated in 1795.[52] Schelling's source, therefore, was the *Bhagavad Gītā,* which was not a part of the *Upanishads,* but Vedāntic and available from 1785 onward. We may assume from his *Magisterdissertation* and his mythological publications[53] that Schelling was ignorant of both Indian philosophy and mythology in 1793. However, by 1802–3, he shows a knowledge of Indian literary texts,[54] and by 1804 nondualism had become a part of his philosophy.[55] At this time, he wrote not only about the sloughing off of the ego but also the destruction of the affective life through an ascetic ideal.[56]

Thus, Karoline's inspiration came either from an interpolation of Schelling's material or from her own pessimistic reading of the *Bhagavad Gītā*. Clearly, the "Geschichte" 's call to renounce the bonds of action reflects an understanding of the *Bhagavad Gītā*. Similarly, the individual soul's union with the All-Soul, addressed in "Ein apokaliptisches Fragment" and the "Geschichte", are essential constructs of that Sanskrit text. Günderrode's conception of a reabsorption of the soul into an *Urkraft* offers a simplification of the *Gītā's* enunciation of the Sāṃkhya doctrine.[57] These themes will continue to be crucial and resonate throughout our study of the reception of Indian thought. The point at which both Schelling and (to a much greater extent) Günderrode stray from Hindu orthodoxy is this: The *Bhagavad Gītā* most assuredly presents the *karma mārga* (the path of action) as superior to the *jñāna mārga* (the path of knowledge). Knowledge has value only insofar as it leads to action. Neither Schelling nor Günderrode understood this fundamental Hindu truth. In the "Geschichte" and the "Briefe," Günderrode presented salvation in death. Clearly, she believed what she wrote.

At some indeterminate point, a superficial knowledge of exotic fatalism became belief for Günderrode. Unlike Leopardi's, Günderrode's pessimism could not provide her with the strength and resignation to combat her personal pathology, nor, as we see from the preceding discussion, could it be harnessed in a cogent body of poetic expression. Most important, Günderrode's pessimistic misreading of Indian religious theories of being-in-the-world became a rationale for actions arising out of tendencies inherent in the poet's own nature and reactions to the vicissitudes of life. In her work, she presented a belief that death is an escape from life, and she justified this belief with the partial view of Indian philosophy available to her. That she chose to die young, in a theatrical manner, in nature and at sunset, is consistent with her desire to transform her fatal resolution into narrative form.

It is indeed curious how the poem of Bhartṛhari, which was to herald the hoped-for riches of Sanskrit literature, became, through its use by Günderrode, an alibi for despair. Indian religious themes moved from being an ideal of spiritual strength apart from daily life in the world to a rationale for death, with the view that death equals transcendence of earthly pain and reunification with the Absolute.

2

Rationalist Heroes and Irrational Victims: Satīs, *Bayaderas, and Pariahs*

I

Exoticism sought to transcend limits and redefine structures. In a theological sense, it provided a virulent critique of Biblical revelation and a challenge to abuses of the Church. On the social level, it neutralized the political power of the nobility. Beginning in the seventeenth century, social analysts had examined, through the idealizing myth of the noble savage, human survival in nature. Primitives, by virtue of the fact that they were freed from political and religious restraints, functioned as ideal projections of modern man. Calling into question the equation of culture and progress, exoticism thus satirized the origins of power. As Hayden White noted in *Tropics of Discourse,*[1] the exotic effected not so much an elevation of the primitive as the metaphorical *mise à mort* of the noble. European travel literature, as well as poetry and drama set in India, exhibit this tendency in exoticism to redefine socio-religious structure through satire.

Three marginal figures—the self-sacrificing widow, the ritual prostitute, and the pariah—exhibit this tendency more than anything else native to India. Continuing a tradition begun in the eighteenth century, India was used to mask a sharp critique of Western mores, politics, and belief. The widespread appearance of these characters in European artistic representations suggests the extent to which European exoticism satisfied a nostalgia for lost values and innocence. By questioning the status of the *satī,*[2] bayadera,[3] and pariah, authors could criticize Europe's own social ills without fear of censorship. Of course, the very choice of these characters catered to European tastes for the lascivious, grotesque, and barbarian. Thus, on the more general level, the emplotment of these figures supports the conceptual framework of doubleness articulated in the Introduction.

II

Depictions of exotic characters and locales did not only serve as a critique of European corruption. The exotic provided models for self-definition. Shortly before Günderrode took her life, she composed "Die Malabarischen Witwen." This poem depicted the *satī*'s self-immolation on her deceased husband's funeral pyre as the pinnacle of eroticism:

> Women go to the banks of the Indus
> For a death by fire,
> They go with their husbands, in their youth,
> Without hesitation and without song,
> Adorned in finery,
> As in bridal costumes.
> The custom understood the meaning of love,
> Released them from the harsh humiliation of separation;
> They consecrated death itself as their priest
> And gave immortality to their marriage bonds.
> Even separation did not threaten such a union,
> Since the previously disunited flames of love
> Fall together ardently into one.
> Death becomes a sweet festival of love;
> It unites the separated elements.
> The end of existence becomes the pinnacle of life.[4]

Considering the ritualistic contours of Günderrode's death, it is not surprising that she imbued that *satī*'s act with devotional meaning; nor is it absurd to suggest that, with her own death, she masqueraded as a *satī*. In "Die Malabarischen Witwen," Günderrode employs the exotic to ennoble her own despair and valorize her own imminent suicide.

It is clear that Günderrode had no orthodox understanding of the *satī*'s act. She incorporated the widow's sacrifice as part of a personal distortion of Indian religious belief. The *satī* functioned as a symbol of transcendence, self-immolation being only one path among many. Death on the Rhine was equally symbolic. What was important was that, for Günderrode, the *satī*'s act consolidated honor after rejection, brought about an eternal union with the beloved in death, fulfilled a vague religious longing for integration, and, most significantly, provided the erotic pinnacle of earthly existence. Even in light of the hypertrophied emotionalism that was endemic to German Romanticism, the melodramatic message of this poem is simply excessive. However, Günderrode's distortion of the *satī*'s ritual was not the unique expression of her despairing mind but was consistent with European discourse on suttee. The texts upon which this discourse was constructed consisted of eyewitness accounts, by Western voyagers and missionaries, that were either recorded directly or related secondhand. In other words, these texts were neither objective nor free from distortion.

One of the earliest comments on suttee, made by the Italian Hieronimo di Santo Stefano in 1499, presents the *satī*'s sacrifice as a common practice among Indian wives.[5] Another Italian voyager, Ludovigo di Varthema, in 1510 relates in greater detail the celebration surrounding the *satī*, her ritual clothing, the feast, the music, the dancing, and the act of immolation itself. Varthema comments that the women are often drugged into submission by priests who are "clothed like devils" and may coerce them into killing themselves.[6] In disgust, he notes that the fire is accelerated by adding balls of pitch. If the *satī* does not die quickly, she is recognized by her family to be a whore. The Genovese traveler Pietro della Valle in 1626 describes a woman who wished to burn herself out of love for her husband. Della Valle and Varthema in no way sentimentalize the *satī* or her self-sacrifice. However, another Italian, Nicolo de Conti, refers to self-immolation as a means by which wives gain honor and make themselves more acceptable to their husbands. He too places blame upon the brahmin priests who exhort the women to hold life in contempt. These same priests, he notes, are even capable of throwing a woman into the flames if her courage fails.[7] De Conti romanticizes the *satī*'s martyrdom by describing it as a burning (in the sense of passionate) embrace that the *satī* bestows on her husband. Although imbuing the *satī*'s act with sexual overtones, de Conti, along with his compatriots, condemns it as cruel torture. In these early accounts, the tension between erotic fascination and moral repugnance that will remain a central dynamic of the Western representation of this ritual is already present.

The Portuguese travelers ignored the erotic potential and the barbarism of the *satī*'s act and tended to focus on the issue of honor. Tomé Pires, writing in 1512–13, notes that only honorable wives become *satīs*. Although the brahmin officiants are known to coerce them, some women recoil before the flames. The refusal to become a *satī* results in dire consequences: The woman is forced to live the remainder of her life as a temple prostitute.[8] Duarte Barbosa in 1514 makes this same point. Not only does the *satī* establish her honor, but this sacrifice allowed women of lesser value and social standing to upgrade themselves.[9] While alive, husbands owe respect to their wives because they are potentially capable of such devotion. Women, likewise, should learn from the *satī*'s act and respect their husbands in emulation of it. The erotic undertones and moral didacticism prevalent in the travel literature found its way into subsequent emplotments of this figure.

Pierre Sonnerat's *Voyage aux Indes orientales*, first published in 1765,[10] contributed significantly to the dissemination of information concerning widow-burning. His widely read and richly illustrated travel account relates an instance of self-immolation as a trial of love. Sonnerat's rendition of the tale was particularly titillating to his readers by virtue of the fact that his *satī* was not a devoted wife but a *fille de joie* whose feelings overcame her professionalism. In this manner, the *satī* narrative converges with that of the bayadera, or ritual prostitute.[11] The surprising devotion of the bayadera/*satī* does not go unrewarded. The man for whom she is willing to sacrifice herself is, in fact, a god who bestows the gift of immortality upon her. This particular myth, as told by Sonnerat, captured the European reader's fancy, although similar renditions of the tale were recounted earlier, by Rogerius in *Offne Thür zu dem verborgenen Heidenthum* (1663)[12] and subsequently, by Dorville in his *Histoire des differens peuples du monde* (1770).[13]

The interest that Sonnerat's rendition elicited was perhaps due to his emphasis that true love and devotion could be found in any woman no matter how low she had sunk. In fact, with typically irreverent Gallic wit, Sonnerat commented that Indian society could not be all bad if they had such a high estimation of whores that they immortalized them. (The use of the term *whore* is intentional; other historical accounts use euphemisms, but Sonnerat consistently uses the word *putain*.)[14] These historical accounts differ from earlier treatments of the custom in that they use a myth to rationalize what was too strange an act for Westerners to comprehend.

By framing the ritual in a mythological context, Sonnerat, Rogerius, and Dorville displace disgust from the act itself and exploit its comic and romantic potentialities in much the same manner as did Voltaire in *Zadig* (1747). In the chapter entitled "Le bûcher," Voltaire has Zadig convince Almona not to throw herself into the flames. She admits that she seeks self-immolation only to gratify her vanity and in deference to religious prejudice. Zadig then asks the chiefs to abolish the custom or en act a law forcing widows to spend an hour with a young man before they decide to sacrifice themselves. Although in this instance Voltaire seemed to make light of the practice, he was actually quite incensed by the *satī*'s fate. He condemned it elsewhere, most notably in the *Questions sur l'Encyclopédie* under the rubric "Bracmanes, Brames." Voltaire sympathized with the *satī* less out of concern for her suffering than out of moral outrage; she represented the ideal victim of religious superstition.

Herder, equally a vociferous critic of Indian social customs, deplored the practice of widow burning. Voltaire's contention that it existed as one of the evil consequences of the Hindu belief in metempsychosis was also echoed by Herder in the *Ideen*. Herder noted that the *satī,* by her act, gains entrance into heaven for both her self and her husband. He attributed the origin of the practice to the lack of compassion endemic to Hinduism and Indian social organization.[15] Herder strongly criticized the *satī*'s motives: She was either aping some false conception of holiness or submitting to death as punishment. He blamed the brahmin priests for having ennobled such an unnatural practice and for willfully deceiving the *satī* with the promise of rewards in a future life. In fact, he saw the institution of widow burning as a cheap trick to make men's lives—and consequently, men themselves—more valuable to women. Herder's comment raised a larger ethical question: Was love, even in its most intense manifestation, worth possessing if it was elicited by deceit? Voltaire's anticlerical diatribes and Herder's moral critique reverberated in subsequent emplotments of the *satī* figure. Poetically, she evoked pity, displayed moral courage, or expressed the need for social change and the end of religious tyranny, as in Goethe's poem "Der Gott und die Bajadere" (1797).

Goethe presents a Christ-like Indian god who descends to earth in order to test the quality of human love. A young bayadera, with the allure of a prostitute,[16] offers him hospitality. The god's fatigue is soothed and his heart stirred. The bayadera falls in love, and what had previously been commerce becomes devotion.[17] Goethe's poem then becomes a simple tale of redemption. The bayadera awakens the next day to find her lover dead beside her. Despite the priests' protests, she enters the flames of the funeral pyre. This act of selfless love redeems her otherwise unworthy existence. In thanks, her divine lover rises up out of the flames, and together they ascend to heaven. In a journal entry dating from 6–9 June 1797, Goethe acknowledges that "Der Gott und die Bajadere" was inspired by a German translation of Sonnerat's *Voyage,*[18] which he read in 1785. However, Goethe altered his source material considerably, as can be seen by comparing his poem with the original tale.[19]

As we have noted, the strength of Sonnerat's tale resides in its ironic use of a sexually licentious woman as an exemplar of fidelity. Goethe's poem inverts Sonnerat's message by shifting the emphasis from the issue of a whore's faithfulness to that of an absolute, self-sacrificing love bordering on religious devotion that is realizable in all women, no matter what their station. Goethe's unchaste *satī* represents *das ewig Weibliche,* recast as an Indian Mary Magdalene. There is even some speculation among Goethe scholars that the figure of the *satī,* presumably seen by the poet as a sexually loose, low-class woman, symbolized Goethe's common-law wife, Christiane Vulpius. Christiane's rejection by Weimar culture was thus symbolically represented by the *satī*'s rejection at the hands of authoritarian brahmin priests. The tension between the sexually active female and the male authority figure, once embedded in the *satī* narrative, assumed parameters of the exotic model functioning as a vehicle of social and religious satire.

On the dramatic level, the European representation of the *satī,* borrowing its style from pseudoclassical tragedy, was both picturesque and sentimental, as in Metastasio's opera *Alessandro nell'Indie* (1730). Here, too, the *satī*'s love for her dead husband, which was so intense that it could only be sublimated in death, dramatically succeeded when it became a manifestation of unbridled sexual passion. Thus, the association of the *satī* with the bayadera and her subsequent perversion into a "prostitute with a heart of gold," which occurred in the historical literature and in Goethe's poem, was retained in subsequent dramatic and operatic presentations.

In 1801, the then-valued composer Charles Simon Catel wrote the music for an opera entitled *Les bayadères* from a text by Joseph Étienne, *dit* de Jouy. Here, too, the *satī* is a fallen woman who evinces absolute love for a superior male. A king has to choose a wife from among the three best women in his realm. He loves the bayadera Lamea, but cannot approach her because she is consecrated to a god. The plot develops through intrigues, the betrayal of a leader, and the imprisonment of the king. Having promised the enemy that she will kill the king, Lamea rescues and spirits him home to victory and celebration. The king, although desiring to marry Lamea, is prevented by her religious obligations. Only when he is believed moribund, and no woman except Lamea will agree to enter his funeral pyre, does her selfless love become apparent to all. A religious procession leads her to the pyre, where she finds the king alive and they wed.[20]

Another *satī*/bayadera opera, *Dieu et la bayadère ou la courtisane amoureuse,* composed in 1833 by Auber, with a libretto by Scribe, enjoyed tremendous success with 148 performances. This opera further exploited the ironic theme of the *satī* as prostitute. The God Brama (*sic*), dramatically portrayed as the *mystérieux étranger,* elicits the love of a bayadera. He has descended to earth in order to regain his divine status through the experience of faithful love. Condemned to the flames for having protected the disguised God, the *satī* is miraculously saved and ascends to heaven wrapped in Brama's arms. The *satī*'s unselfish love has purified her of wanton desire.

When *Dieu et la bayadère* was reprised in Paris in 1837, Théophile Gautier wrote a critical review.[21] His interest in the character of the bayadera changed considerably when, in the following year, he saw a troupe of authentic *devadāsīs* perform in Paris.[22] He found their dancing an endless enchantment. The bayaderas' performance was to give him the criterion by which he could "authoritatively" judge any aspect of India. The troupe appeared again at the Théâtre des Variétés in August 1838;[23] the spectacle was successful on both an artistic and a financial level. For Gautier, the mere term *bayadera* evoked a range of images.[24] Bayaderas are artifacts of the phantom India found in our dreams. They comprise a poetic fantasy come to life, *l'amour teint en noir:*[25] savage, perfumed, and capable of driving men to excesses.[26] Amani, the most beautiful of the troupe, particularly inspires Gautier's grandiloquence. She moves like a sparrow. Her skin is the color of a female panther's fur. To the touch, it is like rice paper and colder than a lizard's belly. Amani was an inexhaustible source of inspiration.[27] Whenever Gautier subsequently looked at an Indian, he thought of Amani, although he never saw her again.[28] Shortly after her visit to Paris, she hung herself in London "*par un excès de spleen.*"[29] She is the artist doomed to destruction. However, as the poem that introduces this volume suggests, the bayadera is also the erotic figure who beckons at the edge of the abyss for a generation of poets enthralled by the exotic.

It was in her death that Amani most inspired Gérard de Nerval. He would end his life in the same manner. The bayadera appears on several occasions in Nerval's work. The name *Amany* (*sic*) glossed a manuscript of his poem "Erythrea."[30] Nerval had attended the same private performance that had so entranced Gautier. In his review, Nerval associates[31] Amani with Vasantasenā, the rehabilitated courtesan of the *Chariot d'enfant,*[32] and Mamia, a bayadera depicted by the voyager Haafner. The latter was a charming *fille d'amour* who was rehabilitated and died saving her lover, Haafner, from drowning. For Nerval, also, the bayadera is an aesthetic object: She incarnates "*la poesie matérielle et vivante.*"[33]

Whether an aesthetic ideal or art itself, the bayadera is a figure charged with tremendous eroticism. Nerval alone expresses exactly how she was perceived, when, with remarkable candor, he wrote:

> Yes; we have seen the Bayaderas,—we have even *touched* the Bayaderas; but in the most proper sense of the word, and only to convince ourselves that their skin was really *golden black* and not dyed with some mixture of licorice juice. . . . Yes, they are certainly Oriental beauties, and their face bears the unimpeachable traces of a primitive and unmixed race. You would have perhaps imagined them to be whiter, but not better built, livlier or more seductive.[34]

Let us ignore for a moment the fact that she was an Indian dancer; the fact that she was a prostitute sufficed, and allowed her to be encoded in the general representation of the prostitute in French literature. In a recent study, Charles Bernheimer has shown how nineteenth-century French literature dealt with the integration of the impure yet compassionate prostitute into society.[35]

A "male" plot effecting redemptive revirgination through love also occurs in conjunction with the portrayal of the sexually debased woman as the pure child of nature.[36] The configuration of the prostitute, virtue, and nature prevalent in this literature set the stage for the arrival of the bayadera. As noted already, in French literature and art, women of such qualities and skills had become clichés. In the flesh-and-blood figure of the bayadera, it was almost as if nineteenth-century French authors had found the "real thing."

The bayadera's power as a poetic image derived from the tension she posed between race[37] and the erotic. Flaubert, in his *Dictionnaire des idées reçues,* wrote under the rubric *Bayadère*—"A word which carries away the imagination. All Oriental women are bayaderas (see odalisques)."[38] The full scope of the bayadera's evocative potentiality is reflected in Flaubert's correspondence:

> I dream of bayaderas, frenetic dances and all the din of color.[39]

> Up until now, one understood something shimmering, roaring, empassioned, halting. One only saw bayaderas and curved sabers, fanaticism, voluptuousness, etc.[40]

> One day when I have some imagination, when I would have thought . . . about bayaderas on the banks of the Ganges I will intercalate the most beautiful page ever written; but I warn you in advance that it will be superb, monstrous, horribly lewd.[41]

> Dance, dance, bayadera, daughter of the Ganges, twirl your feet around and around in my head! Like a snake, she curls up and makes her arms more supple, her head moves, her hips sway, her nostrils flare, her hair comes undone.[42]

Even Emma Bovary is likened to a bayadera:

> You were there also, sultans with long pipes, swooning under the bower, with the arms of a bayadera.[43]

> Sarabandes that just wouldn't stop rolled around in her head, and, like a bayadera on the flowers of a carpet, her thoughts sprang up with the notes, swayed from dream to dream, from sadness to sadness.[44]

In European literature, the bayadera/*satī* is always saved by love, either divine love in the form of grace or mortal affection that results in marriage. When she escapes death with the aid of a man, the man is either a pariah who has nothing to lose or a European who is empowered by reason, as in *La veuve du Malabar ou l'empire des coutumes.*

This popular *tragédie-manifeste* by Lemierre opened in 1770. The Enlightenment battle against the power of religious superstitions and customs is set against the backdrop of European imperial designs. The French, led by the handsome General Montalban, besiege Malabar in hopes of liberating it from the tyranny of brahmin priests and their murderous laws. Concerned with civilian conditions, the general sends scouts into the city and discovers that the priests are preparing for a *satī*'s sacrifice. Horrified, he invades Malabar and saves the would-be *satī,* only to learn that she is an Indian whom he loved in his youth. *La veuve du Malabar* was so popular that it inspired several operatic adaptations[45] and parodies.

When not employed as a vehicle for political or religious satire, European dramas featuring the *satī* easily degenerated into sexual farce. In Hervé's parody of *La veuve du Malabar,*[46] a Parisian merchant seeks his fortune in India. He succeeds to such an extent that he can marry the Indian princess of Lahore. However, the parvenu bourgeois discovers that she is none other than his Parisian mistress who has been exiled to India. When the merchant is believed to have been killed, there is a clamor for the false princess to burn herself on the pyre. Then, in a scene reminiscent of Aristophanes, the Indian women rebel against the ritual and prevent it. Another operatic parody of *La veuve du Malabar*[47] presents a Frenchman in India who has become trapped in marriage by an indigenous *cocotte*. The wife desires to rid herself of her husband and move to Paris. She feigns drowning in the hope that her husband will throw *himself* on *her* funeral pyre. While the authors of these parodies were primarily interested in depicting the *satī* of the café-concert, they contributed to the literature by bringing the feminist militancy, always underlying the self-sacrificing courage of the rebellious *satī*, to the forefront of their narratives.

We can isolate several major themes of the eighteenth-century emplotments of the bayadera/*satī* figure. Even when the narrative plot appears most absurd, the bayadera/*satī* literature expresses the conflict between Voltairean enlightened reason and the fanaticism of religious customs, usually personified by the brahmin priest. A recent study of exoticism in German opera has shown how "Indian" operas always present brahmins as incarnations of evil. In numerous cases, Hindu religious fanatics condemn the innocent to death only to have their designs thwarted by the "good" European colonialist.[48] While a case can be made for situating the bayadera/*satī* solidly within the discourses of Enlightenment anticlericism and Western misogyny, it would ignore her role within this literature as a courageous rebel against social rigidity. The bayadera/*satī* not only animated the libidinous reveries of certain nineteenth-century authors and was a sympathetic victim of religious superstition, but she effectively challenged societal values. In this sense, she often functioned in conjunction with, and in the same way as, another character popular in nineteenth-century exotic literature and artistic representation, the pariah. Although lacking the rampant sexual charms of the bayadera/*satī*, the pariah was no less forceful a character. Together they support our claim that this literature was primarily social.

III

Bernardin de Saint-Pierre's short novel, *La chaumière indienne* (1790), tells the story of an Englishman who, having traveled the world over in search of truth and happiness, finds himself in Bengal. There he is thwarted in his quest by the ignorant pride of brahmin priests. Upon leaving them, the Englishman is caught in a storm and graciously received by a pariah and his would-be *satī* wife, who relate the story of their romance. The pariah had first met his wife mourning the death of her *satī* mother. Together they weep over this victim of religious prejudice, recognizing that a *satī* is even more unfortunate than a pariah. On a subsequent encounter, the pariah learns that the young woman herself is destined to suffer the ignominious fate of her mother on the pyre of her own aged and unloved husband. Upon the pariah's entreaty, she breaks the bonds of superstition that bind her to society. As a supreme act of rebellion, she runs off to live with the pariah and bear his children.

These outcastes then proceed to answer all the Englishman's questions on the nature of existence. Their resemblance to the self-sacrificing heroes of the author's masterpiece *Paul et Virginie* suggests to what extent these exotic figures owe their characteristics to the Romantic image of the noble savage. They possess intelligence from nature, which has been their temple, book, and refuge. Through them, the Englishman understands that truth resides not in a mind troubled by desire and hunger for power, but in a simple heart devoid of selfishness and purified by its contact with nature. For Bernardin de Saint-Pierre, the pariah and wife have become evangelicals: They love their enemies and practice poverty. Most importantly, they are living proof that there can be no happiness for a man without a good wife—in this case, the *satī,* who has renounced social prejudice and chosen life over a senseless death. Here both are clearly disenfranchised victims of religious prejudice, displaying a sense of social protest reminiscent of the hypothetical legislators of Rousseau's social contract.[49] Bernardin de Saint-Pierre explicitly identifies the *satī*'s fate with that of the pariah, an idea that was only implied by other European authors. In this context, the outcastes are abstract symbols of the oppressed.

Michael Beer voiced his own discrimination as a German Jew in his depiction of the Indian pariah's plight. The hero of *Der Paria* (1821) has also rescued a *satī* from death and married her. Their unholy union[50] is later discovered. Lest they be tortured and killed, they eat poisoned fruit. Like Bernardin de Saint-Pierre's pariah, Beer's outcaste is extremely articulate, and given to philosophizing.[51]

In Casimir Delavigne's drama *Le paria* (1821), an ambitious outcaste leaves home seeking to improve his lot beyond the confines of the forest. Disguised as a respectable Hindu, he goes to Benares and successfully leads troops against the Portuguese. His talents gradually raise him to the rank of supreme commander and gain him the love of the high priest's daughter. The pariah confesses his true status to her, and they plan to wed. His beloved, although at first shocked by his revelation, renounces her prejudice upon hearing the impassioned plea that all persons are equal in God's eyes. However, before the marriage can take place, the pariah's identity is discovered. He is abandoned by his people and stoned to death. Disgusted by society's murderous prejudice, his beloved renounces civilization and retires to the forest.

Beer, Delavigne, and Bernardin de Saint-Pierre present characterizations of spiritually enlightened pariahs that neither capture the reality of the Indian context nor are acts of appropriation true to their objects. Obviously, these authors' intention was not to depict Indian life realistically, but rather to present consistently drawn, idealized "savages" who emphasized positive traits that were felt to be sorely lacking in European society. In fact, they exhibit uniquely meritorious qualities: Prostitutes are faithful unto death, and pariahs are wise, long-suffering, and forgiving. In the face of torture and death, these exotic figures console themselves with platitudes and offer lofty philosophical thoughts.

The pariah characters, although their virtue can never be faulted, lack a certain psychological depth. Goethe's "Paria" trilogy,[52] however, revitalized what had become a trite and sentimental image. Written in 1824, Goethe's poetic triptych consists of a legend that is framed by a prayer of supplication and a prayer of gratitude. The legend itself is a subtle expression of innocence and guilt, representing the bifurcation of human nature between the spiritual and the physical.

A brahmin wife fetches water daily without the aid of a vessel. Her magical power is a result of her purity. One day, while collecting water from the Ganges, she sees the form of a young god mirrored in the water. The "impure" lust that this glimpse of the god engenders and the subsequent guilt deprive her of magical power. Upon the wife's return home, her husband discovers her "sin" and decapitates her. Their son attaches his mother's head to one of two corpses he happens to find, and seals the wound magically before he realizes that he has connected his mother's head to a pariah's body. She possesses the wise head of a brahmin wife and the necessarily depraved body of a pariah. Reassembled according to the imaginary prescriptions of a male subject, Goethe's recreated woman must now seek to mediate between conflicting desires.[53] Through God's grace, this reconstructed woman eventually succeeds in reconciling the dictates of the spirit and the flesh. The pariah, for whom she has become a paradigm, recognizes the parable's truth. In the prayer of gratitude, he reaffirms human equality.[54]

It is not without significance that "Der Gott und die Bajadere" and the "Paria" trilogy, both composed late in life after many years of reflection and interest in Sanskrit literature, were Goethe's only incursions into the Indian domain. That Goethe chose to write about these two figures alone reaffirms not only their parallelism but also suggests the ultimate significance of the bayadera/pariah literature.

IV

Viewed as a whole, the European representations of these figures illustrate various functions of the exotic. The artificial introduction of the plight of the bayadera/*satī* and pariah foregrounds a larger European intellectual concern with the moral ramifications of transmigration. By stressing evident social evils, Europeans expressed their moral abhorrence of the belief in transmigration that created these customs. In fact, the bayadera/pariah literature intentionally subverts this pivotal issue, disregarding the function of transmigration as the philosophical rationale for caste exclusion. The Indian system incarnates, therefore, societal and religious prejudice that can be put aside with an act of will. Secondary Indian characters become true children of the Enlightenment when they sympathize with a European moral stance. In Delavigne's *Le paria,* the brahmin wife, although initially shocked by the revelation of her husband's pariah status, quickly renounces prejudice.

The Hindu doctrine of transmigration—that one is reborn in a form commensurate with one's actions in a previous existence—was not unknown to the nineteenth-century Europeans; they were familiar with it through their reading of classical[55] and travel[56] literature. Moreover, a collective interest in death and the afterlife was particularly prevalent in Germany of the Enlightenment and the post-Enlightenment. Speculations about a continued life in a future state can also be attributed to conventional conceptions of immortality. The writings of Klopstock and Wieland and the poetry of Young, Grey, and Ossian fed this fixation on death. In eighteenth-century works dealing with death, even when reincarnation was not specifically suggested, there appeared an optimistic expectation of reunions in the afterlife.[57] If the *satī*'s sacrifice aimed at nothing more than the reunion of husband and wife in a future life (an idea that was attractive to literary sensibilities), why did it warrant the condemnation that it engendered in French and German literature? Clearly, Europeans could not view the *satī*'s death as a matter of romantic wish-fulfillment. Nor was its brutality the primary cause of censure. As we have seen from this literature, the cruelty of the act was not overly emphasized. A more likely reason for its condemnation was that its determined self-affliction and disrespect for life was seen as symptomatic of a dangerously fatalistic Indian worldview. Indeed, as we shall see in subsequent chapters, fatalism became an increasingly fateful lure for artists and writers. Similarly, what European readers found abhorrent was not the pariah's condemnation to a life of inequity, but, rather, the fact that his fate precluded both divine grace and forgiveness.

Some European writers speculated on the positive effects of metempsychosis,[58] but for the most part this concept was seen as too deterministic. In *Zerstreute Blätter,* Herder presented his thoughts on metempsychosis in Christian terms as a primitive expression of penance.[59] When he wrote *Palingenesis* some twelve years later, Herder rejected his earlier conception of metempsychosis; he now saw it to be a delusion of the senses[60] and blamed it[61] for a plethora of India's social ills, including the pariah's and the *satī*'s status.[62] He noted, however, that a great lesson could be learned from this delusion—that one should be ruled by reason.[63] Was not this rationalist imperative at work in the use of the exotic in general and the *satī*/pariah cliché in particular? Just as Herder's comments on metempsychosis sounded the clarion call of the Enlightenment, so did the European *satī*/pariah literature echo a condemnation of religious prejudice and social rigidity. From Voltaire on, this literature allowed authors to articulate their hatred of the Church as hypocritical and brutal, without the Church being French or Catholic, and with its prejudiced clerics being brahmins and not Jesuits. Indian characters such as the *satī,* pariah, and bayadera became true children of the Enlightenment when they sympathized with this critical moral stance.

The abundance and rich intertextuality of the bayadera/*satī*/pariah literature supports the contention that the exotic was fashioned in neither a hasty nor a negligent manner. Indian exoticism served the dual purpose of introducing the strange and unknown and challenging bourgeois values and sensibilities. Consistently drawn and idealized characters, emphasizing positive traits that were felt to be sorely lacking in European society, suggest that the exotic did not merely seek to enrich poetic vocabularies with tableaux of hypertrophied landscapes. Goethe's "Gott und die Bajadere" exemplified the sophisticated use of the exotic to displace the reader in time and space in order to draw universal conclusions about mankind.

These various exotic poems, dramas, and operas follow the consistent paradoxical pattern we have attributed to exoticism. While prodding the reader to question certain sociosexual presuppositions, this literature simultaneously expresses a darker message. Günderrode pushed the *satī* metaphor to its natural conclusion, one that was implied in the *satī* narrative's expression of obsessional devotion and fatal eroticism: A male India of fanatics and despots incarnating superstitious fatalism and arbitrary power confronts the female India of sexual license and matrimonial rigor. In response, the bayadera/*satī* transforms her desire into an oblation. Sex produces "the supreme poetry of the néant-vivant."[64] It represents erosion, loss, absence, and death. The motive of suicidal disgust with life was met by a temptation to overcome that disgust through some extraordinarily foreign agency. "Die Malabarischen Witwen" and, to a greater extent, Günderrode's suicide reflect the morbidity of desire and passionate fidelity that this literature espoused.[65]

The strength of the bayadera/*satī* comes from the absolute and selfless love she evinces for the king/god. The pariah embodies a Christ-like ideal and incarnates the virtues of a model husband and father. Their status as exemplars of bourgeois virtue is more salient because it arises from ironic character traits: The bayadera is righteous in her unchastity and abnegation, and the pariah's sophisticated wisdom develops from a simple heart and contact with nature. However, they live their lives in direct violation of European taboos. The pariah does not know his place and leads would-be *satī*s astray. The bayadera represents promiscuity incarnate. Her exemplary behavior questions the moral implications of rigid gender roles. "La Veuve du Malabar," like the other European representations of the *satī,* is forced to redefine her moral stance and allegiance to duty in order to gain redemption.

The *satī* and pariah further controvert social structure by espousing the radical ideal of disobedience to religion and state. Pariahs and prostitutes are exemplars of virtue, but integral members of society they are not. Only in the rejection of and by society can the bayadera and pariah find their strength and wisdom. Marginality alone ensures their privileged status.

This literature catered to the popular desire to believe in the power of natural goodness, to expose corruption, and reform social inequities, while playing upon the cliché of the aggressively sexual women as irremediably evil and polluted. In her initial impulse to become a *satī,* a woman is an exemplar of virtue; in her decision not to, a child of the Enlightenment. In these narratives, the Enlightenment's liberal concern for women's rights did not demand that these women be brought back to society. Rather, it allowed them to recover their natural power over men, which derived from their submission as loving wives and mothers.[66] At all times, the bayadera supports a conservative patriarchal ideology: A loving prostitute suggests the possibility of exciting sexual encounters while exemplifying the renunciation of predatory female sexuality. The virtue of the bayadera, *satī,* and pariah, and the fact that their virtue is embedded in acts of transgression, suggests the extent to which the exotic serves to elucidate the human condition and suggest alternative modes of behavior.

Travel literature and primitivism had long since conditioned the reading public to question some of the more vaunted achievements of rationalistic culture. Kant had proclaimed that the modern State resulted from the progressive development of humanity. How was one to reconcile such theories with the perception that many primitive peoples are happier and better off than inhabitants of the civilized world? In accordance with popular Enlightenment propaganda, one could simply render these noble savages as more sophisticated than their modern counterparts and recognize their wisdom to be a direct expression of their feelings. The *philosophes* believed in the unity of mankind and held that all individuals subsisted under the same natural law of right and reason. They supposed that all men would participate alike in progress and that the outcome of history would be one of uniform civilization in which all peoples and races would share equally. The Enlightenment's unquestioned belief in the potential similarity of all human beings and in freedom from intolerance and ignorance had not been realized. As Herder would maintain in the *Ideen,* even without the benefits of Western culture, one has the potential of ascending to the ideal of infinite perfection. The bayadera/*satī*/pariah literature set out to prove this very issue by presenting the ethical theme of *Humanität,* the knowledge of good in evil, guilt in innocence, and the recognition of common suffering among mortals, regardless of caste, sex, or position.

Certain early-nineteenth-century authors recognized that the European caste system was such that it did not immediately accept the existence of any cultural values in the *Stände* below the middle class.[67] The belief that the lower classes were barbaric vestiges of the Dark Ages still prevailed. Moreover, the artists realized that an effective integration between society and their self-understanding no longer existed.[68] Sensing themselves, to a greater or lesser degree, displaced in bourgeois, industrialized society, these artists created in the pariah/bayadera literature an ideal, primitive, and fictive society that became a metaphorical locale for the expression of values of justice and equality that remained unfulfilled in the rational West. In this manner, European writers used the exotic to attack the complacency of the age, which seemed to believe that all sociosexual progress was complete. Indian exoticism thus satisfied a specific bourgeois intellectual desire—to emphasize, by means of a metaphorical spatial displacement, the need and possibility of a new social geography. However, as this cluster of exotic clichés suggests, Indian exoticism did not merely provide a positive model for effective social satire. Simultaneously, this literature exhibited a strategy linking artistic self-reflection to images redolent of sexually and politically charged fantasies signifying structural collapse and moral decay. The need for a source of inspiration beyond the boundaries of the European cultural milieu and the projection onto India as the locus of a darker truth were expressions of a significant dynamic inscribed within the exoticist project. They were not confined to the tortured psyches of poets or to what was dramatically effective. In part II, we will see how the tension between these creative impulses articulated itself in early nineteenth-century scholarship.

PART II

THE POLITICS OF LANGUAGE AND THE POLITICS OF EXOTICISM

Introduction

Out of the *Aufklärung,* with its affection for similarity and belief in the brotherhood of all mankind, there developed a progressive sense of individual self-identity, freedom of interpretation incommensurate with the rigid and confined social reality, and the promise of gradual reform within the context of the *Standestaat.* Historical *Sprachwissenschaft* could not have emerged in the period between 1765 and 1780 without the precondition of historical self-consciousness, the idealistic progressive system of values provided by the Enlightenment. Many historical works of the Enlightenment sought answers to the question of human origin. While the valorization of the German language always played a role in the ideology of origins, one should not judge this discourse as an initial expression of chauvinistic, racist, or fascist teaching, nor should one forget that the *Humanitätsidee* provided a conceptualization of humanity as equal, albeit separate.[1]

The problem of human origin stimulated interest in the roots of language. By studying Indo-European linguistic roots, scholars sought to discover humanity's earliest ancestors, their words and their deeds. In the eighteenth century, debates on the problem of the origin of language can be found in the works of Rousseau, Diderot, Court de Gebelin, Condillac, Turgot, and Maupertius. Typological arguments (regarding historical or geographical connections between peoples, with common descent accounting for grammatical structures) were confused with historical arguments. Sanskrit figured prominently in European attempts to discover the universal language. Much of this linguistic paleontology sought to decipher this lost language and its unknown people, who lived in a mythic-poetic age.[2]

Recent studies in the history of science, particularly the work of Foucault[3] and Feyerabend,[4] have departed from the assumptions of traditional historical research and concerned themselves with the relationship between theoretical and societal conditions essential to a critical reconstructive history of science. However, as Habermas has noted, a detailed interfacing between scholarly research, institutions of the production and distribution of knowledge, the subject these produced, and the relation to other subsystems in the public sphere has never effectively been investigated.[5] I shall not attempt this, to my mind, nearly impossible task. Rather, I would like to examine, with reference to the problem of institutionalization, how certain internal and external factors converge in the social-scientific construction of the discipline of early Indology. I limit my remarks to the issue of language theory rather than the more developed and specialized science of linguistics; my remarks are restricted to the study of Sanskrit as a field of inquiry. I shall chart the inception of Sanskrit studies in the emergence of the Romantic theory of language through the initial development of philology as a discursive institution with a specific historical organization of knowledge and textual strategies. Because the emergence and development of philology in the nineteenth century were primarily German phenomena, special emphasis will be placed on the German discourse on language.

Our investigation begins in 1786, the year that might be considered the beginning of historical lingustics. In this year, in an address to the Royal Asiatic Society in Calcutta, Sir William Jones established the historical kinship between Sanskrit, Latin, Greek, and the Germanic languages.[6] Before Jones's pronouncements, others had speculated on the similarity between the Sanskrit language and European tongues. B. Schulze and Père Coeurdoux had earlier made the same discovery. In 1538, the Jesuit Thomas Stephens had noticed a structural relationship between Sanskrit and Latin. The Florentine Filippo Sassetti had commented on the similarity between Sanskrit and Italian.[7] In 1686, Andreas Jäger had discussed the relationship between languages of what we today term the "Indo-European" family. It was, however, Jones who—with his translations from Sanskrit and speculative articles in *Asiatick Researches* (beginning in 1786)—brought the linguistic affinities between Sanskrit, classical, and European languages to a larger audience of learned Europeans.

Speculation concerning the original language centered on the issue of language's origin. In 1704, Leibniz proposed that an understanding of language held the key to understanding the origins of nations.[8] In 1746, Condillac devoted the second part of the *Essai sur l'origine des connaissances humaines* to this problem, as did Rousseau in 1755 in the *Discours sur l'origine de l'inégalité* and in his posthumous (1782) essay on the origins of language (*Essai sur l'origine des langues*). Condillac held that language represented the genius and character of each people. Once language became associated with the idea of nationhood, it was identified as the source of national character.[9] Both Condillac and Rousseau held that language originates in eidetic and imitative gestures and natural cries, with the phonic element becoming gradually dominant.

In his *Preisschrift* for the Prussian Academy in 1759, Michaelis maintained that language was present at the birth of things and was able to give us the best description of their essential qualities.[10] By 1770, however, the assumptions leading to the Enlightenment conception of language as an arbitrary sign system in service of the representation of ideas or as an external organon for the transference of representations were coming under attack by Herder.

Herder criticized the semiotic and rhetorical distinction common to Enlightenment views between ideas, signs, thoughts, and expressions, and diverted the focus from the arbitrariness of the sign to the reciprocal relationship between language and thought. The Königliche Akademie der Wissenschaft posed the question: Could humanity have developed language unaided, and, if so, how was it accomplished? In the prize-winning essay "Abhandlung über den Ursprung der Sprache" (1770), Herder subscribed to the position of British Enlightenment thinkers John Locke, Adam Smith, and Horne Tooke—that humans themselves had fashioned language. In this fundamental essay, Herder rejected the thesis of Süssmilch, who in 1754 had postulated a divine origin for language.

Herder maintained that language was the result of a conscious human effort to find *Merkmale* for objects, images for things imprinted on the soul by the senses. The original language could not long remain a unity. Groups split off from the main body. Different climatic conditions and geographical surroundings of the language population brought about further changes in the developing languages.[11]

For Herder, who was always guided by the Lutheran theology of Providence,[12] the development of language as well as humanity itself was determined by the successive chain of generations rather than by the individual links.[13] Nevertheless, Herder also placed importance on the role of the individual in this process. Individuals must be aware of the duties and consequences of their actions. This conception of the individual's human, as opposed to social, value led to a new conception of history, which can be seen in Herder's *Ideen*.

Without Herder's critique of historical meaning and semiotic representation, the institutional birth of philological-historical hermeneutics would have been unthinkable. Between 1770 and 1790, traditional philological criticism was transformed by the infusion of conceptions and practices of interpretation. It became established and institutionalized as an independent, comprehensive, scholarly activity that was no longer subordinated to theology and jurisprudence and no longer viewed as an auxiliary discipline for epistemological concerns.[14] This period marked a profound movement away from *Altphilologie* as mere text criticism toward a genuine hermeneutical science, interpretive philology. This shift in orientation initiated a self-reflective encounter with texts and history.

Herder's theory of language's origins, combined with the multiplicity of languages—each contributing to the self-formation of individuals in specific ways[15]— formed the basis for a program of individual education. Herder resisted viewing linguistic constructs as being comprehended in a single moment and as complete, ready-made works (*Kritisches Wäldchen*). Rather, he asserted that they must be continuously interpreted in a process of ongoing self-reflective understanding. Thus his criticism of the purely semantic interpretation of language was implicitly political insofar as it questioned the rulership of ideas and the rational privileged grasp of reality.

Herder's ideological statement, that language opens up for us "ein unermessliches Land von Begriffen,"[16] was not unrelated to progressive political reform. Because language and thinking were interdependent, the thoughts and popular literary patterns of different peoples could be properly understood and studied only through their language.[17] Although such opinions had been discussed before, their reintroduction and elaboration at the beginning of the German Romantic era, when the forces of European nationalism were about to become a dominant theme of the nineteenth century, found a ready audience. Similarly, assertions positing the individuality of a nation's speech and its intimate bonds with national thought, national literature, and national solidarity were particularly resonant.

In the *Osnabrücksche Geschichte* (1768), Justus Möser placed central importance on the origins and development of national character. He found it present in everyday life as a product of the past. Because the future is shaped by the present, Möser maintained that one can shape the future by considering traditional lines of development through appropriate language, sagas, and mythology. Toward a similar end, Bodmer (1698–1783) and Klopstock (1724–1803) tried to introduce Germanic mythology in their work. In the *Horen* of 1796, Herder called for the rejuvenation of national mythology. Thus the belief in the existence of a national character, which was important to individual as well as national growth, gradually became linked to the development of language. One must emphasize the philosophical nature of these discussions; the initial scholars were cosmopolitan in their views with no notable political aims—that is, until the French Revolution.

The Enlightenment concern with similarities, as well as historicism's quest for causality, led to the juxtaposition of language with race. In the early decades of the nineteenth century, speculation concerning linguistic families brought about an erroneous identification of linguistic communities with racial communities. Linguists such as Friedrich Schlegel, Bopp, W. von Humboldt, Klaproth, Burnouf, Lassen, and Abel Remusat all held to this error. The erroneous identification of language and race categories was supported by knowledge gleaned from evolutionary science. In turn, language became an indication among other indices for determining physical and racial characteristics. Although a universal outlook largely prevailed in Enlightenment and Romantic linguistics, nineteenth-century linguists nevertheless sought data to determine racial and cultural development and potential in the organic growth of language. The connection between race and language later degenerated to the level of vulgar propaganda, and an interest in language in general narrowed to a single focus on the German language. This shift in the ideology of philology and humanistic study occurred in response to changes in the political climate. Resistance to French armies and the subsequent need for liberation from Napoleonic oppression spearheaded the rejection of French cultural domination. The progressive, dynamic characteristics of individual expression, criticism, and self-cultivation, which were essential to philological activity at its inception, were subverted and used for other ends–exploited as weapons of patriotic education of a German-speaking nation against Napoleonic tyranny.

In the fourth lecture of the *Rede an die deutsche Nation* (1808), Fichte drew distinctions between the French and German characters and attributed these distinctions to differences in linguistic development. Friedrich de la Motte Fouqué used race theory as a guiding principle in his plans for the reorganization of Germany. He characterized race by an attitude of mind passing from generation to generation. The attitude of mind of each generation is defined and maintained by the tradition of a given language community.[18] Thus French, Spanish, and Italian could be viewed as having broken with the original language, or as *verwelschte Germanen*. Other influences such as environment also effected the distancing of language from the original German. It was the duty of all Germans to protect themselves from foreign taint and *Verwelschung*. In 1813, this meant opposition to Napoleon and a rejection of French as an elite language. However, these ideas were applicable not only to the specific crises of those years; much of German history can be viewed as a struggle to keep the German spirit intact.

In the preceding chapter, I tried to show how the progressive political reform common to intellectual spheres in the late eighteenth century was expressed in the popular exoticism of the time. In the following two chapters, I will concentrate on a crucial period, the end of the eighteenth century and the beginning of the nineteenth century, when *Sprachwissenschaft* entered its modern period and differentiated itself as a relatively autonomous scholarly subsystem resting on specific forms of institutionalization and professionalism. As the primary concern of philological discourse shifted from the issue of language's origins to questions of translation, certain thinkers discovered in this development the opening of an area in which their own religious and philosophical ideas could gain legitimacy. In the following pages, I will examine how speculation concerning the origins and nature of the Sanskrit language influenced early Sanskrit translations, the reception of Indian philosophy, and translation theory in general. I will focus on several important actors in the drama of nineteenth-century philology as an emerging nationalistic academic discipline.

3

The Politics of Exoticism: Friedrich Schlegel's Metaphorical Pilgrimage to India

> The spirit of nations expresses itself in its language, and the descent of nations from each other, when physiognomy has not already passed sentence, almost always follows from the similarity of their languages.[1]

As a pioneer in the study of the Sanskrit language and author of the first direct translation from Sanskrit into German, Friedrich Schlegel played a major role in the history of early German Indology. Like others of his generation, he idealized India and its culture as the source of the aesthetic and spiritual absolute. In the *Athenaeum,* Friedrich Schlegel wrote: "Im Orient müssen wir das höchste Romantische suchen."[2] Toward this end, Schlegel devised linguistic theories, many of which were immediately disproved by the publication in 1810 of the first edition of Pāṇini's grammar. This *vyākaraṇa* (analysis), dating from the early fourth century B.C. and compiled in eight books of four thousand rules, resumes the etymological and morphological principles of some sixty earlier Sanskrit grammarians. Armed with Pāṇini's grammar, later nineteenth-century linguists such as Bopp and Böhtlingk revised Schlegel's theories on the nature of Sanskrit.

Schlegel has recently reemerged as a controversial figure in present-day critical discourse on Orientalist scholarship. His errors concerning the structure of Sanskrit and its position in respect to other languages have been condemned as contributing to modern racism,[3] developing the concept of the Aryan race,[4] and harboring far-reaching reactionary implications.[5] Uninitiated readers may not recognize in the sweeping generalities of such criticism a style that has come to characterize these discussions concerning the scholarship and literature growing out of the European encounter with the Orient. As we have noted in the Introduction, the critique of Orientalism views Western literary approaches to the East in terms of political discourse. The critical debate that Said initiated centers on the following formula: The Orientalist's scholarly frenzy was nothing but a deliberate attempt at cultural hegemony. However, Said's fundamental premise that Western writers, believing in the efficacy of their "imperial selves,"[6] approached the Orient first as nationals and second as individuals[7] is highly questionable, as is the implicit belief that all European nationals approached the East for identical reasons. It is not historically sound to think that Germans brought the same prejudices to their encounter with the Orient as did the French or the British. However, Said, mentioning the Germans in a cursory manner, associatively links them with those notorious "Orientalists" who comprise the object of his inquiry.

The fundamental message of *Orientalism* is that no European is ontologically (as is no European critic) capable of producing true knowledge about non-Europe.[8] Said's concept thus consigns the Orientalist work to a secondary position, and it becomes merely a function of political forces rather than an expression of the private motives and desires that inspire the individual artist or scholar. Said's argument disregards the testimony of a text's language, reception, and character as narrative, poetry, translation, or scholarship. By linking texts with certain cultural practices, Said imposes a systematized coherence on the historical past that presupposes the political experience of the twentieth century.

Said contends that Western Orientalist literature views the Orient as a static, fixed, and artificial object of discourse. However, his own analysis of Orientalist writers and scholars demonstrates an equal inability to see them as individuals who respond to particular motivations and whose conceptions of the Orient undergo change. He views their work solely as a function of ideology. As a result, all Orientalists become indistinguishable. In fact, they are static, fixed, and artificial objects of Said's own discourse. In *Orientalism,* Gramsci's inventory of traces, a metaphor Said cites,[9] is significantly separated from other sorts of inventories and traces. Nowhere is there a personality or cultural location upon which these traces are woven.[10]

Said isolates two major traits of Orientalism—"a newly found scientific self-consciousness based on the linguistic importance of the Orient to Europe and a proclivity to divide, subdivide, and redivide its subject matter without ever changing its mind about the Orient as being always the same, unchanging, uniform, and radically peculiar object."[11] He further notes that Schlegel "illustrates these traits together." While one can clearly perceive how Said ascribes importance to Schlegel's Sanskrit scholarship, it is hard to fathom (and fathom one must, since such assertions are not substantiated) how Schlegel's work illustrates the subversive tendency to dissect and stereotype the Orient. Most disheartening, however, are those instances when Said does isolate important issues but his polemical attitude does not allow him to recognize the value of these insights. For example, he correctly articulates the significance of Schlegel's disenchantment with India; but rather than question the crucial issue of enchantment versus disenchantment as a cornerstone of cross-cultural reception, he uses it as an occasion for further anti-Orientalist rhetoric.[12]

Less strident in tone but similar in intent, Martin Bernal supports many of Said's judgments on Schlegel's Indological scholarship. In the first volume of *Black Athena,* a work asserting the Afroasiatic roots of Greek culture, Bernal sees a racist Schlegel abetting the deafricanization of Hellenism by his false suspicion that Egyptians descended from Indians. Bernal accuses Schlegel of being old-fashioned for viewing Sanskrit as a perfect language.[13] In this respect, however, Schlegel's designation corresponds with Indian belief: After all, the term *Sanskrit* does mean "perfected." Schlegel may not have understood the migrations of Aryan warlords, but his knowledge of Sanskrit was sufficient for him to know that Indians believed their language to be perfectly formed. One questions Bernal's ability to judge Schlegel's linguistic premises when he himself lacks any knowledge of the language in question. The same criticism may be applied to Said's critique of Schlegel's Indological scholarship.

If this genre of criticism proves nothing else, it does show that Schlegel's reception of India (and, by extension, that of other thinkers) would be better understood if viewed within the larger context of religious, philosophical, and philological concerns. Such issues rarely enter into the debate centered on Orientalist discourse, which is all too dependent upon its own critical categories and dismissive of other "inventories and traces." By raising these issues, I hope to extend the present-day lines of inquiry beyond the rather narrow, albeit significant, course of political investigation.

Schlegel attempted to learn the Sanskrit language with no personal experience of India, its people, or its culture. One suspects that this was less an issue of contempt for India than an aversion to visiting the land in which his eldest brother, Carl August, died.[14] Earlier European pioneers in the acquisition of Sanskrit learned the language from its brahmin custodians or through grammars written in other Indian vernaculars. Due to this distance from the cultural context, Schlegel's understanding of Sanskrit was necessarily impressionistic. His progress in its acquisition was all the more difficult because manuscripts were few and dictionaries and grammars were not yet available in Europe. The lack of pedagogical tools, and the particular linguistic idiosyncrasies endemic to Sanskrit language and poetry, further complicated the task. Nevertheless, even before learning Sanskrit, Schlegel was anxious to be its unique prophet. In a letter to his brother August Wilhelm, Friedrich wrote of his desire to keep Goethe away from India, which he saw as his personal scholarly domain.[15]

Mythology had been revitalized by writers of Schlegel's generation[16] and was now recognized as a largely untapped reservoir of poetic inspiration.[17] Since the modern Occident had no mythology, "one would have to be invented."[18] The inspiration for this new mythology, and hence for the new Romantic poetry, was to be found in the Orient,[19] by which Schlegel meant India.[20] However, it is not only the poet's task to reveal the great truths of mythology, but the translator's as well. Schlegel characterized the translator as both an artist and a prophet addressing the lamentable intellectual and cultural state into which his country has fallen: "a nation which is always becoming more brutal and dull."[21] In fact, the entire argument of the *Gespräche über die Mythologie und symbolische Anschauung* calls for the renewal of German poetry with the help of the Indian muse.

What the West recognized as religion, mythology, and poetry originated in the Orient. Classical Indian culture exhibited in a pure, undiluted form that which in the West was a mere vestige of the union of philosophy and poetry. Just as one would go to Italy to learn about art, one should now go to India to learn about God and poetry.[22] Schlegel the translator clearly saw himself as the guide for this aesthetic and religious pilgrimage. The unique fruit of his metaphorical journey, *Über die Sprache und Weisheit der Indier,* appeared in 1808, six years after he began to study Sanskrit. Instead of articulating a newfound wisdom, this small volume expressed utter disillusionment with Indian thought. In the interval between his initial enthusiasm for India and the publication of this work, Schlegel had totally rejected the Indian model and supplanted it with a more congenial theodicy.

Analysis of Schlegel's writings from his early study of Sanskrit to the publication of *Über die Sprache* reveals an idiosyncratic perspective.[23]

His interpretation of Indian philosophy, as found in his Cologne Lectures of 1805, was marred by a lack of source material. Either consciously or unconsciously, he ignored what other Westerners had perceived as India's pessimistic worldview.[24] It may even be argued that Schlegel reworked Indian philosophy in an attempt to construct a Hinduism without the fatalism that other Western thinkers had projected onto the doctrines of emanation,[25] predestination, and the eternal return.[26] All of these beliefs detracted from Schlegel's sought-after idea of the Absolute, but also led to what he viewed as moral stupefaction and intellectual indolence. In a rectified Indian philosophical system, Schlegel could still discover the union between the finite and the infinite,[27] spirit and matter,[28] and God and Man.[29] Schlegel could even add to his system what he found most positive in Western philosophical thought. By introducing the concept of progress,[30] Schlegel effectively limited the negative principles of emanation: Evil was rendered accidental and transitory,[31] eternal return was circumvented, and the hope for a better world was kept alive.[32]

However, in the process of translating the poetic and philosophical selections for *Über die Sprache,* Schlegel discovered other unpleasant byproducts of emanation (astrology, superstition, and materialism) that were less easily dismissed. Śaivism, initially unknown to him, united voluptuousness with death; its god was worshiped in the form of a phallus. This was not Schlegel's conception of religion.[33] If emanation annihilated free will by arousing a feeling of ultimate culpability, then Śaivism rejected the idea of human responsibility in any form. While in the Cologne lectures of 1805 Schlegel argued that certain faults could be mitigated by an Oriental-Occidental synthesis,[34] by 1808 a syncretistic solution was no longer possible. Schlegel "discovered" that what he considered to be the land of primitive revelation had, in fact, degenerated into an atomistic and materialistic India that he could not accept. Although traces of divine truth could still be found in Indian philosophical systems, Schlegel concluded, they had been inextricably mixed with error.

Having approached India in search of truth and revelation, and finding neither, this hierophant *manqué* sought salvation in Catholicism. *Über die Sprache* appeared several days after Schlegel's conversion to Roman Catholicism on 16 April 1808.[35] In fact, Schlegel's gradual religious conversion process ran parallel to his Indic studies.[36] The book was received with sarcasm. Both Heinrich Heine[37] and Goethe[38] judged it as a Catholic manifesto presenting the Church as the only refuge. Since Catholicism and Romanticism shared many traits,[39] it is not clear on what criteria Goethe and Heine justified their claim. However, a detailed examination of the translations found in *Über die Sprache* reveals emendations in which Schlegel resolved the theistic and pantheistic imagery of Hinduism in Christian terms.[40]

The speculative chapters, composed subsequent to the translations, betray Schlegel's disenchantment with Indian philosophy. As we have noted, Schlegel's initial dream was to effect a philosophical and aesthetic revolution via India.[41] The initial chapters show how this project was not feasible. In the remainder of the volume, therefore, Schlegel emphasized the complexity of the Sanskrit language and his mastery of it. Schlegel's approach differed significantly from methods of language comparison previously used. Traditional methods sought to demonstrate the superiority of one language over another—that is, to distinguish languages from each other by superficial differences and to view such differences as manifestations of the diverse national genius of individual populations. Not relying upon superficial similarities among Greek, Latin, German, Persian, and Sanskrit roots, which the standard methodology would have emphasized, Schlegel sought, by analyzing grammatical structures, conjugations, and declensions, a criterion for the relationship between languages in morphological comparison.

However, Schlegel erred in his insistence on linguistic polygenesis. He broke languages into two groups—inflected (root internally modified) and agglutinative (affixing an external particle to the word).[42] The former had spiritual origin; the latter, animal.[43] Using the then-popular analogy of botany, he saw inflected languages as linguistic vegetation.[44] Just as a stem, branches, and leaves develop from a plant's root, so nominal and verbal forms come from the linguistic root.[45] Schlegel postulated that German and other languages developed from Sanskrit because they possessed inflection.[46] He believed that other languages, such as Chinese and Hebrew, lack this inflection and are agglutinative by means of affixes joined to the roots.[47] Because of inflection, Sanskrit and its derivative languages were seen as living organisms capable of penetrating intelligence.[48] Agglutinative languages were labeled "mere agglomerations of atoms."[49] These erroneous linguistic theories in particular are the source of Schlegel's current disrepute. A hidden agenda is perceived in Schlegel's categorization. Orientalism's critics contend that he sought to brand agglutinative languages as inferior[50] and promote an intentional anti-Semitic project.[51]

Certain factors belie such criticisms. For example, Schlegel denied any intention to distinguish between superior and inferior languages.[52] Further, it would seem contradictory that a man who was neither socially nor politically anti-Semitic[53] and who praised the lofty power and energy of the Hebrew language[54] would contrive a linguistic edifice merely to voice anti-Semitic prejudice. Finally, Schlegel's repudiation of his system of linguistic classification in the Vienna lectures of 1828 counteracts any imputed racist intent.

To determine the motivating factors shaping Schlegel's linguistic theories, one must, unavoidably, examine his involvement with Indian thought. Schlegel's writings on India and, in particular, the whole of *Über die Sprache* state his motivation very clearly. India emerges as the cradle of humanity, and Sanskrit as the mother tongue of Indo-European languages. In the philosophical, religious, and translation sections of *Über die Sprache,* Schlegel presented India as a problematic locus of the Divine. He formulated his linguistic theories in a consistent manner, as a metaphorical edifice constructed to isolate Sanskrit from other languages and thereby support his belief in its perfection and divine origin. The larger plan was to salvage palatable aspects of the Divine from his abortive Indic studies. He projected onto Sanskrit what he could not find in Indian philosophy and religion. Through his analysis of Sanskrit, Schlegel sought to orientalize the Catholic *Logos.* Unfortunately, the divine status that he accorded to inflected Sanskrit necessitated a less-than-divine origin for what he perceived as the agglutinative languages. This was clearly a negative by-product rather than a motivating factor.

Schlegel's linguistic theories were inextricably bound up in his spiritual and aesthetic encounter with India. His professed motivation was to prove the German language capable of mirroring the spirit of the Sanskrit original and to prove himself a poet capable of translating it skillfully.[55] However, the quality of the translations included in the appendices to *Über die Sprache* attest to the fact that he had acquired neither a deep nor a comprehensive knowledge of the language.[56] Schlegel himself must have realized this, because the more ambitious translation projects to which he was deeply committed never materialized.[57] By espousing the Indian belief in the divine origin of the Sanskrit language and, most importantly, by elaborating scientific theories to that effect, Schlegel may well have sought to allay his sense of creative failure in not having mastered the language. However, by setting out to compete with Sanskrit poets, Schlegel doomed himself to artistic failure, just as his spiritual idealization of Indian religious philosophy had led to disillusionment. In the end, Schlegel did not have the poetic genius to succeed in manipulating this "antidiluvian" language, nor did he find in India a repository of religious truth.

The case of Friedrich Schlegel provides a cautionary model for viewing the dynamics of East-West reception. His search for inspiration in Indian models implied a questioning of the dominant Western cultural values as well as a dependence on what culture ostensibly assures in terms of self-realization. Although his quest manifested an arrogance that was endemic to his Europeanism, it would be wrong to view Schlegel's reception of India solely in light of his political entitlement. It should be recognized that he also exhibited a will to be spiritually converted and empowered by India. His linguistic theories developed from a conscious search for a unifying principle, a confused longing for filiation with a highly religious culture, and, as we may surmise from his translations, an incomplete understanding of its language. These motivations are certainly less sensational than those currently ascribed to his work. Indeed, they lack the shock value of attributing to Schlegel a racist or imperialist agenda. The sad truth of the matter is this: Schlegel went to India not as a fanatic, but under the banner of an ultimately faulty science.

Scientific theory can become codified as can the objectives it sets for legitimate inquiry without any attention paid to its prehistory. In a world where the concepts of the text and author have been seriously challenged, it is curious that the process of theoretical formation remains mythologized. In the preceding discussion, I have tried to point out some personal influences relating to biographical data and intellectual limitations that might have contributed to Schlegel's reception of India and the linguistic theories he devised. I fully realize the disrepute of such methodology in literary critical circles. However, in engaging in such analysis, I wish to deflate the sanctity accorded to theory formation. Without wishing to sound facetious, I think the following analogy can be drawn between the theorist and the grocer of quality goods. With no deceit intended, the grocer does not inform his patrons of the provenance of certain fine fruits. So too does the theorist offer indications and references without ever divulging the key impetus behind his theory. It is not to denigrate the theory or the theorist that such accountability might be desired. One must, of course, respect one's *maîtres*. Yet, without undue reticence, the provenance of their theories may be questioned, not in order to better understand those same theories but rather in an effort to demythologize theoretical knowledge. It is out of a desire to continue such demythologization that we now turn our attention to the canonical interpretation within nineteenth-century European philosophy of the *Bhagavad Gītā*.

4

Scholarly Collusion and the Ethos of Despair: The Initial Reception of the Bhagavad Gītā

I

It has been noted that the latter decades of the eighteenth century witnessed a concerted effort to gather diverse material on unknown or little-known languages. We have also seen that general theories of a purely abstract nature concerning the origins and development of language were being promulgated at this time. Furthermore, it has been clearly shown that this theoretical speculation was being developed with an absence of adequate data. The discoveries of explorers and missionaries regarding language and the efforts of linguistic theorists developed separately and in a parallel fashion in the years just prior to the discovery of the relationship between Sanskrit and the major languages of Europe. These efforts coalesced in the first two decades of the nineteenth century under favorable academic circumstances that allowed for the integration of language theory and linguistic and literary data. Therefore, propitious circumstances contributed to the burgeoning historical study of Indo-European languages. Indeed, linguistics in the first half of the nineteenth century was largely limited to Indo-European studies.

Recent criticism views Indological scholarly productions as aiding and abetting Western political trends.[1] It has been asserted that the European discovery of India's philosophies, in addition to marking the beginning of modern Indology, parallels the establishment of European hegemonic designs.[2] Europe's reception of Indian philosophy has been interpreted as supporting the belief that India has nothing worthwhile to teach the West. Its tradition, inimical to historical progress, never reached the levels of philosophy and science that are uniquely European achievements.[3] The nineteenth-century scholarly critique of Indian intellectual models plays a significant role in the totality of the reception of India and the intellectual climate in which this reception evolved. The Western scholarly reception of the *Bhagavad Gītā*, in particular, has been singled out as contributing to the institutional philosophical and political refusal to take India seriously.[4] In the following pages, we will examine the scholarly reception of this poem. I have suggested that the search for models in an Indian exotic ultimately collided with a vision of fatalism that certain Europeans projected onto a fictive India or read into its literature. What parallels, if any, did the philosophical discourse on India have with the dynamic of exoticism as we have defined it?

In 1785, Charles Wilkins translated the *Bhagavad Gītā* from Sanskrit into English. Wilkins's rendition was the most important Sanskrit philosophical translation of its time.[5] The view of Indian philosophy that European intellectuals would initially form was based on Wilkins's work. Of this work, Sir William Jones wrote: "If they wish to form a correct idea of Indian religion and literature, let them begin with forgetting all that has been written on the subject by ancients or moderns, before the publication of the Gītā."[6]

Forty years elapsed before the next significant treatment of Indian speculative thought in the West. In 1823, A. W. Schlegel published the original text of the *Gītā* along with a Latin translation.[7] The following year, H. T. Colebrooke wrote a five-part essay on Indian philosophy that would set the standard for the European exploration of the field.[8]

Colebrooke's essays[9] present a clear and nonjudgmental exposition of the major Indian philosophical systems.[10] He relies on the Sanskrit sources that he cites at the beginning of each essay and does not seek to draw from this material any theoretical argument on the nature of Indian philosophy. He equally eschews speculation regarding the relationship between art, religion, and philosophy. Colebrooke introduced the schools as systems with one goal: to explicate the path to eternal bliss. On the whole, Colebrooke approached the classical schools of Indian thought in a straightforward, if somewhat simplistic, fashion.[11] His exposition is surprisingly nonpolemical.

In the same year that Colebrooke wrote his essay, the French Sanskritist A. S. Langlois wrote a scathing review of August Wilhelm Schlegel's Latin translation of the *Bhagavad Gītā*.[12] Between 1825 and 1827, three thinkers who were to have a significant influence upon the pedagogical projects of their respective countries entered the fray. First,

Wilhelm von Humboldt reacted in detail to Langlois's attack on Schlegel's translation.[13] Humboldt then followed this response with an essay on the *Bhagavad Gītā*,[14] to which G. W. F. Hegel responded in an extensive review article in 1827.[15] Hegel commented specifically on Schlegel's view, seconded by Humboldt, that the *Gītā* was the only classical Sanskrit poem with philosophical content. Victor Cousin then made the *Gītā* the subject of his philosophical lectures of 1828.[16]

It is misleading to see (as does Halbfass in his recent study) this initial reception of the *Gītā* as a purely philosophical debate. Rather, the discussion revolved in large part around issues of a philological nature—namely, the problems of translation, artistic commensurability, and value. The discussion of translation centered on the presentation of the philosophical concepts promulgated in the *Gītā*.

There is no need to summarize here the plot or the epic context of the *Gītā*; it is a text familiar to most readers, given the exoticism of our times. Moreover, the Sanskritists' arguments over specifics (origin, age, homogeneity), which continue to this day, must remain peripheral to our discussion. As I have maintained throughout this entire study, a "correct," "Indian" interpretation of any text in question is not the purview of this investigation. Given the tools and the multileveled distortion already imbricated in the European reception of India, the process of proving that these Europeans erred would not further our understanding. We must, however, provide a working definition for the principle terms that engendered the debate (*sāṃkhya* and *yoga*), for no other reason than to mark out the "garden paths" along which these European thinkers strayed. The Sāṃkhya doctrine may be described as a path to perfection reached with the reasoning intellect. The more important path, as defined by the *Gītā*, is that of *yoga*—self-concentration through nonintellectual meditation. Principally at issue in the initial reception of the *Gītā* was the understanding of the concept of *yoga*. In his translation of 1785, Wilkins defined *yoga* as "junction, devotion, bodily or mental application of the mind in spiritual things." In the essay "On the philosophy of the Hindus" (1824), Colebrooke obliquely referred to *yoga* as the "meditation on special topics." In his translation, Schlegel chose as the primary "equivalent" the Latin term *devotio*.

In the following discussion, I will supplement recent critical analyses of the *Gītā*'s reception by focusing on the philological and literary parameters of the debate. I will look at specific assessments of problems in comprehension and the issue of translation that this reception raised. I agree with a recent study by Humboldt scholar Helmut Gipper that suggests that the scholarly contours of this debate arose from conflicting theories of translation.[17] I shall also try to place the institutional discussion of Indian philosophy instigated by the translation of the *Gītā* within the larger context of the European cultural reception of India. As it cuts across national, disciplinary, and institutional boundaries, this reception provides an excellent opportunity for a broader understanding of the European reception of India.

II

Wilhelm von Humboldt, the minister of state for Prussia, was a Sanskrit scholar and a philological authority of his time. Provoked by Langlois's virulent criticism of August Wilhelm Schlegel's Latin translation of the *Gītā* (1823), Humboldt responded on 17 June 1825 in a letter to Schlegel commenting on Langlois's severe and, as we shall see, unjust criticism.[18] Humboldt's letter to Schlegel investigates the specific issues of translation that Langlois's review had raised. Langlois's main dissatisfaction stemmed from Schlegel's translation methodology. Langlois felt that each word in the original language should have been rendered by a single term in the target language. Rather than the many renderings that Schlegel gave to the term *yoga*—*destinatio, exercitatio, applicatio, devotio, disciplina activa, mysterium, facultas mystica, maiestas, mysterium,* and *contemplatio*—Langlois preferred the single term *dévotion*. For the *yogī,* he favored *dévot,* disregarding the pejorative implications of the latter in French.

Humboldt initiated his response with the assertion that translating is, in principle, an impossible undertaking, because different languages do not constitute synonyms of identically structured concepts. A good translation, he maintained, was only an approximation in terms of replicating the beauty and the sense of the original. Ideally, in the best of translations, a reader with knowledge of both the original and the target language can recognize the original term from its correspondent in translation. Humboldt felt that, in Schlegel's translation, such recognition was possible. Moreover, he felt that Schlegel had captured other important qualities of the original, such as its syntactical simplicity, brevity, emphases, lightness, and elegance. Humboldt raised the important point that, especially in the Sanskrit language, terms (and especially philosophical terms) are multifaceted and defy translation into one word. For this reason, Humboldt felt that Schlegel's decision to render a term with representations of its different aspects as appropriate to each occasion of its use provided the only reasonable solution for translations from the Sanskrit language.[19]

Humboldt then discussed the specific problem addressed by Langlois (and subsequently reiterated by Hegel and Cousin) concerning the translation of the term *yoga*. He reiterated that he found it impossible to find in any language a single translation suitable for this term. While he readily admitted having problems with certain choices that Schlegel had made, Humboldt noted that "anyone who knows the Sanskrit word *yoga* through translation cannot grasp its true meaning." Furthermore, he felt that it was impossible to eliminate every blemish in a translation.[20]

Humboldt saw, therefore, that in translating one could chose from two methods, of which only one could be adopted. Either the translator did what Langlois demanded and sought in the target language one word corresponding to the original concept and aided comprehension by appending a commentary, or the translator could do what Schlegel attempted—render an original term by different words in the target language that approximate the different uses of the original term. Humboldt recognized that the latter method might be detrimental to philosophical exactness and depth, because the common link between the various applied meanings and the original concept is lost. Moreover—and this is important in Sanskrit—he felt that the nuance of each word originating from the same source is also lost. These comments addressed pertinent issues concerning translation conventions of nineteenth-century Germany.[21] More importantly, however, Humboldt's letter to Schlegel raised larger concerns: The problem of translation, and the particular difficulties in translating Sanskrit, entailed discussions of nineteenth-century philosophies of language.

With Humboldt, the connection drawn between a *Volk* and language reached its first acme. Humboldt carried Herder's conception of the parallel development of thought and language one step further with the assertion that "a people's speech is their spirit and the spirit is their speech."[22] According to Humboldt, language was the outgrowth of a nation's spiritual strength.[23] The national character of a language rested on its disposition (*Naturanlage*). This does not suggest that Humboldt believed that racial differences had an influence on language formation or even whether such a determination was possible. He did not divide languages according to race or nations.

Humboldt's theory of language stresses the creative linguistic ability inherent in the speaker's mind. He identified language not with products of acts of speaking, but with the living capability by which speakers produce and understand utterances. Humboldt qualified language as *enérgeia*. In German, he referred to it as *Tätigkeit* and *Erzeugung*. He viewed the capacity for language as universal. As with Herder, the individuality of each language represents the peculiar property of a given speaking group. We have already noted that later nationalist arguments would misuse such linguistic identifications. Humboldt, however, is not to be charged with personally initiating this trend. He himself was not as interested in German as he was in other languages. He viewed German as one language among many.

Humboldt viewed every language as containing a specific and exclusive worldview. Thus, an extralinguistic world is transformed into language in a particular way, when extralinguistic realities become linguistic structures. Humboldt viewed the act of translation as a continuous transposition from one worldview to another. A philosophical poem such as the *Bhagavad Gītā* would entail further contextual values. Thus, he deemed Langlois's demand for one-to-one correspondence in translation to be totally out of the question.

In summary of Humboldt's philosophy of language, note that he viewed all languages as separate organisms that differ from one another both in unique grammatical structures and in specific semantic structures. He viewed linguistic diversity not as a matter of sounds and signs but as an issue of worldview.[24] Humboldt perceived language not as an object but rather as an activity (*enérgeia*).[25] Its inner form consists of structures articulating specific thought principles or strategies. He felt that the existence of such specific *Sprachstilen* could be corroborated by anyone who had practice in translating. Thus, when Humboldt spoke about translation technique, he also addressed the nature of language, its origins and development, and its relationship to national identity. Moreover, Humboldt's philosophy of language and its relation to the formation of national identity reflected concerns not unique to this thought. Similar attitudes concerning translation and the philosophy of language were voiced by Schlegel in response to Humboldt's letter.[26]

August Wilhelm Schlegel, the first chair of Sanskrit at the University of Bonn, translated the *Bhagavad Gītā* into Latin because he considered it a particularly suitable language for translating the subtlety of meaning found in the Sanskrit language.[27] His foremost concern in the translation was to retain the context-dependent semantic variants, as in the case of translating the term *yoga*. Schlegel was an experienced translator whose renditions of Dante, Caldéron, Ariosto, Petrarch, Camoẽs, and the Classics had set the standards for European translations of the time. He was well aware of the pitfalls of translation. Schlegel felt that sublimity could not be translated, because the translator would have to re-create what the first author had achieved and would have to use the same tools and materials as that author had used. In his response to Langlois's review, Schlegel questioned where, even were those tasks possible, the translator would find the fullness of sound, the flow or "happy succession" of consonants and vowels, that originated together with the original idea and formed part of its essence. In India, particularly, he noted, the development of language and the formation of ideas were immeasurably different from anything with which Europeans were familiar. Thus, Schlegel also believed that language mirrored the soul of a nation and that the national *Geist,* embodied in a nation's literature, could not be perfectly communicated. Schlegel responded to Langlois's demand for word-to-word correspondence with the comment that such a method best suits the process of translating geometry textbooks. In poetry and philosophy, one cannot treat the "poetic representation of the mind's innermost conceptions of itself and the eternal" like a "collection of algebraic signs."

As a competent practicing translator, Schlegel had explored all options he felt were available to him, given the literary conventions of his day. He compared their shortcomings and weaknesses and selected the one that seemed to him the most acceptable. Given the choice of retaining a Sanskrit term because it was untranslatable—a method used by Wilkins and the Persian translators of the *Upanishads*—he found this option unprofitable. Such indirect translations require contextual assistance that burdens the narrative flow. He deemed Langlois's demand for a convergent translation unfeasible, because often no equivalents present themselves in the target language, and when equivalents are found and used, the richness of the original is lost.[28] Schlegel chose, therefore, the third option, refractive translation, whereby a complex expression in the source language is rendered, according to context, by various expressions in the target language. He was not blind to the disadvantage of this method in terms of its inadmissible arbitrariness. However, he felt that it allowed the many-sidedness of a term to be grasped quite well. Of all the terms to be translated, *yoga* presented him with real difficulty; he found it truly "Protean."[29] Thus, Schlegel admits struggling and forcing the term *yoga* "to reveal its secrets."

As they were formulated, both Humboldt's letter (*Über die Bhagavad Gītā*) and Schlegel's response clearly reframed Langlois's individual criticisms of the *Bhagavad Gītā* translation into the larger translation problem—that of the transferability of meaning from one worldview to another. In fact, Humboldt's concern with this specific problem of translation may be seen as forming the matrix of his subsequent discussions of the *Gītā*.

In the essay "On the Episode of the *Mahābhārata* known by the name *Bhagavad Gītā*,"[30] Humboldt addressed the ways of thinking that he found peculiar to India and drew attention to what might seem to Western nonspecialist readers to be the text's apparent contradictions. It was this latter essay that inspired Hegel to reexamine the *Gītā* more closely and write his own critical assessment.

As did F. Schlegel, Humboldt posited the doctrine of emanation as the main doctrine of Indian philosophy.[31] However, with the term *emanation*, Humboldt specifically referred to the Sāṃkhya school of philosophy. His interpretation of Sāṃkhya,[32] based partially on Colebrooke, is lucid in its major contours. He correctly stated the workings of *prakṛti* (nature), *puruṣa* (being),[33] and the *guṇas* (natural qualities).[34] He described the *Gītā* as presenting human nature as imitation and the particularization of the divine model, which creates bodies and permits them to be destroyed by entering or leaving them.[35] God then joins the Self to mortal bodies that perform actions (*Bhagavad Gītā,* 15.7–9). This involvement, however, in no way taints the Divine (*Bhagavad Gītā,* 9.8,9). In discussing Sāṃkhya and Yoga, Humboldt addressed both their moral and their intellectual implications. He cited the *Gītā* to the effect that Sāṃkhya calls for the application of rational understanding.[36] Humboldt clearly distinguished Sāṃkhya from Yoga, which places God in his independent infinitude at the summit of all things and offers a means for reaching bliss through the concentration upon God's Being.[37]

According to Humboldt, Colebrooke's presentation of Patañjali's system of Yoga agrees with the doctrine expressed (with less sophistry and mysticism) by Krishna in the *Gītā*.[38] Humboldt maintained that the poem's philosophical system pivots around two main dicta: (1) that the spirit is simple and imperishable by nature, and separate from the body, which is complex and perishable (*Bhagavad Gītā,* 2.14, 18) and (2) anyone who strives for consummation must perform any and all acts "without regard for their consequences and with perfect equanimity" (*Bhagavad Gītā,* 2.26–30).[39] From this assertion, Humboldt concluded that the *Gītā* teaches the inconsequentiality of death and action. Although death concerns only the perishable body, actions in and of themselves are not without weight. Humboldt correctly maintained that actions, once freed from passion and intuition, function as mere products of nature or precepts of duty.[40] However, he did not perceive the whole system of Indian thought as resting upon pure intellectuality. Rather, he cited *Bhagavad Gītā* 3.3 to support the view that there are two operative systems, one of action and the other of insight. Humboldt recognized well that the *Gītā* warned about the bonds of action rather than actions themselves. In this essay in particular he acknowledged the weight given to action as preferable to nonaction and reaffirmed that the poem does not suggest anything as vain as the suppression of action.[41]

As in the earlier essay (the letter to Schlegel), Humboldt defined *yoga* as a process whereby spirituality can be controlled through immersion in the godhead or the personalized God.[42] By choosing to translate *yoga* as *Vertiefung* (immersion), Humboldt hoped to convey the mystic mood characteristic of the *yogī*. Humboldt felt that A. W. Schlegel's translation (*devotio*), while adequate, lost too much of the original meaning of "connecting."[43]

Moreover, he felt that the Latin term was too narrow and inapplicable in those instances where *yoga* should be understood as active energy. Humboldt noted that the term *yoga* derives from *YUJ*, which means to connect or tie. It expresses a link between one thing and another. Humboldt glossed that *yoga* signifies a constant orientation of the mind toward the deity. The mind has withdrawn from all other objects, thoughts, movements, or bodily functions.

Humboldt correctly noted that through Yoga (as well as Sāṃkhya), action is negated. What is attained is *nirvāṇa*, understood by Humboldt as nonthinking or a wafting away of the earth spirit. Humboldt warned that *nirvāṇa* should not be interpreted as the suppression of all earthly thoughts[44] or as a permanent state defining man's entire contemplative life. Rather, he emphasized the importance that the *Gītā* always places upon action and reminds his reader that the setting of the poem, after all, is a battlefield. Humboldt elucidated how Krishna's message proceeds from the principle that truth cannot be found by means of discursive or rationalizing reason. To find truth, one must prepare the mind, purify it of taint, call upon insight in order to control it, animate an inner feeling for truth, and direct the spirit to the point in which the Self connects with things as part of them. Such a doctrine—which teaches direct insight through inner perception—demands firmness, exertion, and steadfastness of spirit. Two paths present themselves, primarily because humanity is composed of countless dispositions; some proceed in accordance with reason and others through action.[45] Both paths, however, ultimately aim at the transformation of human nature into godly nature, and Humboldt reiterated that this goal cannot be obtained merely through intellectual exercise.[46]

Thus, Humboldt's explication of the *Gītā* defended Indian philosophy against any accusation of fatalism and predestination independent of the will.[47] Humboldt suggested that the Hindu combination of ethical freedom with the concatenation of mutually determinative natural events and actions presents a task no more philosophically insoluble than that of any other religion. Humboldt concluded that, from an absolute point of view, ethical freedom remains safe in the *Gītā;* the godhead participates causally in no human action, good or evil. All action originates in the character that performs it. In this sense, *yoga* appears to Humboldt as founded on the necessity of ethical freedom, since perseverance and steadfastness of will function as its final aim and can spring only from absolute freedom, which, in turn, opposes itself to all strivings of finite nature. He denied the theme of quietism that Hegel imputed to Indian philosophical thought. In no way did Humboldt posit insight (*Erkenntnis*), as Hegel would, as the foremost of all human efforts promulgated in the *Gītā*.[48] However, in his response essay, Hegel will discount Humboldt's reading of the *Gītā* and seek to cut Indian philosophy to fit his own schema.

III

Whereas Humboldt, knowing Sanskrit, worked from the *Gītā* itself, with reference to Colebrooke, Hegel worked primarily from Colebrooke's essay. Hegel's judgments on Indian thought evolved during the process of rewriting his lectures on the history of philosophy, and they became more detailed in later versions. In the 1825–26 version, he added a section on India, after having read the first of Colebrooke's two essays dealing with Sāṃkhya and Nyāya-Vaiśeṣika. Although that section was ostensibly a response to Humboldt, Hegel dealt less with his colleague's interpretation of the *Bhagavad Gītā* than with the acceptability of the Indian philosophy purportedly promulgated in the poem.

Hegel's analysis of India was intimately bound up with his criticism of the Romantics. He responded negatively to their infatuation with the Orient[49] and sought to demythologize India's prestige in romantic Europe. Hegel felt that the Romantic emplotment of India represented a theology of origins.[50] Initially his comments were directed against Friedrich Schlegel. Hegel rejected Schlegel's ideas on revelation, primitive peoples, or an original unified state of humankind.[51] Although, as we have seen, Schlegel eventually became disenchanted with Indian philosophy, he continued to adhere to the view that India remained a source of spiritual force and orientation. Hegel could not accept this position. What rankled Hegel most was that Romantic Indomania articulated both a sentimental nostalgia for origins as well as a blatant disregard for the present. According to Hegel, the Orient represented vestiges of the past. It was of no use in deciphering the present.[52] Thus, Indian philosophy is embedded within his more general critique of the notion of an *Urvolk,* the belief in an Asian origin of European mythology,[53] and the neo-Catholic belief, defended by Friedrich Schlegel, of continuous revelation.[54] In fact, one cannot disregard the connection between his reception of Indian metaphysics and his more general attack upon Christianity. Hegel's emplotment of Indian philosophy enabled him to attack the Romantic ego-centered concept of faith.[55] Most importantly, for our purposes, Hegel's reception of India reflected his views on the relationship of Sanskrit to Latin, Greek, and other European languages.

We have seen how Schlegel's linguistic theorizing, his search for a new mythology, and his desire to enrich the biblical catechumen through Indian mythological formulations all eventually led to disillusionment. However, his Indological research supported and popularized the ideology of an *Urvolk, Ursprache,* and *Urreligion* in Germany between 1800–1830. As a consequence of this trend, Hegel felt that a strong response was necessary.[56] Humboldt's essay on Indian philosophy offered Hegel the long-awaited opportunity to attack Romantic enthusiasts of antiquity and modern pietists.

Hegel viewed philosophy itself as occurring within a process of unfolding, with his system as the complete realization of this movement. In the dynamic movement of history, earlier developments are taken up (*aufgehoben*) into what succeeds them.[57] The study of the history of philosophy thus parallels the study of philosophy itself.[58] In Hegel's estimation, the Orient represents the first stage and any investigation of India is coeval with the examination of the roots of the Western tradition. It was this function of Indian philosophy within the European present that Hegel found deeply problematic. For Hegel, European history embodied the dynamic of progress, and the European present was its highest manifestation. If India was "static," as Hegel maintained, what role could it possibly play in the European past or present? Clearly, Hegel's argument rests on the identification of India as a "static" entity. How did Hegel reach this conclusion?

Hegel viewed Hinduism as the prototype of the religion of substance, with *Brahman* as the Ultimate Substance.[59] He maintained that the acme of Indian speculative thought consisted of a "sinking" into *Brahman* (the universal soul), "annihilation" of the subject, and "unconsciousness."[60] Before Brahman everything else is accidental and nothing.[61] Therefore, religious action is contentless and inessential.[62] Since *Brahman* as substance is abstract, in order to be united with it, the Hindu renounces everything pertaining to life and the world.[63] Thus, for Hegel, the Hindu union with God consists in destroying and benumbing all self-consciousness. Rather than understanding union as a liberation, Hegel sees it as entailing a process of emptying.[64] The individual escapes into nothing and has no freedom.[65] Since there is no freedom for the subject, Indian philosophy cannot present true philosophy in the Hegelian sense of the word.

Hegel's reading of Colebrooke[66] did not radically transform his assessment of Indian philosophy,[67] except for the fact that he had previously taken for granted India's exclusion from the history of philosophy and "real" philosophy's European origins.[68] After reading Colebrooke's article, Hegel realized that a real philosophy did exist in India of which Europe was ignorant.[69] He also realized that he had to address the existence of this philosophy. For the purposes of the present study, we are examining Hegel with a specific purpose in mind. The moral dilemma of fatalism that we have attributed to the Western reception of Indian thought in general found its first systematic articulation in Hegel's essay responding to Humboldt.

The *Gītā* instructs that the individual soul's (*Ātman*'s) recognition of its intrinsic identity with the Universal (*Brahman*) effects salvation. As Halbfass has noted, Hegel disregards the pivotal identification of *Brahman* with *Ātman,*[70] and in doing so he ignores the single most affirmative aspect of Indian theology. Instead, Hegel described the union with *Brahman* as a permanent state of abstraction, a union where the self "plunges into itself,"[71] and an intuition of nothing (*das Anschauen des Nichts*).[72] To reach union with *Brahman,* Hegel maintained, the Indian extinguishes all awareness of content and attains abstract unity through utter stupefaction and insensibility.[73] Hegel read into the *Gītā* a constant call to immobility and inaction.[74] "The Indian soul's union in emptiness is rather deadening."[75] It leads to no truth, since it is without content.

Hegel gave primacy to the *Bhagavad Gītā* within Indian philosophy and posited *yoga* as its central theme,[76] attributing an abstract character to the yogic path.[77] Correcting Schlegel's translation of *yoga* as *devotio* and Humboldt's translation as *Vertiefung,* Hegel defined *yoga* as abstract devotion because it moves upward to complete the fusion of subject and object and, in doing so, moves toward the absence of consciousness.[78] He argued that the term *devotio* implied divine orientation, content, and meaning—all of which *yoga* did not possess. Similarly, *yoga* could not be *Vertiefung,* as in art or science, because it lacks image, idea, and definite thought.[79] Moreover, *yoga* could not adequately be rendered by the term

Vertiefung, because the absorption of *yoga* is into nothingness. It consists of emptying the mind and renouncing thought. For Hegel, the *yoga* described in the *Gītā* falls into the contentlessness of subject and object and leads to a loss of consciousness.[80] At best, *yoga* encourages one to perform work senselessly and stupidly.[81] It exemplified for Hegel the negative attitude of the Indian mind[82] as well as the negative nature of religion.[83] Hegel diametrically opposed *yoga,* interpreted as a quietistic exercise, to his historical orientation.

Contrary to his initial dismissal, Hegel now conceded that India, with the concept of *Brahman* as pure substance, had developed an idea of the Universal and hence could be said to have a religion and philosophy. However, he noted that the Indian concept of *Brahman*[84] was in no way comparable to our idea of God. Moreover, he did not recognize in Indian speculative thought any return to the concrete particularity of the world; Hegel found that Hinduism lacks the essential mediation (*Vermittlung*) of the abstract Universal with the particular, and therefore it negates the dialectic of subject and object necessary for the creative development of humankind within history.[85] The finite becomes lost in the infinite; the world becomes absorbed in *Brahman*[86]—which Hegel identified with pure nothingness. If God contains all finite and particular beings as nonessential modifications, then humanity must, of necessity, possess neither identity nor dignity.[87] Abstraction, by precluding mediation,[88] also abolished freedom.[89] In fact, Hegel's definition of an Indian Absolute precluded the possibility of a free individuality manifesting itself in India.[90]

For Hegel, therefore, Indian substantiality presented the opposite of European reflection and the vanity of the subject.[91] As onerous as this vanity is, Hegel found it to be of greater worth[92] than its Indian alternative,[93] where the subject is obliterated and humiliated, where individuality disappears, and where eternal happiness is understood as the loss of the Self.[94] With the absolute void as the substructure of the Indian worldview, the Hindu vision of humanity appeared to Hegel as a large anthill closed to historic existence, with *nirvāṇa* giving life its only value. For Hegel, Hindus can empower themselves only in this negative sense;[95] knowledge, happiness, and human value are all equally impossible.[96]

Although Hegel felt that with A. W. Schlegel's translation of the *Gītā*[97] and Colebrooke's essay he had the necessary information to take on Indian philosophy,[98] he evidently did not, or rather chose only what suited his preconceived argument. As noted, Hegel had used only the first two parts (on Sāṃkhya-Yoga and Nyāya-Vaiśeṣika)[99] of Colebrooke's five-part essay. Although Colebrooke treated Sāṃkhya merely as an example of a sectarian doctrine, Hegel presented Sāṃkhya as the primary school of the Indian system.[100]

Sāṃkhya can be described as "dualistic realism." Its doctrine identifies two ultimate realities, *prakṛti* (matter) and *puruṣa* (self or spirit). The *puruṣa* denotes pure consciousness and pure subject. It differs completely from the ego, senses, and intellect. The *puruṣa* is passive and unchanging. The manifold objects constituting the universe arise from *prakṛti*. Before this evolution occurs, *prakṛti* is in a state of constant transformation, with the *guṇas* (components) constantly balancing each other. Evolution occurs from a disequilibrium of *guṇas*. *Prakṛti* transforms into gross elements, which further disintegrate into subtle elements, which in turn disintegrate, resulting in the undifferentiated and homogeneous *prakṛti* in dynamic equilibrium. *Prakṛti* develops with a purpose. It evolves for the sake of the *puruṣa* and requires contact with the *puruṣa* for evolution. The distinction *puruṣa/prakṛti* is essentially that of subject and object; they are radically different from each other. How, then do they interact? Michel Hulin claims that this issue is answered unsatisfactorily in the form of an analogy appearing in the *Sāṃkhya Kārikā* 21[101] and that Hegel forms his opinion largely from this particular *kārikā*.[102] What is important to note, for the purposes of a literary examination of the *Bhagavad Gītā*'s reception is that Hegel based his interpretation upon a partial and idiosyncratic reading of the verses in question.[103] Hulin notes that Hegel, in his analysis of the Sāṃkhya school,[104] omits and misreads the two significant passages upon which his entire analysis rests. First, he disregards *kārikās* 19 and 20 translated by Colebrooke in this manner:

> From the contrast between soul and the other principles, it follows . . . that soul is witness, bystander, spectator, solitary and passive . . . by reason of union with it, insensible body seems sensible and though the qualities be active, the stranger (soul) appears as the agent.[105]

Both knowledge and action have value in this system. Knowledge allows one to recognize one's bondage. It is by actively subduing the senses and suppressing the emotions that knowledge of one's true nature is gained. Thus, *yoga* provides the method and techniques to break through the veil of *māyā*. This very significant point is lost in Hegel's editing. Furthermore, as Hulin reveals, Hegel misreads *kārikā* 21. Colebrooke translated this strophe in the following manner:

> It is *for* contemplation of nature and *for* abstraction from it, that union of the soul with nature takes place, as the lame and

> the blind join for conveyance and for guidance: (one bearing and directed, the other borne and directing). *By* that union of soul and nature, creation, consisting in the development of intellect, is effected" (emphasis mine).[106]

Hegel, however, renders it: "It is *by* contemplation and *by* abstraction . . . that the union of soul and nature is effected . . . *by* this union of nature and soul, creation is effected."[107] As Hulin notes, Hegel thus identifies contemplation with abstraction and with the union of nature and soul.[108] Through what Colebrooke correctly identifies as "proximity,"[109] *puruṣa* enables *prakṛti* to surge forth and create the world. It is this proximity that effects liberating knowledge of what belongs to *prakṛti* and what constitutes the *puruṣa*. This knowledge, in turn, terminates their proximity. Hegel, however, omits the passage referring to proximity.[110]

Through such emendations and omissions, Hegel effectively presents Sāṃkhya as masking monism.[111] Furthermore, he is able to attribute to Sāṃkhya the same fatal binary of blind practice over and against abstract reflection that dominated his analysis of Yoga and, indeed, all of his interpretation of Indian thought. Indeed, Hegel's treatment of *kārikā* 21 is illustrative of the manner in which he supported his interpretation of the *Bhagavad Gītā*. His partial reading of Colebrooke and the *Gītā* allows Hegel to project onto Indian philosophy a despairing quietism that tallied with his earlier negative assessment of Indian thought, paralleled his interpretation of Buddhism and supported his judgment of Hindu religious observances.[112]

For Hegel, the absolute of Buddhism was *Brahm* (*sic*), cut off from deployment in the multitude of differences, a calm unity, not differentiated, the pure retreat into Self or the void.[113] Hegel posits this nothingness as the single principle from which all diverse individual persons and things proceed and whence they return. Completely subtle, absolutely simple and pure, this void consists of nothing other than the substantial, which is identical to itself.[114] It does not produce the world by generation. By autodivision, in the manner of Brahma, it lets the self *distractedly* emanate from itself like an evanescent appearance.[115]

Hegel imposed a similar negative characterization upon Indian cultic practices, which he described as the physical destruction of concrete vitality through macerations, et cetera.[116] Everything is petrified into distinctions, and caprice holds sway. There is no ethical life or human dignity. The spirit wanders in the world of dreams and the highest value is annihilation.[117] Hegel consistently viewed Indian ascetics as placing themselves beyond good and evil.[118] They tear themselves from nature through a process of depersonalizing ascesis, instead of using their intellect to situate themselves as individuals within the world.[119] Through the paths of cult and ascesis, Indians raise themselves above the finite only to lose themselves without return "in the night of Brahm [*sic*]."[120]

A number of scholars and philosophers have addressed Hegel's idiosyncratic interpretation of Indian philosophy, and have theorized about his motivations for forming his arguments. As the preceding discussion suggests, the manner in which Hegel went about his critique of India is of more than passing interest. His method relates to the general reception of India in the nineteenth century, not only in terms of the themes he chose to emphasize but also in the manner in which he legitimized his choices. In this regard, the issue of translation plays a pivotal role both on the level of problems originating in the *Bhagvad Gītā* as a translated text and also on the level of Hegel's translation theory in general. Hegel's ability to draw the conclusions that he did depended to a large extent on the use he made of translations and the justification for such usage. It is, therefore, pertinent to touch upon this purely "literary" dimension briefly.

Hegel's understanding of the *Bhagavad Gītā* was to a large extent shaped by the problem of adequately translating the term *yoga*. Hegel felt that Humboldt's reservations about rendering *yoga* by the French *dévotion* or the Latin *devotio* were misplaced. Humboldt had asserted that these terms failed to denote particular features of *yoga*. They were too narrow to represent the overall concept; they expressed only a derivation not contained in the meaning of *yoga*. Hegel preferred *Vertiefung* (in the sense of "absorption"). He found it more appropriate, but felt that it did not go far enough in defining *yoga,* since the Sanskrit term possesses a specific meaning beyond "absorption." Wilkins's gloss—"that junction and bodily or mental application"—could be generally used as a theological term to express the application of the mind in spiritual things and the performance of religious ceremonies. However, Hegel felt that as a translation, Wilkins's gloss proved unwieldly. Hegel's difficulty in finding an adequate translation for the term *yoga* was not due to mere semantic quibbling. It stemmed from far deeper theoretical concerns. Indeed, Hegel's reading of the *Bhagavad Gītā* and his reception of Indian thought in general is problemematized by the very issue of the (im)possibility of translation itself.

Hegel cites as an authority on translation Guignault, the French translator of Creuzer, who held that Schlegel's general method of translation altogether fails to convey the originality, exactness, and local color of a text. In this judgment, Guignault articulated a theory of translation that Hegel fully espoused, namely, that translation does grave injustice to terms that are sacrosanct in their own context. For Hegel, meaning is not transferable; original theological and mythological sense are, of necessity, lost.[121] Thus for translation in general, Hegel posed a fundamental epistemological problem: A translation cannot articulate specific meaning. How then can one possibly translate in any precise manner a term such as *yoga,* which denotes a concept so essential to the understanding of Indian religion? One cannot. Hegel maintained that it was impossible, for example, to render *yoga* into the German language, since the concept did not exist in German culture and religion.[122] Hegel noted that one cannot demand that an expression in a source language, with its specific mentality and culture, be rendered by a corresponding expression in a target language. A word in our language is given our specific conceptions and not that of other people with their own conceptions.[123]

Hegel, therefore, agreed with Humboldt with reference to the impossibility of translation. However, his reasons were different. When Humboldt talked about the impossibility of translation, he was making an aesthetic judgment rather than positing a philosophical pronouncement. Humboldt focused on the loss of philosophical depth and exactitude, as well as on the aesthetic parameters in terms of "blemishes," associated links, contextual values, and the nontranslatability of worldviews. Humboldt, like Herder, eschewed any temptation to compare; for both, their universalism rejected arguments of commensurability. However, Hegel's theory of translation was predicated upon the need to judge incommensurability. It corresponded well with his need, expressed throughout his discussion of the *Gītā,* to set value judgments upon Indian philosophy in light of his own philosophy. The discussion concerning the inadequacy of translating the term *yoga* led Hegel to postulate a theory concerning translation that asserted that translation was impossible due to the incommensurability of source and target languages.[124] He constructed his reading of the *Gītā,* and the conclusions he drew from it concerning the value of Indian philosophy, to highlight this incommensurability.

The impossibility of exact translation opens up the possibility of alternative and creative translations. Thus, Hegel was unconstrained in offering imprecise and fragmentary renditions that also happen to support a judgment on Indian philosophy that was grounded in a defense of his own philosophical system. In this manner, Hegel employed an idiosyncratic translation to support a vision of fatalism and a denial of Indian morality. A text retains little legitimacy when subject to such a theory of translation. The hermeneutical process breaks down, the reader's prejudices are never called into question, and the text functions as a mold into which these prejudices are poured.

It is indeed ironic that Hegel, the virulent critic of the Romantic emplotment of India, produced a reading no more authoritative than that of the Romantics he sought to debunk. Although their respective projects differed radically, India was no less a conscious fiction in Hegel's normative reading than in Schlegel's flights of fancy. Whereas nascent philology proved to be Schlegel's undoing institutional philology (in the form of translation theory and technique) provided Hegel with a potent weapon, which Cousin would subsequently wield with great aplomb.

IV

Victor Cousin excelled as a persecuted liberal hero. His courses at the École Normale Superieure were suspended in 1818–19. In 1824, he was arrested in Berlin by order of the French police, only to be released upon Hegel's intervention with the Prussian minister of the interior. Cousin resumed lecturing in April–July 1828 and was incredibly popular with the students. Viewed as a cult figure, Cousin issued pronouncements in his lectures that were hailed as acts of insurrection to the unpopular regime of the restored monarchy. Cousin's set goal was to open up philosophy, especially German philosophy, and Hegel's work in particular, to the French. His lectures drew many auditors. The content of those lectures alluded to the contemporary political issues and were fully publicized. In newspapers, the appearance of *comptes rendus* received the same attention as did parliamentary debates.[125] By defending a form of spirituality autonomous from revelation and faith, Cousin's message found a ready audience.

Between 1818 and 1825, Cousin devised a schema for the history of philosophy that he later published in *Histoire générale de la philosophie* (1863). He presented philosophy as the history of the human spirit, which could be broken down into four distinct categories:[126] sensualism, idealism, skepticism, and mysticism. In the fifth and sixth lessons of the *Cours de l'histoire de la philosophie* (1829),[127] Cousin applied this schema to Indian speculative thought. In fact, the primary purpose of the *Cours* was to prove the universality of his system. If, with the help of Colebrooke's essay, Cousin could discover elements of his schema operant in ancient India, how could his method be contested? Similarly, one cannot reject a universal system of philosophy once it has been discovered nascent in

India,[128] the cradle of civilization[129] and philosophy.[130] It was in this context that the fifth and sixth lessons of Cousin's *Cours* contributed to the diffusion (via Colebrooke) of Indian philosophy in Europe. Goethe's mention of these lectures to Eckermann is indicative of their popularity and circulation abroad. Whereas Humboldt, assuming a unanimity between Patañjali's system of Yoga as explained by Colebrooke and the *Gītā,* worked directly from the Sanskrit text of the *Gītā,* and Hegel worked primarily from Colebrooke, Cousin based his lectures on both Colebrooke and the Latin translation of the *Gītā*.

As Roger-Pol Droit has shown, in order to incorporate the Indian philosophical schools into his system, Cousin first alters Colebrooke's account of their developmental order.[131] The Vedas are dropped from consideration because, as revelation, they are precluded from the domain of philosophy. Cousin also omits Mīmāṃsā because he considers it primarily theological, as he does Buddhism.[132] He equates Nyāya with Idealism[133] and discovers traces of Sensualism in Sāṃkhya, because it arrives at the Sovereign Good through sensation, perception, and inference rather than through religious practices or intellect.[134] Furthermore, Sāṃkhya presents Cousin with three incompatible traits: skepticism, sensualism, and mysticism.

While Cousin recognized indifference and skepticism throughout the Indian philosophical systems,[135] he found it particularly prevalent in the Sāṃkhya tradition, which he felt advocated fatalism, absurd fanaticism, and pure mysticism.[136] As a champion of liberal spiritualism, Cousin viewed the issue of Sāṃkhya's blatant mysticism as most problematic.[137] Cousin understood the *Bhagavad Gītā* as both the literary monument of Sāṃkhya[138] and the paradigm for mysticism in Indian philosophy. Therefore, his analysis of the poem attempts to expose the moral and metaphysical excesses of Indian philosophy.[139]

To understand Cousin's interpretation of the *Gītā,* we must understand his definition of mysticism. Mysticism entails the primacy of intuition over discursive knowledge and the superiority of faith over works. Most importantly, however, mysticism leads to inaction and indifference. Cousin views mystics as individuals who have separated themselves from science, turned from regular study, and embraced contemplation.[140] The entire thrust of Cousin's reading of the *Gītā* is aimed at proving it to be a text promulgating mysticism in his sense of the term. Cousin supports his interpretive reading of the *Gītā* with translations of excerpts that are contextually unsupportable and fragmentary. Thus, Cousin's reception of the *Gītā* is strangely reminiscent of Hegel's treatment of the text, in both its emphasis on quietism and its manipulation of translated material.

To establish the mysticism of the *Gītā,* Cousin must first establish its demand for *recueillement* and interior contemplation, which for Cousin are the prolegomena of mysticism.[141] Cousin sets the stage for this reading by interpreting the *Gītā*'s call for disinterested action as disdain for book knowledge, belittlement of the Vedas, and mockery of ceremonies. In Krishna's criticism of the type of ritual action that aims at the enjoyment and exercise of power (*BG* 2.43), Cousin sees a condemnation of action in general that is not supported by Schlegel's Latin text.[142] In those instances where Cousin is forced to acknowledge Krishna's message of disinterested action, he fabricates a subtext. According to Cousin, the author of the *Gītā* has Krishna teach disinterested dharmic action only in order not to shock the common sense and virility of a young *kṣatriya.*[143] Cousin allegedly exposes the subterfuge inherent in this teaching: Because one cannot be sure about the disinterestedness of any action, one would tend to abstain from action in general, which in turn engenders inertia and, finally, the ideal of complete inaction. To support this interpretation, he cites verse 4.18:

> He who perceives inactivity in activity, and activity in inactivity, he among mortals knows.[144]

And when the final *pāda* of this verse (*sa yukta kṛtsnakarmakṛt,* he disciplined, doing all action") contradicts the quietist interpretation, Cousin omits it. One cannot even conclude that this omission stems from any ambiguity in the Schlegel translation ("is devotus cunctis operibus peragendis aptus est"). As Cousin edits Schlegel, the central injunction to perform all actions with discipline is consistently lost, and Cousin can erroneously conclude that the *Gītā* teaches the superiority of contemplation over action and works.

For Cousin, the mysticism of the *Gītā* extends to the point of degrading works, both good and bad. Although he cites verse 2.50 to support this claim,[145] here too he omits its final *pāda* (*yoga karmasu kauśalam,* "*yoga* is skill in actions"), found in Schlegel as "Quare devotioni te devove: devotio dexteritatem in operibus praebit."[146] From this misreading, Cousin concludes that such disdain of works easily leads to any madness, even the most perverse forms.[147] Moreover, if the Hindu God only counts faith and disdains action, then he must be indifferent to good as well as bad actions.[148] In such a religious system, Cousin concludes, the individual can arrive at sainthood regardless of sin. Supporting the notion that the *Gītā* promulgates actions beyond good and evil, Cousin asserts that verse 9.30 teaches the destruction of all liberty and all morality when he translates it as:

> The most criminal, if he serves me without division is purified and sanctified by it.[149]

In the Sanskrit original, as well as Schlegel's rendition,[150] it is an issue less of being beyond good and evil than of the power of *bhakti* (faith or devotion) over moral effects.[151] The *Gītā* does not teach, as Cousin would have us believe, that the individual is destined to advance beyond good and evil, as well as error and truth and good and bad philosophy.[152] Rather, Krishna enjoins Arjuna to fulfill his *dharma* as a warrior.

Objectively, there are those instances where Cousin's predisposition to read fatality into the *Gītā* was abetted by Schlegel's translation, as in verse 5.13:

> The moderate one among mortals, whose soul, bound by action is completely released, remains in the city built with nine doors, he himself neither acting nor the teacher of those acting.[153]

The Sanskrit specifically refers to the individual who sits as a ruler and through control has removed all actions "with his mind." Although Schlegel clearly expresses that the individual is restrained (*temperans*), he has omitted translating *manasā* (with his mind), which ultimately refers to the *yogī*'s ability to perform desireless action. Cousin will render this passage:

> Delivered from all cares of action, the true devotee remains tranquilly seated in the city with nine doors (the body) without moving himself or others.[154]

In a similar fashion, Schlegel's correct translation[155] of verse 2.58 conveys the yogic agenda of distancing the self from involvement and controlling one's thought.[156] The Sanskrit literally refers to the drawing together (*saṃharate*) of the senses. Unfortunately, Schlegel has chosen to render the verb *SAM-HṚ* as *asbtraho,* which leads to Cousin's choice of the term *se recueillir,* evoking the process of retiring within oneself. Hence, the quietist rendition:

> He retires within himself, like a turtle who retracts into itself.[157]

Other examples can be brought forward, such as Cousin's rendition of *abstinens* (for the Sanskrit *saṃyamin,* "a man of restraint") as "le sage" in *Gītā* 2,69. Here, too, the translation does not adequately express the status of abstinence as an action that Sanskrit text suggests.[158]

Although an argument can be made for the mysticism of the *Gītā,* Cousin's thesis that the poem promulgates absolute quietism, indifference, renunciation, and contemplative immobility is simply not justifiable:

> Let action alone be thy interest, never its fruits. Your motive should not be fruits of action, nor an attachment to non-action.[159]

Rather than recognizing the Hindu mystical identification of the individual soul (*Ātman*) with the All-Soul (*Brahman*), Cousin chose to view this recognition as a wholly passive act. To a certain extent he was led astray by Schlegel's translation of *yoga* as *contemplatio* and established the fundamental theme of the *Gītā* to be that of quietism. Moreover, the message of the *Gītā* is not particularly simple. It teaches a complex game of action, detachment, and devotion. The individual is enjoined to behave according to one's own *dharma* (*svadharma*). Action ought to be completed, once one has renounced the fruits of that action. By the unification of the senses and thought, with desire, hope, and fear dispelled, action is pursued. Renunciation separates the actor from the act. The action, in which the subject is not implicated, is then offered to God. The *Bhagavad Gītā* clearly does not promote the issue of inaction. Neither Hegel nor Cousin was willing to read this message in the *Gītā*.

V

It is indeed curious how Humboldt, Hegel, and Cousin, three thinkers who were to have a profound effect on the institutional instruction of philosophy in their respective countries, set out to decipher Indian philosophy for the West. Hegel and Cousin, in particular, paint an extraordinarily contrived and negative vision of the *Gītā*'s philosophy.

Humboldt intentionally read the *Gītā* in isolation from other religious and philosophical texts. With his translation of *yoga* as *Vertiefung,* he sought to convey the nuances implied by the root *YUJ* (to bind): *Frömmigkeit* (piety), *Weihung* (devotion), *Widmung* (dedication), and *Anstrengung* (effort). Humboldt viewed Hegel's response article as directed solely against him and believed that Hegel's point of departure was to show that Humboldt could be called everything but a philosopher.[160] To a great extent, Humboldt was correct in his assessment: Hegel refused to appreciate Humboldt's attempt, as a philologist, to *translate* Indian philosophy objectively, without mixing it with Western philosophy, Indian ritual, or contemporary sociological observations.

In turn, Humboldt questioned Hegel's philosophical method. Indeed, Hegel based his knowledge of Indian thought on Upanishadic, epic, and Purāṇic fragments, and the testimony of British military officials.[161] Although he was virulent against his fellow Germans who sought to discover religious purity in India, in his own research he was not especially critical of the variety or objectivity of his source material. While he railed at the Schlegels and Humboldt because they did not think conceptually, he never challenged his own historical perpective: Hegel himself mixed philosophy with fable, and modern scholars with missionaries, travelers, and military officials.[162] In fact, his analysis of Indian philosophy was as much a fiction and an abuse of the Sanskrit "sources" as anything done by the Romantics, with the major difference being that Hegel supported his claim by "science" and the Romantics relied on intuition.

Hegel's belief that India was immutable with no possibility of creative originality perhaps justified (in his own mind) his method of inquiry. By cutting away everything that did not suit his argument, Hegel retained from Humboldt's reasoned discussion only the negative, engulfing, emptying aspect of devotion.[163] To a certain degree, Schopenhauer's assessment of Hegel's attempt to understand world history—that it was naive and trivial[164]—would not be a gratuitous dismissal if it were based on Hegel's interpretation of Indian philosophy.

In his own analysis, Cousin imitated Hegel's method of legitimizing a normative reading with the pretense of scholarly method. His method consisted of supporting Hegel's negative assessment and imposing his own philosophical schematization through a distorted dissemination of Schlegel's Latin translation in French. Hegel's accusation of *Substanzualität* became Cousin's campaign against mysticism. For Cousin, the *yoga* (*dévotion*) of the *Gītā* consists of union through ecstasy: Inaction is preferable to action, and faith to works. Through the indifferent renunciation of all actions, one gives oneself over to the immobility of indifference.[165] This theme of quietism, embedded thus in the mysticism of the *Gītā,* encapsulated Cousin's judgment on Indian philosophy in general. Although Cousin does not explicitly mention Hegel's articles, his lectures voice a similar critique of the abstract character of pure Being. Cousin differs from Hegel only in his belief that this abstraction is a universal trait of mysticism, whereas Hegel views abstraction as historically circumscribed to India.[166]

In conclusion, we might compare these three thinkers' reception of the *Bhagavad Gītā* in terms of their overarching thematics and styles. In reference to the seminal theme of inaction, Humboldt offers a sober explication, highlighting the role of action in the *Gītā* while pointing out its problematic relation to the path of contemplation. Although Hegel does not specifically identify the renunciation of the fruits of action with inaction,[167] his response to Humboldt levels a sharp condemnation of Indian passivity and fatalism. Cousin follows Hegel in his condemnation of Indian inaction, which he identifies with mysticism. By attributing a mystical agenda to all Indian philosophy, Cousin, although he works from the *Gītā,* avoids any ambiguity inherent in the text.

However, the greatest mistake in Hegel's and Cousin's interpretations of Indian thought consists of their imposing upon Sāṃkhya a Cartesian agenda wherein the individual appears as the point of departure and ultimate term of reference. Given this perspective, Indian philosophy necessarily fails when it disengages the *puruṣa.* Belief in this Self that is impassible and inactive strikes them as nihilistic, given the Western metaphysical grounding in subjectivity, of which Hegel's philosophy is the exemplum.

Thus, an image of despair runs throughout Hegel's and Cousin's treatments of Indian philosophy, an image that was at no time confirmed by Schlegel's Latin translation of the *Gītā,* Colebrooke's essay on the Indian philosophical schools, or Humboldt's commentary. This misconception[168] can best be summed up by Hegel's opium metaphor: that Indians could only attain a dream world and the happiness of insanity through opium.[169] Viewed in this light, Indians place themselves beyond good and evil at the price of total destruction of their concrete individuality. Neither Hegel's criticism of European vanity of the Self nor Cousin's radical liberalism deter them, however, from their Western-centered arrogance. Europe represents progress and remains superior to all other nations of the world. Hegel and, to a lesser degree, the persecuted liberal hero Cousin appear as advocates of this ascendancy and the colonialism that such an intellectual posture fostered.[170]

By focusing on the literary dimension of the initial reception of the *Bhagavad Gītā,* I have suggested that nineteenth-century translation theory and hermeneutical concerns played a role in the critical dismissal of Indian philosophy in the West. Humboldt read Colebrooke in conjunction with the *Gītā* in the original Sanskrit. His reading is syncretic; in order to avoid misreadings of Indian philosophy, he points out how Indian speculative thought differed from Western philosophy. He felt such misinterpretations would mask the universality of the message, and his primary concern was to highlight this universality. His "enlightened" approach places him in direct opposition to the hermeneutical position articulated in the narratives of Hegel and Cousin. In this sense, this initial reception of the *Bhagavad Gītā* heralds the ideological shift I have advanced for the general emplotment of India in the West, the movement away from Enlightenment universalism to later epistemological categories (subject/object) or psychological categories (Self/Other).

Hegel compared Colebrooke's thoughts with the Schlegel translation. Although he was as well versed in the fledgling field of Indology as any nonspecialist of his time, he never allowed its message to challenge his own philosophy or system. To the end, he insisted on the radical alterity of East-West representations. Cousin, however, attempted a direct assimilation of Indian philosophy. But his method erred in two important respects. First, he did not even suspect that the Latin translation might pose problems. Second, in the most egregious fashion he toyed with the translation to support his reading. His metaphysical psychology suggests that Schlegel's refractive Latin translation gives access to the letter of the text without diffraction or effraction. Cousin thus presupposes the possibility of total translation, a negation ("foreclosure") of the act of translation.[171] Whereas Schlegel and Humboldt spoke of the figurative impossibility of translation, Cousin predicated his argument upon the immateriality of translation. Languages and their representations are interchangeable. Cousin was content to reposition the Other to fit his view of the Western model.

Hegel's relation to the text was predicated upon the incommensurability of cultures. He worked from the vantage of the superior position he ascribed to Western philosophy, with his own philosophy as its acme. As J. L. Mehta noted, Hegel originated the idea that the Orient can be superceded in order for the West to understand it. By contrasting "Western" truth to that of the Orient, he was the first systematically to set out and prove the Orient deficient in terms of this truth.[172] Hegel's project consisted, therefore, of a good deal more than merely distancing India, negating the Other, and avoiding the temptation of viewing the Self in "an Aryan mirror."[173] Yet, despite his assumption of superiority, there is clearly a defensiveness that works as a consistent subtext. The exotic (and equally the Romantic) must be discredited in order to prove that truth is rational and develops historically, even broadening its scope through the only means devised to explicate its meaning—institutionalized philology and philosophy.

This initial reception of the *Bhagavad Gītā* foregrounded the hermeneutical problems involved in addressing the Other. In their remarks concerning the translation of the *Bhagavad Gītā,* each of these thinkers questioned how philosophical thought can be understood outside its own tradition. In a critical detour from Enlightenment universalism which still held sway in the nineteenth-century hermeneutic tradition (and was supported by the work of Humboldt), Hegel foreclosed the very possibility of such understanding when he rejected the notion of a common standard of meaning and inflicted the standards and methodological apparatus of one culture upon another. The impossibility of understanding the Other with a European mode of understanding is nothing more than a movement to colonize the consciousness of the Other. Any hermeneutical project is thus aborted.

If, as Hegel maintained in his discussion of the translation of philosophical terms, understanding is impossible, how are we then to interpret any venture into the exotic? We learn from Gadamer the impossibility of objectively understanding the Other in its own identity. Gadamer posits two essential processes in understanding: the historical reconstruction of the original context as well as the discovery of a message beyond a text's content. The second step necessitates a willingness to accept the message. In the circular movement of hermeneutical understanding, the text imposes flexible expectations, sharing (in the form of play) in the common meaning of tradition and interpretation. This movement allows for the anticipation of meaning. Within the reader's desire to communicate with the text, there appears strangeness as well as familiarity in the form of prejudices which facilitate or thwart understanding. Thus, the distance between the reader and the text does not appear as an unbreachable obstacle, but rather as what sets the hermeneutical process in motion. As noted earlier, it is precisely this process that is shortcircuited in these exotic quests. The hermeneutical process does not run full cycle; it stalls at intervals for a variety of reasons. The reader may refuse to engage in the play or in alternative forms of inquiry. Delectation with some dominant fiction or master narrative may ultimately be more gratifying than mere understanding. The ensuing privileging of the self beyond the quotidian may simply be too seductive.

An examination of the initial European reception of the *Bhagavad Gītā* bears witness to these procedures. Advancing the truth claim of

Western philosophy is inseparable from defending the preeminent position of the individual Western philosopher and translator. An unfortunate result of this ambition was that the scholarly reception of Indian philosophy was repressed and marginalized. The resulting lacuna could only be filled by popular notions of the esoteric and occult East. Scholarship abrogated its responsibility when it capitulated and codified Indian philosophical concepts in a bastardized form. The field was opened for a revitalization of Romantic irrationalism with an important difference. The Romantic emplotment of India had not been effectively legitimized by science (in the form of philosophical and philological discourse), as subsequent master narratives on India would be.

PART III

THE POETICS OF DESPAIR: IRRATIONAL RESPONSES TO EXOTICISM

By waves swept on, I learned to ride the waves;
I served my masters till I made them slaves;
I baffled death by hiding in his graves,
His watery graves, Nirvana.

—Sidney Lanier, "Nirvana"

Introduction

In *The Crisis of German Ideology,* George Mosse[1] contends that themes such as *karma* and rebirth are components of the theosophical and occult influences upon National Socialism. However, long before the Nazis came to power, such ideas were known to Germans through a long tradition of Indological scholarship, the reception of India in German literature, and a general identification with India that was supported by racial and linguistic theories.

As we have seen in previous chapters, with the earliest translations from the Sanskrit, India became a great source of aesthetic inspiration, and its influence permeated German thought. The works of Herder, Goethe, and the Schlegels attest to the scope of these influences. India was used to voice Germany's hopes for a cultural invigoration from without—so much so that the argument made for the idealism and absolutism that animated Germany's search for inspiration in classical models can equally be posited for Germany's metaphorical journeys to India in the nineteenth century. However, as in the case of Greece's tyranny over Germany (to use that wonderful phrase coined by E. M. Butler), it was not so much India's tyranny over Germany as the tyranny of Germany's ideologizing of Indian metaphysical concepts. Let us take, for example, the case of Philipp Mainländer.

The day after the appearance of *Die Philosophie der Erlösung,* Mainländer shot himself, stepping into the abyss through which he sought to pass into *nirvāṇa*. Mainländer's effort was the logical conclusion of Schopenhauer's philosophy, a conclusion before which Schopenhauer himself recoiled. However, Mainländer's act shows to what extent Schopenhauer's reinterpretation of Buddhism had given rise to a movement that, although celebrated as Indian, would ultimately reveal itself as the dark underside of the *Zeitgeist,* noteworthy for its blend of pessimism, irrationalism, and atheism. Enthusiasm for Schopenhauer's philosophical synthesis of Buddhism and Brahmanism became a permanent fixture of the spiritual landscape. Many perceived in Schopenhauer's premises an absolute void in which one might escape personal despair, whereas others rejected pessimism to affirm a view of life as prevailing over all pain.

In the 1870s, a group of writers produced what might be termed a German "*nirvāṇa* literature," embodying the Romantic, exalted interpretation of the peculiarly "Indian" philosophy of the individual soul's extinction. The designation *nirvāṇa literature* is perhaps misleading, and these works might better be classified as *karma-saṃsāra-nirvāṇa literature,* since they dealt with the themes of ethical retribution, the illusory nature of the world, and the destruction of individual consciousness, respectively.

In part 2, we saw how the philosophical reception of India, grounded as it was in imperfect philology, ratified a fatalistic interpretation of Indian religious thought. Nineteenth-century European philosophy and philology were used as weapons to prove "Indian" quietism. This vision of quietism was then rejected. In a parallel process that developed throughout the remainder of the nineteenth century, the emplotment of Indian metaphysical thought fluctuated between its roles as a model to be ultimately discarded and an alibi to be embraced and transmogrified. In part 3, I will examine this creative process. I will first focus, in chapters 5 and 6, on how this vision of quietism attains a lyrical focus in the German and French quests for *nirvāṇa.* I conclude this study with an examination, in chapter 7, of the appropriation of "Buddhist" and "Hindu" themes as components of a new Aryan faith. In chapter 5, I begin by distinguishing the vision of *nirvāṇa* found in Schopenhauer from its Brahmanic and Buddhist connotations. I then assess the body of German *nirvāṇa* literature as attempts to support or refute Schopenhauer's pessimism. For Schopenhauer, his disciples, Wagner, Nietzsche, and others, the lure of *nirvāṇa* held out above the ruins of theism the tantalizing promise of an exotic humanism.

5

The German Quest for Nirvāṇa

I

Monier-Williams defines *nirvāṇa* as a blowing out or extinction of a flame, dissolution, death, final emanicipation from matter, and reunion with the Supreme Spirit. For Buddhists, *nirvāṇa* is absolute extinction or annihilation of individual existence or all desire and passions. It is also defined as perfect calm, happiness, and beatitude.[1] Clearly, it is a term fraught with varying and even contradictory significations. It has no simple primordial meaning.

For the Vedāntin, *nirvāṇa* is eternal life and the end of the illusion of individuality. After the suppression of individuality, the Vedāntin comes face-to-face with *Brahman,* the Absolute. Brahmanical salvation consists of union, perfect knowledge, and the identity with *Brahman*. In early Buddhism, *nirvāṇa* is reality without any consciousness. Hīnayāna Buddhism understood *nirvāṇa* as relative nothingness and the extinction of individuality. The Lesser Vehicule never denied the empirical reality of the world; both *saṃsāra* and *nirvāṇa* are real and oppositional. In Buddhism of the Great Vehicle, or Mahāyāna, *nirvāṇa* is absoltue emptiness about which there can be no predication. The Madhyamaka philosophy views *saṃsāra* and *nirvāṇa* as both separately unreal. In Vijñānavāda philosophy, *saṃsāra* is unreal and *nirvāṇa* is real.[2] This summary of the various theories of *nirvāṇa* suffices to show how problematic a concept it is in the history of Buddhist and Brahmanical thought. Such canonical distinctions are not, however, crucial to our understanding of the German reception of *nirvāṇa*. The authors we will examine did not have access to primary sources. They culled their information from an identifiable corpus of secondary materials which were themselves distorted.[3] For the sake of this study, let us accept the working definition of *nirvāṇa* as an unqualified deliverance, deliverance as a state about which we have no right to predicate anything. It is the cessation of rebirth and a deliverance from transmigration, disease, old age, and death.

With Arthur Schopenhauer (1788–1860), Buddhism became a real force in the intellectual life of Germany. Schopenhauer's Indian *Schwärmerei* is a fascinating example of East-West philosophical reception. He wrote at a time when European Indological research was in its infancy, and pedagogical and scholarly tools were scarce. However, Schopenhauer made good use of what was available. Perhaps no other Western philosopher has been influenced as much by Eastern religious thought as Schopenhauer. Nevertheless, we must ascribe to his system a definite independence even though he recognized Buddhists as his *Glaubensgenossen*[4] and took great satisfaction in having come to similar theories before actually having studied Buddhist philosophy.

> If I wished to take the results of my philosophy as the standard of truth, I should have to concede to Buddhism preeminence over the others. In any case it must be a pleasure to see my doctrine in such close agreement with a religion that the majority of men on earth hold as their own. . . . And this agreement must be yet more pleasing to me, inasmuch as in my philosophizing I have certainly not been under its influence.[5]

When he wrote the first edition of *Die Welt als Wille und Vorstellung* in 1818, Schopenhauer had a fragmentary knowledge of Buddhism and as complete a knowledge of the *Upanishads* as could be garnered from a tertiary translation. He incorporated ideas that were suggested by a rudimentary and incomplete pedagogical apparatus into a system firmly grounded in the tradition of continental philosophy. Schopenhauer claimed that his philosophy developed from a reaction to experiences similar to those that inspired the Buddha. He wrote in his *Nachlass:* "When I was seventeen years old, without any scholarly education, I was as moved by the misery of life as the Buddha was in his youth when he perceived sickness, old age, suffering and death."[6] The Buddhist idea of existence as impermanent is clearly present in Schopenhauer's argument. The *Parerga und Paralipomena,*[7] articulates that happiness is unattainable. Schopenhauer's postulate that striving after happiness ends in disillusionment echoes the Buddhist doctrine that the desire to live, the thirst to exist is the source of all suffering.[8]

Thirst is the underlying force that drives the empirical world of *saṃsāra*. The will, that for Schopenhauer animates the phenomenal world, deeply resembles this Buddhist concept of thirst. Both thirst and the will engender suffering, but thirst is purely an aspect of the empirical world, while the will is something beyond it. This will is unconstrained in its freedom and has a subjective expression. It can just as easily be called "*Brahman*" or "the universal soul."[9] Immanent in all, the will has all being as its objectification; it is the *Ding an sich*.

The will can be known, and it can also, and indeed should, be denied. Schopenhauer enjoins us to extinguish the will so that all phenomena and the world as we know it might come to an end.[10] His call to negate the will serves the same function as the Buddha's injunction to extinguish thirst. They both aim at the removal of desire and the end of suffering. While the method whereby the will, through its phenomena (ideas and representations), can will its own extinction remains obscure in Schopenhauer, in Buddhism, these aims are attained through the experience of *nirvāṇa*.[11] It is within this context that Schopenhauer develops his appropriation of the themes of *nirvāṇa* in the supplement to the fourth book of *Die Welt als Wille und Vorstellung*. The world is the worst of all possible worlds. The Judeo-Christian concept of original sin is false; the true original sin is one's birth. Life in the world is inseparable from guilt because it means acceptance of the actions of the will and the notions of individuality that are attendant upon it. Schopenhauer offers no refuge in this world nor salvation in the next. The possibility of salvation exists only through the negation of the will in a state where all striving ceases.

> The great fundamental truth contained in Christianity as well as in Brahmanism and Buddhism, the need for salvation from an existence given up to suffering, and death, and its attainability through the denial of the will, hence by a decided opposition to nature, is beyond all comparison the most important truth there can be.[12]

Where does this deliverance lead us? To nothingness? Philosophy has the ability to represent the world to us. In so doing, it can decisively influence our values and actions, but it cannot offer transcendence.

Initially, in accord with Buddhist teaching, Schopenhauer defines *nirvāṇa* negatively.[13] It is not four things: birth, old age, sickness, and death.[14] It is important to note that, for Schopenhauer, *nirvāṇa* cannot be death. Death is the cessation of physical life but does not alter the nature or insistence of the will to live; it merely cuts the will short. Therefore, death provides an inadequate solution. Upon this point Schopenhhauer's more determined disciples disagreed with him.[15] While Mainländer, at least, equated death with deliverance, Schopenhauer believed that death was in no way an extraordinary feat. The cessation of life, unlike *nirvāṇa,* comes to everyone. Suicide, Schopenhauer noted, was the *Meisterstück der Māyā.*[16] Schopenhauer's *nirvāṇa* is both the denial of the will and the condition that follows such a denial of the will:

> He willingly gives up the existence that we know; what comes to him instead of it is in our eyes nothing, because our existence in reference to that one is nothing. The Buddhist faith calls that existence Nirvana, that is to say, extinction.[17]

Although seemingly absolute, this nothingness is to be welcomed, not feared:

> We have to banish the dark impression of that nothingness, which as the final goal hovers behind all virtue and holiness, and which we fear as children fear darkness. We must not evade it, as the Indians do, by myths and meaningless words, such as reabsorption in Brahma, or the nirvana of the Buddhists. On the contrary, we freely acknowledge that what remains after the complete abolition of the will is, for all who are still full of the will, assuredly nothing. But also conversely, to those in whom the will has turned and denied itself, this very real world of ours with all its suns and galaxies, is—nothing.[18]

However, with time, an absolute quality of Schopenhauer's *nirvāṇa* was tempered. In the "Epiphilosophy," it became a relative nothingness. Schopenhauer's modification of *nirvāṇa* was probably due to a more profound knowledge of Buddhism. In the edition of 1818, four pages were devoted to *nirvāṇa*. In the "Epiphilosophy," *nirvāṇa* is not the absolute nothingness of his youth, not merely pure negation, but capable of being the ground from which the will arises.[19]

It would seem that negation of the will could produce only an unqualified nothingness, yet Schopenhauer is unwilling to posit a nothingness completely devoid of all qualities. He denies the absolute in favor of an irreconcilable tension between being and non-being. With the suppression of the will, "we see that peace that is higher than all reason, that ocean-like calmness of the spirit, that deep tranquility, that unshakable confidence and serenity . . . ," yet it is also "empty nothingness."[20] What is the reason for this seemingly paradoxical definition?

The ambiguity of Schopenhauer's nothingness echoes the teaching of the Prajñā-Pāramitā literature, and, in the note to the abovementioned passage, Schopenhauer acknowledges his indebtedness to this system of thought.[21] The Prajñā-Pāramitā scriptures of Mahāyāna Buddhism were not well-known in Schopenhauer's time. Their principle theme is *śūnyatā* (emptiness) and they present *nirvāṇa* as *śūnyatā* itself. In fact, both *śūnyatā* and *nirvāṇa* are thought constructions and devoid of any reality. *Saṃsāra,* at times, is identified with *nirvāṇa*. The subtle dialectic of the Prajñā-Pāramitā, balancing between being and nonbeing, allowed Schopennhauer to maintain his equivocal stance and, as it were, remain above this abyss of nihilism. However, disciples such as Mainländer and Hartmann rejected this dualism. In their popular combination of Schopenhauer's pessimism and Hegel's teleology, they drew unequivocal conclusions from Schopenhauer's premises when they defined *nirvāṇa* as absolute nothingness.

Edward von Hartmann's *Philosophie des Unbewussten* (1869) returned to the tenets of Buddhism finding, not Schopenhauerian quietism,[22] but a rationale for a heroic kind of modern pessimism. Schopenhauer sought deliverance by negating the will to live; Hartmann proclaimed that will. Although rejecting Schopenhauer's absolutist claims for Indian religion, as well as those of Hegel for Christianity,[23] Hartmann nevertheless sought to incorporate Schopenhauer's understanding of *nirvāṇa* in his interpretation of the development of Western religion.

Hartmann developed a conception of the unconscious that posited the initial unity of reason and will. Reason battles with the will and needs to be emancipated. Once separate, the will determines the melancholy career of the unconscious. When enough of the will is enlightened by reason to recognize the misery of existence, a collective effort to will nonexistence must be made so the world can lapse into nothingness. In his essay "Was ist Nirwana?" Hartmann defines this nothingness: It consists of both deliverance and the nothingness behind the illusory phenomenal world.[24]

Mainländer saw the world as moving in a process of dissolution. He interpreted Schopenhauer's philosophy as a teleology of decay with the will to death masking a will to live.[25] Both Mainländer and Hartmann emphasized the possibility of world-*nirvāṇa,* a concept they borrowed from Schopenhauer.[26] Buddhists generally believe that all sentient life will eventually attain *nirvāṇa* with the help of those elite few who forstall their own entry into this state. Schopenhauer and his disciples, however, suggest that *nirvāṇa* is open to all who seek it.

Because Schopenhauer viewed history as a farce,[27] he discredited the linear view that tied redemption to a unique event.[28] Schopenhauer's will functioned as the most knowable entity[29] whose negation involves not destruction but, rather, a subjective act or an event of self-transformation through withdrawal from the world. Schopenhauer's interpretation of the concept of *nirvāṇa* allowed him to question the adequacy of objectifying knowledge.[30] His soteriological agnosticism enabled him to view *nirvāṇa* not as knowledge *stricto senso,* but as ascetic detachment pushed to an extreme, as a soupçon of deliverance itself.[31]

II

Rushing, roaring wheel of time,
You knife of eternity;
Shining spheres in the broad Universe,
Which surround the world
Original eternal creation, stop,
Enough with becoming, leave me alone!

Stop, you generating power,
Original thought, which eternally creates!
Stop your breath, calm the urge,
Be quiet for only a second!
Swelling pulse, catch the beat;
End, the will's 'eternal day!'

. . .

Far in craved desire
Spread out your arms,
And embrace prisoners of delusion
Deserted emptiness of vain horror.[32]

Mathilde Wesendonck,
"Wesendonck Lieder"

At the conclusion of the *Götterdämmerung,* Brünnhilde prepares to mount her beloved's funeral pyre. In the tradition of European operatic *satīs,* she uses the occasion of her martyrdom to expound upon the intensity of her love for Siegfried. Ecstatically enjoining her horse Grane to accompany her, she explains how love has overwhelmed and enslaved her.

> Greetings Grane, my horse,
> Do you know, friend,
> Where I am leading you?
> In the blazing fire
> Lies your master,
> Siegfried, my late hero.
> Do you neigh happily
> To follow our friend?
> Do the laughing flames
> Lure you to him?
> Feel how my breast also burns;
> Bright fire
> Seizes my heart:
> To embrace him,
> To be enclosed by him,
> To be wed
> In the most Powerful Love!—
> Hi-ho! Grane!
> Greet our friend!
> Siegfried! Siegfried!
> Let my greeting bless you.[33]

These final lines of the opera were most probably written while Wagner was occupied with *Tristan und Isolde,*[34] and they address the theme central to both operas:—the loss of self through the experience of love. However, in an earlier manuscript of *Die Götterdämmerung* dating from the summer of 1856, Wagner has his heroine sing a different tune. In this version, when Brünnhilde ascends the pyre, she is no longer a pawn in Wotan's plot for world conquest; rather, she is answering Schopenhauer's call:

> If I now journey no more
> To Walhalla's feasting,
> Do you know, where I go?

I leave the Land of Desire,
I flee the Land of Illusion forever;
I close behind me
The open door
Of eternal Becoming:
Now, she who is wise journeys
    To the desireless and delusionless
    Holiest chosen land,
The goal of world-wandering,
Freed from rebirth,
    Everything eternal
    Blessed end,
Do you know, how I have won it?
    The deepest suffering
    Of sorrowful love,
My eyes opened:
I saw the world end.[35]

Here we leave the domain of old German sagas and enter into the realm of exoticized Buddhism when Brünnhilde seeks to break the bonds of rebirth and escape the domain of Kāma and the snares of *māyā*. Brünnhilde leaves behind the world of vain cravings and illusion, and her wandering through countless existence ends, as suggested in a variant of the preceding version.

Sorrowful love
Deepest pity
Opened the gates to me:
Who, above all things, respects life
Turn your eyes from me!
Who, out of pity
looks after the departing one
To him redemption dawns from afar
which I have attained.
With this greeting, I part from you, O world.[36]

In the final aria, both these verisons were stricken. In the version that Wagner retained, the theme of love's redemptive power assumes prominence. For the purposes of this study, it is important to note that pity

(*Mitleid*), not love, initially formed the final thematic of the *Götterdämmerung*. As Brünnhilde lights the pyre, she turns to those around her and wishes them an end to their rebirths.

In these ultimately omitted versions of the final scene, Brünnhilde equates the world of the living with the dwelling of the restless. The wise one, recognizing this world to be one of deceptive illusions, realizing its worthlessness, leaves it gladly. By closing the doors of eternal becoming, the initiate escapes future rebirths and attains an eternal end. Brünnhilde here does not refer to an individual cessation of existence. These lines, written at the height of Wagner's *Schopenhauerwendung,* express the heroine's longing for *nirvāṇa* as Wagner understood it via Schopenhauer.

At first reading, Wagner found the implications of Schopenhauer's philosophy unacceptable.[37]

> But on the other hand, the final summing-up regarding morals alarmed me, as, indeed, it would have startled anyone in my mood; for here the annihilation of the will and complete abnegation are represented as the sole true and final deliverance from those bonds of individual limitation in estimating and facing the world, which are now clearly felt for the first time. For those who hoped to find some philosophical justification for political and social agitation on behalf of so-called "individual freedom" there was certainly no support to be found here, where all that was demanded was absolute renunciation of all such methods of satisfying the claims of the personality. At first, I naturally found his ideas by no means palatable.[38]

However, Wagner came to appreciate the philosopher's exegesis of Buddhism, especially when it served the poet-composer's ideological concerns, as in his oft-cited criticism of "narrow" Judaism.[39] For Wagner, as well as others of his generation, the study of Buddhism provided material for the then-popular critique of Judeo-Christian religious institutions.[40]

As Wagner became a more dedicated disciple of Schopenhauer,[41] his fascination with the esoteric aspects of the philosopher's thought increased.[42] In the winter of 1855, Wagner began to study Buddhism itself,[43] through Eugène Burnouf's *Introduction à l'histoire du bouddhisme indien* and Karl Friedrich Köppen's *Die Religion des Buddha*.[44] In a letter to Liszt, Wagner described *nirvāṇa,* the "Land of Being-No-Longer," as an amalgamation of Christianity, Schopenhauer, and German Romanticism.[45] It entailed the dissolution of the self, preceded by the abdication of the will and its reabsorption into a larger, depersonalized stream. Wagner was so impressed with this newfound faith that he planned to use the theme of *nirvāṇa* for the projected opera *Die Sieger.* This opera did not develop beyond a sketch.[46] In it, Brahma, the supreme god, is embodied in this world and finds salvation through saints, such as the Buddha, who, by a perfect negation of the will, sympathize with all suffering and enter *nirvāṇa.* Although Wagner's vision of a Schopenhauerian *nirvāṇa* never materialized in *Die Sieger,* it can be found in the early version of the suttee in *Die Götterdämmerung,* as well as in *Tristan und Isolde,* the opera written contemporaneously with the conclusion of *The Ring.* It should be remembered that the sketch for *Die Sieger* dates from 1856, and the poem for *Tristan* from 1856, hence we can place both around the time when Wagner wrote the Schopenhauerian version of Brünnhilde's suttee.

In *Tristan,* Wagner drew an inner connection between the themes of death and redemption (*Erlösung*) and his conception of *nirvāṇa.* In fact, Wagner identified *Tristan's* annihilation of the self and its concomitant *Vergessen* with *nirvāṇa.*

> Everything is strange to me, and longingly I often look to the Nirvana-land. Nirvana quickly becomes again *Tristan.* You know the Buddha's teaching on the origin of the world. A hand darkens the clarity of heaven: it swells, condenses and in impenetrable hugeness, the whole world stands finally before me again. It is my old destiny, as long as I still have such unredeemed spirits around me.[47]

Wagner's fragmentation of the phenomenal world and its ultimate submersion in *nirvāṇa* is attained far more in a Schopenhauerian sense—as an unfettering of the will—than in Buddhist terms. In particular, act 1, scene 5, of *Tristan* presents the process of disintegration. A development from nonbeing by way of being back to nonbeing, what Ulrich Weisstein has called "*Ent-Ichung,*"[48] is reflected in a diminution of the characters' consciousness of the outer world. Weisstein isolated key passages in *Tristan* where the process of deindividualization occurs. In act 2, where the lovers seek to appropriate each other in preparation for the actual exchange of identities, Tristan sings:

> You, Isolde
> Tristan, I,

No longer Tristan!
Not Isolde![49]

This sense of oneness as being no longer tied to the individual culminates in the last act, where the transfigured Isolde sings:

In the Sea of Delight's
Surging waves,
In the fragrant wave's
Resounding sound,
In the World-breath's
Wafting Universe—
To drown,—
To sink,—
Unconscious—
Highest joy![50]

According to Schopenhauer and his disciple Wagner, the world, in as much as it was created by error or as a consequence of sin, must be rejected. The duet "O sink hernieder/Nacht der Liebe" illustrates the lovers' dismissal of the world as illusory:

Tristan: By your magic
Gently encompassed
Before your eyes
Sweetly vanishing;

Isolde: Heart to your heart,
Mouth to-mouth;

Tristan: Of one breath
Of a single bond;

Both: My glance breaks off
Blinded with delight,
The world grows pale
With its dazzle;

Isolde: Which the day deceptively
Brightened for us,

Tristan: Opposed
To the deceptive illusion

Both: Even then I am
The world.[51]

Erlösung as Wagner conceived it in *Tristan* was to give meaning to the theme of *nirvāṇa,* which the composer anticipated for *Tristan's* projected companion piece, *Die Sieger.*[52] For the composer the two projects in their conception were intimately related.[53]

> First, you must have digested my *Tristan,* especially the Third Act, with the black and the white flag. Then, for the first time would *Die Sieger* make sense.[54]

In fact, as Wagner wrote to Otto Wesendonck, the subject of *Die Sieger* initially interested him more than that of *Tristan.*[55] Had *Die Sieger*[56] been written, it would have been the religious counterpart for those themes Wagner treated in a secular fashion in *Tristan.*

Although Wagner associated the two projects in his own mind, it is clear that *Tristan* dealt primarily with death and love, themes far more akin to German Romanticism than to Indian metaphysics. Likewise, the presence of themes such as *Weltschmerz* and *Todessehnsucht* in *Tristan* are more attributable to Romanticism and Schopenhauer than to Buddhism. Nevertheless, Indian religious thought did enter into the opera in the previously mentioned references, most significantly in Isolde's invocation of the "Welt-Atems wehendem All," which marks the tonal acme of the *Liebestod.* Both *Tristan* and *Die Sieger* offered different responses to the same problem. Whereas Tristan and Isolde sought transcendence through their love and death; in *Die Sieger* the protagonists were to attain *nirvāṇa* through the renunciation of carnal love as a precondition for release from earthly bonds.[57] The Wagnerian schema consisted of complete renunciation and the perfection of love in death. It corresponded well to the nineteenth-century misreading of fatalism in Indian metaphysics, as Nietzsche was quick to note.[58] In defense of Wagner's position, however, it must be noted that he received his misperception from the scholarship that was available to him, most notably the work of K. F. Köppen. Guided by Schopenhauer's and Köppen's distorted visions of Buddhism,[59] Wagner projected nihilism onto Indian *nirvāṇa.* Furthermore, concerning its central teaching on reincarnation,[60] Wagner did not understand that there is no soul to transmigrate in Buddhism, a point made very clearly in Schopenhauer.[61]

Wagner found in Burnouf the legend upon which he based the sketch for *Die Sieger.*[62] It is clear from Wagner's treatment of the legend, however, that Burnouf's material merely served as a vehicle for Wagner's own thought. The composer understood reincarnation, redemption, and the spiritual worthiness of women[63] to be central themes of the tale.[64] Significantly, the last two themes appear with some frequency in his other operas. In an extensive diary report dated 5 October 1858, Wagner wrote to Mathilde Wesendonck:

> In the beginning, Śakyamuni was against the acceptance of women into the order of the saints. He repeatedly expressed the opinion that women by their very nature were far too subject to their gender traits as far as temper, obstinacy and their dependency on personal existence were concerned, for them to be able to achieve the composure and broad contemplativeness through which the individual renounces natural tendencies in order to attain redemption.[65]

In *Die Sieger,* Wagner's expressed purpose was to articulate humanity's redemption (*Erlösung*) through the spontaneous *Gefühlserschütterung* and the resulting knowledge and purification that renounce all suffering and desire.[66] However, it was only through Buddha's sympathy with the *Tschandala-Mädchen* that the Enlightened One effects his own final transfiguration. In this respect, Wagner continues the European stage tradition of representing the pariah female as redemptive. However, before *Erlösung* can be attained in *Die Sieger,* the pariah must renounce the world,[67] and she must do so as a proper Schopenhauerian, but one molded according to Wagner's own dictates:[68] Unlike Burnouf's account, where the father of the girl rejects the man's suit, Wagner's heroine herself assumes a personal guilt through her intentional and callous rejection of love.[69] Thus Wagner sets the stage for her transformation, her willingness to put aside the demands of the ego and her need to redeem herself through an ultimate act of renunciation. Although the pariah maiden Prakriti was initially subject to social pressure, Wagner has her reflect the strictures that society and her own self-absorption have placed upon her. To a great extent, she resembles the operatic pariah who populated nineteenth-century French and German opera, and it would be foolish to assume that Wagner was not familiar with this operatic cliché.

However, Wagner "betrays" his thematic when Prakriti's renunciation issues forth from her ever-more-intense love for Ananda rather than from any insight into the truth of Buddhism and its call for renunciation.

The Buddha figure plays a more important role in Wagner's sketch than in the original legend. A Buddha who is conventional, mild, enlightened, and immune to suffering becomes in Wagner's hands rather like an artist: sensitive and vulnerable. The *nirvāṇa* that he obtains in *Die Sieger* has no rapport with Buddhism; in no way does it stem from an understanding of the world and human nature. Rather, it originates in an overwhelming emotional and sensual experience garnered through Prakriti's unreserved love for Ananda. Intense love as exhibited through renunciation is presented here as the elitist path to *nirvāṇa*.

The extant draft of *Die Sieger,* although it embellishes certain dramatic aspects, adds little more to the sketch found in the diary letter to Mathilde.[70] Here Wagner has the Buddha show Prakriti the arduous path to *Erlösung*—leading through suffering, conditioned by the guilt of one's rebirth ("durch das schuldbedingte Leid der Wiedergeburten"), and resulting in eventual freedom and sanctification. The draft and the sketch for *Die Sieger* both anticipate the theme of redemption through love, a theme that would become central to Wagner's *oeuvre* and, indeed, captivate him until his death twenty-five years later. Savitri[71] and Ananda would transmogrify as Brünnhilde and Siegfried and—perhaps even more so—as Isolde and Tristan. At the time of the sketch for *Die Sieger,* however, they just represented Wagner and Mathilde Wesendonck. *Die Sieger's* message concerning the full entanglement of love through renunciation and spiritual union without physical union mirrored Wagner's problematic relationship with Mathilde:

> To become a saint; and as a saint I should say to you: come, leave everything which holds you, demolish the bonds of nature: for this sacrifice I will show you the open path to salvation—Then we would be free: [we will be] Ananda and Savitri.[72]

Later in the same letter:

> So as not to perish, I will look at you . . . help me! Stay close to me! Call, so the farther you disappear; and I am answered: "In this world, where you take on this sorrow, in order to realize your images, in this world,—it does not belong to you! . . . Happy Ananda! Happy Savitri!"[73]

Given Wagner's identification with the character of the Buddhist hero and his projection onto Mathilde Wesendonck of the virtues and failings of the Savitri character, one might suspect that Wagner never wrote *Die Sieger* due to changing fortunes in his sentimental life. However, this explanation does not seem to be the case, as the fantasy of writing *Die Sieger* remained with Wagner for a long time. On 11 January 1878, Cosima wrote:

> R. is working. Around noon he said to me that it was going so well that he wanted to compose Die Sieger right after Parsifal so as not to lose his momentum.[74]

In his notation of 21 March 1879, where he decides that *Parsifal* will be his last *Tonschöpfung,* Wagner reiterates his desire to write the text for *Die Sieger* and have his son Siegfried put it to music.[75] Wagner never really lost his optimism for the project. He told Cosima as he lay in bed, "If you take care of me, dress me well and feed me well, then I will still compose *Die Sieger.*"[76] But his dream never materialized. Cosima, in her compulsive note-taking suggests that a Buddhist opera might cause some "aesthetic" problems.

> In the night, he got up once and read in the Buddha book. We speak all the time about Buddha; recently R. remarked how impossible it would have been for him to compose it, if he would have had to deal with mango trees and lotuses and such.[77]

In a notation of 6 January 1881, Cosima comments that the difficulty with the subject stemmed from the setting and the language ("Die Schwierigkeit ist hier die Lokalität und die Sprache"). Wagner himself confirms these considerations.

> In Christianity, there is noble simplicity, in Buddhism, there is so much education—Education is very unartistic.[78]

We must remember that these comments appear after the completion of *Parsifal,* suggesting that Wagner opted for a Christian expression of those themes that had held his interest in the Buddhist tale.

Indeed, just as Wagner associated *Die Sieger* with *Tristan und Isolde,* so too did he see analogies between *Parsifal,* whose *Prosa-Entwurf* dated from the year after *Die Sieger's* sketch, and Buddhist thematic associations.[79] In fact, for Wagner, the theme of female redemption, which was never realized in *Die Sieger,* both animated *Parsifal*[80] and was fully realized in it.[81] Indeed, *Parsifal* exhibits to the greatest degree those themes that, throughout his career, Wagner most associated with Buddhism.

In Wagner's library at Wahnfried, there was a single translation of a Pali text, the *Suttanipāta*. In this text, desire and sensual pleasure are presented as the fundamental hindrances to consciousness and freedom. These themes permeate the entire opera, and the vaguely Indian Kundry is driven by thirst, another theme central to Buddhism. As Wagner had envisioned for Prakriti, Kundry's redemption is determined by her previous existence.[82] Thus, the Hindu beliefs in *karma* and *saṃsāra* both informed Wagner's development of her characterization[83] and became motivating forces in the narrative. Furthermore, the theme of rebirth, central to the project of *Die Sieger,* appears as a fundamental motif in *Parsifal* and is developed in the characterization of Kundry.

In act 1 of *Parsifal,* Gurnemanz tells how Kundry expiates guilt from a previous life.[84] In the beginning of act 2 when Klingsor spurs Kundry to action, he reflects upon her metempsychoses in earlier incarnations.[85] Near the end of act 2, Kundry herself sings of the curse that has condemned her to rebirth and suffering.[86]

> Do you know the curse, which waking and sleeping,
> Through pain and laughter,
> Steels me to new suffering,
> Torments me endlessly throughout existence?[87]

In the characters of Prakriti and Kundry, Wagner presents renunciation and nonphysical, pure love as the operant paths leading to female redemption. Whereas Prakriti enters the Buddhist community and thereby decides to free herself from *saṃsāra,* Kundry enters the Christian community through baptism. Just as the Buddha receives an entirely new insight through Prakriti, so Parsifal experiences through Kundry the necessary *Gefühlserlebnis*. Of her mediation, Kundry remarks: "So war es mein Kuss, der Welt-hellsichtig dich machte?"[88]

Viewing *Parsifal* from a Buddhist perspective helps us decipher the peculiar and complicated theogony of *Parsifal,* which in many respects is incompatible with the vision of a redemptive figure found in Christian theology. The figure of Parsifal resembles a *bodhisattva,* an ideal with which Wagner was familiar.[89] By carrying the burden for others, Parsifal emulates the *bodhisattva,* who forestalls *nirvāṇa* while there exist other sentient beings still suffering.

And I am that one,
Who caused all this misery!
Ha! Guilt for what sin,
For what crime
Must burden this fool for eternity.[90]

I am sent also for your salvation,
You remain bound to your longing.
The refreshment which will end your suffering,
Does not exhaust the source from which it flowed:
Salvation will never be dispensed to you,
If that source does not close to you.[91]

Wagner's operas—both written and unrealized—offer fascinating testimony for our study of Indian exoticism in European thought. The composer-poet appropriated the exotic clichés of his time: the themes of *karma, saṃsāra,* and *nirvāṇa,* and the figures of the outcaste *Tschandala* and the suttee. He used this exotic imagery both for its dramatic effect and as a vehicle for his own specific thematology. Freedom and sanctification, however realizable in his characters, eluded the artist himself. *Nirvāṇa* could be imagined, it could even be replicated in music, but it was not easily attained. To Mathilde, Wagner wrote:

> My child, the glorious Buddha was perfectly right, when he strenuously excluded art. Who feels this better than I, that it is this unhappy art that eternally delivers me up again to the torture of life and all the paradoxes of existence? If only this wonderful gift, this predominance of artistic imagination, were not in me, then I could through clear judgment and following the stirrings of my heart—become holy . . . then we would be free: Ananda and Savitri!—But such is not to be. See, then! also this, this wisdom, this clear insight—It only makes me again and again a poet, an artist. It stands, in the moment that I gain it, as an image before me . . . I must draw it . . . execute it, give it life as my own creation.[92]

Wagner's artistic gifts may have doomed to failure his personal exotic quest, but he swore that he would give life to the Buddha's insights as he experienced them. What is inexpressible in language is expressible in music.[93] Poetry and the plastic arts labor merely to represent the will objectified in space and time. Only music could manifest the will in the present. In this way, music transcended the world of appearances by becoming the actual and, therefore, perfect representation of the will. Wagner employed these Schopenhauerian conceptions as a groundwork upon which he elaborated a musical edifice.[94] However, his unique insights, like the analogy between compositional technique and the Indian concept of rebirth, provided the real motive force within this structure. While other European thinkers were primarily interested in the moral implications of reincarnation, Wagner was primarily motivated by the musical potentialities of this metaphysical theme.[95] It was in his use of the leitmotif and the reminiscence that Wagner would express the theme of rebirth in art, time and space. Concerning his choice of *Die Sieger* as a subject, he wrote:

> Apart from the beauty and profound significance of the simple tale, I was influenced to choose it as much by its peculiar aptness for the musical procedures that I have since developed. To the mind of the Buddha, the previous lives in former incarnations of every being appearing before him stand revealed as clearly as the present. The simple story owed its significance to the way that the past life of the suffering principal characters was entwined in the new phase of their lives as being still present time. I perceived at once how the musical remembrance of this dual life, keeping the past constantly present in the hearing, might be represented perfectly to the emotional receptivities, and this decided me to keep the prospect of working out this task before me as a labor of especial love.[96]

In 1870, he presented this point more succinctly: "Only music is able to render the secret of rebirths."[97]

In conclusion, we might note that although Wagner renounced his project of an opera based on a Buddhist legend, his decision was not necessarily infelicitous. We can be glad that Wagner put aside his pedantic and self-indulgent wallowing in "Buddhist" window-dressing of Romantic themes such as *Weltabgewandheit* and *Todessehnsucht,* which the foregoing discussion amply documents. Whether they were the products of vicissitudes of his sentimental involvements or a fashionable masquerade, he ultimately chose not to express them in his poetry and, in a confusing schema dating from May 1868, he explains why.

Truth = *nirvana* = night
Music = *brahman* = twilight
Poetry = *samsara* = day

> Brahman becomes desire, as music; the music which is turned towards samsara, poetry; which is the other, the side which is turned away from samsara? Nirvana—untroubled, pure harmony?[98]

Music can express truth. However, exotic truth can be expressed only through music. Although Wagner never completed his Buddhist opera, and his references to Indian philosophical concerns are often misguided, it is clear from his music that his appreciation of such tenets found their proper expression, as he hoped they would, in the form and transcendence of his harmonies.

III

Although surrounded by friends who were professional Sanskritists[99] and in whose work he showed great interest,[100] Friedrich Nietzsche was not in sympathy with the nineteenth-century intellectual malaise that sought its justification in Indian thought. Nietzsche was particularly critical of the cult of Buddhism fostered by the worldview of Schopenhauer and Wagner, which he saw as symptomatic of a general lack of spiritual direction. He deemed Europe's new Buddhism to be a spiritually threatening morality. In particular, Nietzsche overestimated Wagner's role in propagating Buddhism[101] and accused him of exploiting, through his music, "nihilistic instincts."[102] Behind Wagner's facade of Indian metaphysical concepts, Nietzsche saw only a decadent cast of mind.[103] In fact, one may view Nietzsche's life-affirming philosophy as a truly creative subversion of the nineteenth-century European understanding of Buddhism as a philosophical system defined in terms of its life-negating propensities. Nietzsche alone seemed to recognize what was at stake and constructed the philosophy of the *Übermensch* as a rejection of the brand of escapism that sought a justification in "Indian" metaphysics.

Nietzsche was relentless in his attacks upon any system, religious or philosophical, that had as its goal an escape from suffering. He also condemned the popular view that suffering could be eliminated by seeking *nirvāṇa* (*Nihilisierung*).[104] Nietzsche based his polemic on several criteria. He condemned Buddhism's purported call for the total negation of action and phenomenal reality. He viewed its advocacy of pity as a subterfuge to avoid suffering. Following Schopenhauer, Nietzsche represents individual suffering as inseparable from cosmic suffering. Contrary to Schopenhauer, however, Nietzsche does not advocate a negation of human pain,[105] rather, he hails it in its recurrence.

Nietzsche was not without admiration for the rigors of Schopenhauer's philosophy. In the pages of *Schopenhauer as Educator,* one discovers Nietzsche's appreciation for Schopenhauer's ability to avoid being immobilized by a manifest longing for the "other shore of which the Indians speak, *nirvāṇa* or non-existence."[106] However, Nietzsche could only reject Schopenhauer's quest for the cessation of suffering as offensive, suicidal knowledge.[107] He viewed the Buddhist path to redemption as resulting in inactivity.

> "We must not act"—said their more consistent brothers the Buddhists, and then conceived a rule of conduct to deliver man from action.[108]

> In Buddhism this notion predominates: "All desires, everything which creates emotions and blood, calls for actions"—to this extent only one is warned against evil. For action has no meaning.[109]

The entire Brahmanical philosophy denoted a state of deterioration.[110] Buddhism represented the weariness of civilization[111] and Vedānta, confirmed a Hindu indifference to morality: "For the man of knowledge, there is no duty."[112] Nietzsche, inspired to a certain degree by Deussen,[113] did not believe that virtue or moral improvement contributed to redemption in the Indian context. Like the other thinkers we have examined, he too posited a Hindu preeminence of theoretical knowledge over ethical action. Reminiscent of Hegel, Nietzsche understood Sāṃkhya philosophy as articulating a brahmin contempt for works.[114]

Given Hegel's and Schopenahuer's interpretations of Indian philosophy, a good deal of Nietzsche's reception of Indian religious thought was neither new nor revolutionary. With repeated citations of esoteric maxims from the *Upanishads,* Schopenhauer had reinforced the primacy of knowledge over action. In his reading of the *Bhagavad Gītā,* Hegel ratified and embellished this interpretation. Nietzsche subsequently represented Buddhism and the Vedānta in a manner consistent with his conviction that there is a strong antagonism between knowledge and action in the two systems.

Among Germans, Nietzsche was unique in his warning against the incoming Asian "mysticism." What distinguished Nietzsche's reception of India, what positioned him in sharp contradistinction to those entranced by the pessimistic implications of "Indian" morality, was the "constructive" potential that he posited for "Indian" nihilism. By calling for the renunciation of God and supernatural aid in general and freeing the individual from any necessity of "flowing out into God", Nietzsche proposed that the individual could "rise higher."[115] If the individual rejects a higher will, then he has recourse to another will, a human will of one's own. This will, the will to power, alone can truly emancipate humanity.[116] Nietzsche maintained that European pessimism masquerladed in Buddhist garb and could only be surmounted by an ethic that ran counter to the enervating morality of Buddhism.[117]

> Whoever really once, with an Asiatic and super Asiatic eye has actually looked inside and into the most world renouncing of all possible modes of thought—beyond good and evil, and no longer Buddha and Schopenhauer under the spell and delusion of morality—has perhaps just thereby, without really wanting it, opened his eyes to the opposite ideal: the idea of the most vivacious, exuberant and world approving man who has not only learnt to put up with and endure that which was and is, but wants to have it again as it was and is, for all eternity, insatiably calling out da capo, not only for himself, but to the whole piece and play.[118]

Although suffering is not the Buddhist's sole reality, Nietzsche felt it was and thus repudiated Buddhism's "enervating preoccupation" with pain as the exclusive fact of existence[119] to the exclusion of human aspiration and striving. His misconception concerning the role of suffering in Buddhism had been fostered by Schopenhauer's misinterpretation of the Buddhist contempt for superficialities of existence. Nietzsche did not direct his polemic against the Buddhist belief that existence is suffering. Rather he railed against advocating for the elimination of suffering as an aim of existence or any passive acceptance of suffering as the accretion of past action and guilt. Instead Nietzsche called for the embrace of suffering as the fount of human creativity. However, Nietzsche's castigations of Buddhist morality were not merely a response to information culled from Schopenhauer. Since he could not base his knowledge on firsthand materials, he was also dependent on early Western Buddhist scholarship. It is for this reason that Nietzsche, although deeply critical of the uses to which Hinduism and Buddhism were put by his contemporaries, shared the same misprisions to which they were subject.

In particular, Nietzsche based his interpretation of Buddhism principally on the works of Köppen and Oldenberg. One can trace Nietzsche's assessment of Buddhism as a nihilistic philosophy to Köppen's contention that early Buddhism presented an ethos of effacement and annihilation[120] or Köppen's understanding that Buddhism viewed earthly existence as ephemerous and imperfect.[121] One can also find parallels between Nietzsche's totalizing portrayal of "Buddhist" nihilism and Oldenberg's presentation of the Buddhist worldview as constituted completely of suffering to the exclusion of all else.[122] From such misprisions, Nietzsche developed the notion that "Buddhist pity"[123] presented great danger to humankind through its most sublime temptation and seduction—nothingness![124]

> Pity persuades to nothingness . . . One does not say 'nothingness:' one says . . . Nirvana . . . this innocent rhetoric [the pity of Buddhism] from the kingdom of the religious-moral idiosyncracy appears far less innocent as soon as we realize the tendency that shrouds itself here in sublime words: hostility against life.[125]

If, given his source material, Nietzsche misunderstood Buddhism, he did not misunderstand Schopenhauer's mission. Schopenhauer envisioned denial and extinction of the will as natural and ethical responses to human suffering. Brought to despair by suffering in the world of men, the individual should retire into the self, become aware of the true nature of empirical reality, seek transcendence of that suffering self, renounce desire and welcome death.[126] Nietzsche's quest diametrically opposes this abandonment of the self. Nietzsche did not seek to contract out of suffering via *nirvāṇa* as did Schopenhauer and his disciples. Rather, he held that such remedies were not desirable. Human existence is comprised of a cyclical process within a structure animated by pain and creativity[127] and supported by illusion.[128] Apollo, guided by illusion, transforms Dionysian suffering into a joyful occurence[129] through which redemption is gained.[130]

As were his thoughts on Buddhism, so too were Nietzsche's thoughts on *nirvāṇa* conditioned by the scholarship of the time. In his work, *Die Religion des Buddha,* Köppen defined *nirvāṇa* as a blank avowal of nihilism and annihilation.[131] Furthermore, Köppen speculated that *Nirvāṇa* had greater force when found among "stronger and more robust races" who, unlike the "life-weary Indians" were not prone to despair.[132] This concept of individuals who did not cringe before destruction foreshadows Nietzsche's concept of the *Übermensch*. Intimations of the *Übermensch*'s efforts find their parallel in Oldenberg's depiction of the *joyful* striving of the Buddhist after *nirvāṇa*.[133] As a consequence of these readings, Nietzsche envisioned *nirvāṇa* as a state of nonbeing, an obliteration of consciousness and a negation of the will to power.

> In God, non-entity is deified and the will to non-entity proclaimed holy.[134]

> Of course, one does not say 'nothingness' but 'beyond' or 'God' or 'true life' or nirvana, salvation, blessedness.[135]

> The nihilistic flight from life is synonymous with the demand for Nothingness, or for the opposite of existence, for some other existence, Buddhism and the like.[136]

In *Joyful Wisdom*, *nirvāṇa* is defined as "Oriental nothingness."[137]

In direct opposition to the quest for *nirvāṇa*, Nietzsche sought a constructive interpretation and transfiguration of human suffering. While Wagner represented *nirvāṇa* as the acme attained through harmony, Nietzsche took *nirvāṇa* to signify the nadir from which art provided ultimate redemption.[138] Thus, Nietzsche posited *nirvāṇa* as the alternative for those who were powerful. The *Übermensch* did not need to escape into any *nirvāṇa*, he was able to triumph in the world and be creative.[139] *Nirvāṇa* thus functioned as "a substitute desired by some who are incapable of achieving that state of joyous power which they too would prefer if they had the strength to attain it."[140]

Although Nietzsche's use of the so-called Buddhist view of existence differed radically from that of Schopenhauer, it nevertheless echoed the clichés popularized both in scholarship and in belletristic literature of his day. Nietzsche espoused the distinction between the Occidental affirmation and the Oriental denial of reality, as well as the "Buddhist" negation of activity against some image of a Western faithful commitment to duty. These rigid distinctions were explicit both in Indological scholarship that was at Nietzsche's disposal[141] and in popular literature.

As the concept of *nirvāṇa* increasingly became assimilated as a German cultural cliché, both serious thinkers and popular authors severed it from its religious roots. In the hands of certain German authors, *nirvāṇa* became an earthbound nothingness. The *nirvāṇa* model had sufficiently shifted from the "serious" treatment it received at the hands of Schopenhauer, his disciples, Wagner and Nietzsche to a poetic alibi for despair, as in the novel by the Countess Ida von Hahn-Hahn (1875) and the play by Walter Hasenclever (1906), both entitled *Nirwana*.

In these works, *nirvāṇa* is treated an an evocative catch phrase. Hasenclever's play examines the ennui engendered in seemingly sensitive souls by their bondage to social norms. The dramatist takes this despair seriously and ennobles it with this exotic philosophical term. In the process of exotic appropriation, the wisdom of ancient India enables the author to disparage German bourgeois culture. As we have seen elsewhere in this study, India has often served as a foil for social satire; Hasenclever's contribution merely follows a time-honored tradition. In this specific drama, however, *nirvāṇa* functions as a protean concept. It can be a state of deliverance where all wishes and goals are extinguished. Equally, it is the state wherein we experience our hopes attained and our being perfected. Most often, it is also disappointment (*Enttäuschung*). By a simple inversion, *nirvāṇa* has come to denote both the despair from which one seeks deliverance and deliverance itself. Hahn-Hahn's *Nirwana* expresses this same ambiguity.

Little is actually said about *nirvāṇa* in the eight hundred pages of Hahn-Hahn's novel. The author must have been sufficiently secure in her audience's familiarity with the Sanskrit term to assume that the heroine's endless discussions with the local priest on the general meaningless of existence would fit the model of *nirvāṇa* as despair. The heroine's theology is simple: There is no redeemer of humanity. One is bound by chains and bonds from which only the will can set one free. Death is a passage not to an unformed state but, rather, to nothingness. The priest responds that this belief is false. This Schoperhauerian prelate advises the heroine to sacrifice the will. It is by seeking God through illusory paths that one becomes disillusioned and falls into despair. Contrary to the heroine's belief, the will cannot give light, consolation, or strength. Both Hasenclever's play and Hahn-Hahn's novel succeed in one important respect: They present *nirvāṇa* in an utterly pessimistic manner. In these works, *nirvāṇa* moves from being deliverance from life's suffering and becomes a wholly secularized, pretentious alibi for spiritual dissatisfaction.

The literary and philosophical representation of *nirvāṇa* presents a false picture of Indian renunciation that certain German writers thought could be adopted to maintain the belief that the spirit could realize itself only by withdrawal from dynamic reality. This relatively passive despair manifested itself both in the literature and in the authors' asceticism, cults of virginity, and suicides. However, such "passive" attempts at personal and world annihilation developed within the movement from *nirvāṇa's* initial configuration as a metaphor to its later mode as a political agenda. The German *nirvāṇa* literature was yet to reach its penultimate avatar as a revolutionary and political ideal, as in the case of Wilhelm Jensen's novel *Nirwana* (1877), which dealt with the French Revolution, the dramas of Carl Bleibtreu, and the scholarship of Theodor Springmann.

Bleibtreu wrote two Buddhist dramas in which he broke with the Schopenhauerian tradition and saw in Buddhism not a denial of the will to live but rather a denial of the will to self. In *Der Heilskönig* (1901), Bleibtreu uses the narrative form to seek answers to questions concerning fatherland, class, and religious and political freedom.[142] Man is confused by the world and seeks consolation in a distant realm of ethics where one overcomes the thirst to live through a will to self. In *Karma* (1898), belief in the Buddha allows one to overcome the hated world through a will to all. One must recognize oneself as a vessel of transmigration and must expiate past lives in this life through purification. In this manner alone can the chain of *karma* be broken and extinction attained.[143]

The most radical instance of this dynamic and proselytizing vision of *nirvāṇa* can be seen in the work and death of Theodor Springmann, a man who stands out in the annals of German Indology as having taken the translation of *Bhagavad Gītā* he was composing into the trenches of the First World War. For Springmann, *nirvāṇa* had become the vision of the *Siegfriedgestalt*.[144] In this manner, the final destination of the German *nirvāṇa* literature is announced. We are called upon to reevaluate our worth in life and redefine true renunciation. Through the fervor of belief, we must give our deeds some worth. Through a long practice of self-discipline and concentration, we will have the strength to fight our enemies. In the model of the Brahmanical sacrifice, we have a model to sacrifice our entire life. The greatest sacrifice is on the altar of battle. This is *nirvāṇa,* where the doors of heaven stand open to the warrior who possesses this knowledge of the immortality of the soul and its capacity for further development through transmigration. Only by performing one's duty in battle can one attain deliverance.[145] With Springmann, it is no longer a question of prematurely removing oneself from this world, or of despair with the human condition, but rather of fighting in this world and destroying our fellow man.[146] Here German *nirvāṇa* comes full circle from its introduction to the German people at the hands of Schopenhauer. In Springmann's introduction to his translation of the *Bhagavad Gītā, nirvāṇa* is, in fact, the *Schwanengesang* of Aryan knighthood.[147]

What does this literature teach us? In the first place, German *nirvāṇa* literature reflects the specific tensions that we have identified in the nineteenth-century European emplotment of India. Indian religious thought could be used to voice hopes for a cultural invigoration from without as well as to confirm or refute current intellectual trends. These writers, like all metaphorical pilgrims to India, appear to be motivated by contradictory impulses: the desire to exercise *imaginative* expressions fed by a generally exact documentation and the desire to present *faithful* pictures of a reality that apparently is radically different from that of nineteenth-century Europe. However, only in the interstices between a presumably original India and the German pretense of filiation could such curious artistic graftings emerge—and only when the positive foundations of the belief in humankind were shaken.

With the theme of *nirvāṇa,* writers sought an exotic model in a revolutionary age where man was no longer the measure of all things. From the 1870s onward, India was no longer the source of inspiration, as it had been for Goethe, Herder, and the Schlegels. The *nirvāṇa* literature bears witness to this shift in the balance. This second generation of German India *Schwärmer* became enthralled with their "Buddhist" remedy of pessimism and fell prey to the lure of an exalted and exotic interpretation of the individual soul's extinction. It is not without irony that Freud referred to his concept of the death wish as the "*Nirvana-Prinzip.*"

At the height of the Second World War, the German theologian Helmut Thielicke spoke of "technological nirvāṇa," a reflective state where one continues to stand one's ground in the face of questions concerning the meaning of life. There are also times, he noted, of naive nihilism, times when questions of meaning are not negated but are just no longer allowed to appear, when there is a refusal to see life in light of its final purpose or meaning. The nineteenth-century German quest for *nirvāṇa* fits both these categories. Nihilism, in the form of *nirvāṇa,* brought into question the validity of the dilemma of seeking meaning. On a more important level, however, the theme of *nirvāṇa* allowed German writers to avoid two spiritually suicidal options:—abandoning all interest in and hope of finding significance in an objective or religious sense, and trying to find significance in something "wholly other" outside oneself.

In *Der Antichrist* (§ 22), Nietzsche wrote: "Der Buddhismus ist eine Religion für den Schluss und die Müdigkeit der Zivilisation." The "Buddhist" alibi for despair expresses attitudes characteristic of a specific group of German thinkers in the nineteenth century. Yet it also tells us a good deal about the ongoing Western (and particularly strong German) phenomenon of going Eastward in search of some superordinate fulfillment. The search for inspiration in exotic models implies the rejection of one's own cultural and religious norms. It is inevitably contiguous with the larger issue of the individual's conflict with civilization in general. This conflict manifested itself through both a consistent rejection of the dominant cultural values and a dependence on what that culture ostensibly assures—compensatory spiritual and aesthetic satisfaction. Perhaps this is why Indomania flourished in a society like Germany, where there was a desperate need for a new faith, grounded in primitivism and union with nature, that could be used to advocate action. Perhaps this is why it continues to exist in our own day.

Tragically, this new faith, while borrowing heavily from a fragmentary understanding of Buddhism, ignored its reverence for life. Irrational longings, which could find no place in the civilized West, discovered their seeming reflection in the concept of *nirvāṇa*. These German philosphers and writers merely focused upon the concept to which their needs responded, failing to assess the meaning of the whole. Indian religious thought offered a vision of the supramundane that did not posit qualities, was not peopled with deities, and was above good and evil. Both amorphous and paradoxical, it could be cut to fit any model. Certain Germans found it an easy repository for a developing irrationalism.

"Buddhist" pessimism and "Hindu" fatalism, which had been metaphors for *Weltschmerz,* subsequently became elements in a political agenda. Once more-or-less empty symbols, their appearance announced a conscious search on the part of Germans for their Aryan origins. The body of early German Indological scholarship and the philosophy and popular literature inspired by Indian thought provided models for the formation of a new Germany reconnected with the fictive world of the *Indo-Germanen*.

6

Néantisme

> Our sensuality is the desire for oblivion, our shots and stabs, desire for death, desire for voluptuous immobility, that is, desire for death, our laziness, our vanilla sherbets; our meditative aspect is that nothingness that would want to decipher the mysteries of nirvana . . . the novelty, that they attract each other only when they are dead, incapable of giving way to vital currents; from this there is the incredible phenomenon of the current function of myths which would be venerable if they were truly old, but are nothing but sinister attempts to replunge into a past which is attractive only because it is dead.
>
> —Giuseppe Tomasi di Lampedusa, *The Leopard*[1]

In 1826, the noted linguist Silvestre de Sacy[2] exhorted his fellow Frenchmen to transplant "Oriental roses on the banks of the Seine" and abandon representing the East solely in terms of local color. Did the Parnassians respond to his call? Did they expropriate "Oriental roses," transplanting them from an exotic field into their own gardens, or did they appropriate them, set them aside for particular use, exclusive of all other uses? In other words, did Indian exoticism, by offering new, rare, and unexploited imagery, provide French artists with an easy means of obtaining striking aesthetic effects?

Théophile Gautier developed his vision of India as a fantastic land of veils, rose water, hashish, and opium,[3] as well as violence, ruse, and blood.[4] However, India's creations also represented for Gautier an aesthetic ideal.[5] As a chronicler of India, Gautier freed himself from any other preoccupation than to fascinate, move, and amuse a *public bon enfant*. His colorful images of a fictitious India,[6] conjured in a Louis-Philippard Paris, offered vibrant contrasts in tone unknown under Western skies.

This *fantaisiste* emplotment of India should deceive no one. It was certainly not an unconscious motive of the authors themselves, who were quite aware of the dynamics involved in their quest for an exotic ideal. Indian exoticism satisfied a desire to present a fabricated reality. Gautier openly expressed the degree of narcissistic eccentricity that animated his own personal incursion into the exotic.

> The disquiet that has consumed us for a century pushes us, often in spite of ourselves, to seek scattered truth among the populations of the earth. Before each civilization, whether dead or alive, we stop; we question its morality, its religions, its traditions, its efforts . . . then we begin again our task, happy to carry within ourselves a little of this Truth toward which we ceaselessly strive . . . But the great Goddess sleeps in her lair, waiting for time to pass, and we never seize her and we return home sad and discouraged.[7]

If on a poetic level the exotic nurtured nostalgia for a lost and largely imaginary ideal, on a theological level, by its explicit subversion of the bounds of orthodoxy, it suited that generation of Second Empire poets who experienced so acutely a loss of religious faith and whose work articulated so well the despair that this loss engendered.

No other period of French literature finds so many poets who, haunted by the collapse of their childhood faith, present so great a vision of calamity. They expressed a fundamental impasse: the impossibility of reconciling an intense desire for illusion and the horror of its consequences. This crisis of faith fed a desire for escape from the quotidian Parisian life and the scientific spirit of the age;[8] it coexisted with a general intellectual preoccupation with death. Baudelaire saw death as "la délivrance du tout."[9] In "Le gouffre," he complained that his spirit "jalouse du néant l'insensibilité."[10] The fascination with physical death was often equated with the metaphysical state of *anéantissement,* and this *néant* became increasingly associated with the Orient.

In the preceding chapter, we examined the metaphorical use of the symbolic cluster *nirvāṇa/saṃsāra/māyā* in German philosophy, scholarship, and literature. We attempted to chart its course historically and nationally, showing its dynamics and the limitations of understanding within the hermeneutics of exoticism. I would now like to extend this discussion to another Orientalism. Here, as with the German *nirvāṇa* literature after 1870, we are no longer within the parameters of hermeneutics. The writers addressed in this chapter lead us close to Homi Bhabha's conception of the Lacanian lack figured in post-Colonial discourse that determines either a fetishistic or a phobic response to the colonized. The European writers' experience of emptiness leads to an obsession with an exotic that becomes the object of a projected emptiness as well as an aesthetic embodiment and justification of despair. In the following pages, I will investigate the origins and functions of *néantisme*[11] in French philosophical and literary thought, with particular emphasis on the "Indian" poems of Leconte de Lisle.

The suggestion made by Baudelaire in "La belle Dorothée" that the *néant* had an Asian origin[12] was consistent with an understanding of quietism that in French literature can be traced back to the seventeenth century. The noted voyager François Bernier was one of the first Frenchmen to discuss this theme.[13] Bayle, in his *Dictionnaire historique et critique* (1695–97), speculated that for Hindus "la vraie béatitude consiste dans le néant.[14] In the *Encyclopédie,* Diderot attributed the Indians' vision of quietism to their love of nothingness and desire to stupefy and mortify themselves.[15] In the *Esprit des lois* (1748), Montesquieu noted that Indians assimilate the sovereign good to an idea of rest and believe that repose and the *néant* "sont le fondement de toutes choses et la fin où elles aboutissent; c'est ainsi que l'entière inaction est l'état le plus parfait." In 1787, Abbé Grosier noted that Buddhist saintliness consisted of ceasing to be and becoming one with nothingness.[16]

Clearly, nothingness was associated with India in French intellectual circles prior to the development of European Indological scholarship. In the nineteenth century, the study of *sciences religieuses* evolved, revealing (ostensibly from an objective standpoint) the dogmas of other faiths. Indian "fatalism" became accessible as a construct to the educated public through the publication of works such as Burnouf's *Introduction à l'histoire du bouddhisme indien* (1844) and *Le lotus de la bonne loi,*[17] and his translation of the *Bhāgavata Purāṇa* (1840), texts that played a significant role in the religious controversies of their day.

French Catholic thinkers virulently attacked Indian quietist speculation. Ozanam concluded that Buddhism was "only absurdity and infamy." He characterized it as "the greatest religious peril of our day."[18] Edgar Quinet was as receptive to Indian thought as his Catholic colleagues. In *Le génie des religions* (1841), he bemoaned the absence in Indian thought of morality, individuality, and conscience. Quinet viewed inaction as the Buddhist and Hindu prerequisite for salvation.[19] The European fascination with Indian inaction was in Quinet's view the most pressing danger facing humanity.[20] Taine, rather than discrediting Buddhist doctrine, attacked the figure of the Buddha, dismissing him as effeminate.[21] Charles Renouvier condemned the morality of Buddhist contemplation.[22] André Lefèvre maintained that accepting *nirvāṇa* negated any belief in progress. He called for the repudiation of Buddhism and encouraged his readers to march under the banner of science and action.[23] Renan was contemptuous of Buddhists[24] and called for a more heroic response to human suffering.[25]

However, these critics were virtually uninformed regarding questions of Buddhist doctrine. Their negative reactions reflected only to a certain degree their concern with the moral ramifications of Indian metaphysics. Their critique also stemmed from an aesthetic distaste for the "salon Buddhism" that had inundated the literary market in the form of confessional prose and bad poetry. Indeed, the pseudo-Buddhist ataractic was by this time rhetorical, and the writers in question no longer tried to reconcile Christian morality with "Indian" quietism. While offering an "Indian" solution to the problem of evil and world suffering, nineteenth-century esoteric pessimism ultimately provided no solution at all. Nevertheless, the moral implications of "Indian" thought in general and "Buddhism" in particular were troubling due to the very fact that their doctrines were taken up as inspiration by a nihilistic exoticism. As Barthélemy Saint-Hilaire[26] noted, it was this desire for, and adoration of, nothingness that became a religion in nineteenth-century France.[27]

Sully-Prudhomme[28] and Amiel[29] were among those who found legitimization of their fatalistic worldview in Indian thought. In *Fragments d'un journal intime* (1882), Amiel spoke of a "Buddhist" tendency that blunts the human capacity for self-government, weakens the power of action, and reduces one to scepticism.[30] He isolated a "Hindu genius," noteworthy for its lack of ambition, personality, and will. Diametrically opposed to this, Amiel distinguished the Western personality, to which he attributed the characteristics of action, duty, desire to expand individuality, and the willingness to hope and believe.[31] Amiel felt that the Eastern mentality prevailed, and he blamed his personal and artistic failures on what he termed his "Indian affinities." In general, Amiel noted, the "Eastern mind" aborted action; it forced one to cultivate indifference, dissolve individuality, abandon personal duty, and surrender to the weariness of existence. Ultimately, it resulted in universal lassitude.[32]

An equally contrived and exotic vision of personal destruction found its way into the poetry of the time. Louis Ménard regularly composed verses based on the theme of illusion.[33] In the poem entitled "Nirvana," Ménard portrays humans as prey to destructive desire.[34] The poet, disgusted with life, tired of illusion, and seeking loss of self in a cosmic dreamless sleep, invokes divine nothingness.[35] Salvation consists in distancing oneself from life and pleasure.[36]

The poet Jules Laforgue fancied himself a Buddhist and dedicated *Les complaintes* to the Lord Buddha. In "Complainte des voix sous le figuier bouddhique," the poet enjoins the reader to avoid any false perception of reality[37] and make the choice between life and nothingness. Similarly, "Complainte d'une convalescence en mai" describes deliverance from suffering through the nothingness of death. "Inconscient" specifically presents the poet aspiring to refuge in the Hindu state of *nirvāṇa*. In "La lune est sterile," the recognition of the all-encompassing power of illusion (*māyā*) leads the poet to embrace the *néant*.[38]

Alfred de Vigny used Indian metaphysical concepts to question the very possibility of faith. Vigny characterized *absorption* as the basis of Indian thought[39] and projected it as an ideal before which one must not cringe.[40] Vigny was drawn to Buddhism, a "religion of despair,"[41] on account of two characteristic beliefs—the *néant* and atheism.[42] Vigny believed that Buddhists struggle to attain *nirvāṇa,* which he glossed as an *anéantissement complète*.[43] Vigny presented *nirvāṇa* as one's only hope.[44] While *nirvāṇa* does not imply atheism, Vigny nevertheless distilled from it the conception of an indifferent or absent God,[45] a concept dear to him because he grounded his own pessimism in the insignificance of both man and God.[46] In fact, he valued Buddhism's rejection of any compensation for suffering in the world beyond.[47]

For Vigny as well as other French poets employing Indian themes, the thematic interpretation of *nirvāṇa* ultimately dealt with the eternal quarrel between activity and contemplation, which foregrounded the larger discussion concerning the nature of good and evil. Vigny believed that Hindus, in order to arrive at the desired state of inertia, knew how to distance themselves from moral constraints.[48] Although he admired this capacity to function beyond ethical concerns, Vigny did not aspire after it himself. Indeed, his hero Julien turned to Christ in rejection of a "Brahmanical" renunciation of action.[49] In Hinduism's condemnation of action as deceptive, Vigny found support for his own religious doubts. In its denial of God's existence, Buddhism justified his affirmed atheism. However, Vigny recognized that Buddhism's purity and idealism could prove dangerous: In the hands of the vulgar, Buddhist wisdom degenerated into "useless revery, the immobile and useless contemplation of a Fakir or a Dervish."[50] And vulgarization was to be avoided at all costs.

What purpose does the exotic serve if it does not separate one from the rabble? Answers are often less important than how one distinguishes oneself in the quest. Thus, the extreme response to a pessimistic worldview or crisis in faith articulated by the *néantiste* literature can be interpreted as a reflection of the elitism inherent in all exoticist projects. Moreover, the artistic pose adopted by seekers after exotic "truths" tends to obscure any potential for deeper meaning.

Like Vigny, the poet Jean Lahor[51] sought in Indian thought an exotic consolation for his loss of faith. In *La gloire du néant* (1872), a *journal intime* charting his development from pantheism to nihilism, Lahor equated the theme of heredity with the doctrine of *karma*.[52] However, for Lahor *karma* merely rationalized evil and confirmed Darwin's theories.[53] Metempsychosis allowed the soul to participate in all forms of life.[54] But contrary to Hindu and Buddhist orthodoxy, Lahor did not offer the possiblity of deliverance. Indeed, Lahor's speculative message diverged significantly from its Indian source material. In its subject matter and in terms of its aesthetic failure, Lahor's poetry began with death and ended with the abyss.[55] *Karma, saṃsāra,* and *māyā*[56] all led to the *néant,*[57] and Lahor posited the essence of the entire universe as the void.[58]

So great was Lahor's emphasis on the theme of the void that it appeared in even those poems where Lahor describes divinity in the most sensuous terms.[59] "L'enchantement de Śiva,"[60] Lahor's last Indian poem and also the best-received,[61] exhibits this tendency to describe the void in terms of color and texture. "L'enchantement de Śiva" found its inspiration in the *Lalita Vistara* account of an ascetic seduced by female beauty. While wandering the forest, the hero Rāma discovers the hermitage of Kāma (the god of love) and learns of the god's demise at the hands of Śiva.[62] In his poetic rewriting of the story, Lahor substituted *Māyā* (illusion) for the god of love[63] and a female demon for the charming seductress of the original tale.[64] Lahor represented woman as an object of art constructed by a nature characterized by morbid decay and biological decomposition.[65] The reader recognizes in such realism the common cliché of contrasting women and their seductive charm with the ephemerality of human existence.[66] Lahor did not merely repeat the well-worn image of woman as vampire, which was dear to French and Indian poets alike,[67] but his depictions of *nirvāṇa* coalesced into this image, joining an exotic expression of disintegration with one that is erotically charged.[68] For Hindus, the veil of illusion distorts perception of the phenomenal world. For Lahor, illusion expanded to include the primordial essence.[69] Thus, *māyā* did not merely hide reality. Nor did Lahor limit his vision of the void to his plastic experience of reality. The ultimate message of his poetry articulated the notion that even the Absolute is illusory.[70] The gods themselves are mere phantoms of the human imagination.[71]

In reading Lahor's poetry, the reader is initially struck by the pervasiveness of its nihilism and is prompted to question its emotional resonance. To what purpose was the theme of *nirvāṇa* utilized?

In May 1866, Stéphane Mallarmé wrote to Lahor:

> I am the eternal victim of discouragement,
> I must catch sight of real grandeur.
> Unfortunately, in hollowing out the verse to this point,
> I discovered two abysses which make one despair.
> One is the void that I encountered without Buddhism . . .
> the other void is the one I discovered in my heart . . .

To which Lahor responded:

> You know that your ideas on the void are quite nice,
> but they are like certain women,
> beautiful but dumber than their feet.[72]

This pretentious and rather silly dialogue suggests a possible meaning for the appearance of *néantisme* in nineteenth-century French letters. While Indian "nihilism" certainly struck responsive emotional chords among the writers of the time, the lure of the *néant* was often of secondary importance to the *mise en cause* of aesthetic principles. The fact that these writers were initially drawn to the Indian exotic by elitist spiritual concerns did not preclude their exploitation of its poetic potential. An ideal case in point is the distortion of Indian themes in the work of Leconte de Lisle.

The predominant role of exoticism in nineteenth-century French letters has been examined in numerous studies,[73] as have its spiritual and aesthetic components. As the aforementioned discussion indicates, *néantisme* was a particularly pervasive component of this exoticism. We have suggested that aesthetic judgments as well as moral outrage contributed to the negative reception of "Indian" metaphysical themes by the religious critics of the time. The casual and rhetorical exploitation of exotic pessimism on the part of the lesser talents discussed above may account for the dismissal of, or inattention paid to, their work by critics old and new. However, the exotic work of Leconte de Lisle, the only poet of the first order to be significantly influenced by Indian thought,[74] has also engendered a dismissive critical response.[75] His stature as a poet and his sophisticated, systematic use of Indian metaphysical themes do not warrant such dismissal.

In a manner reminiscent of Gautier, Leconte de Lisle reconstructed India's past in terms of an ideal.[76] Of all the poets exploiting the plastic potentialities of Indian exoticism, Leconte de Lisle most persuasively emphasized religious themes with a clear eye to incorporating them into an aesthetic project. He successfully transposed "Western" moral concerns (such as the possibility of faith, the existence of evil, and an ethical response to human suffering) into a dissonant key, where they resonate in an atmosphere of sensuous imagery and create a seemingly paradoxical vision of an illusory phenomenal world grounded in and replete with color and form.

All of Leconte de Lisle's poetry, both non-Indian[77] and Indian, expressed a strongly fatalistic worldview. More than other poets of his generation, Leconte de Lisle discovered in Indian religion a compelling ontology to which his own thoughts on the nature of life instinctively drew him.[78] His view of the evanescence of youth, love, life, and eternally changing divinities might have led him to conclusions consistent with certain tenets of Hinduism even if he had never come into contact with Indian thought. However, his immediate adoption of Indian themes demonstrates the degree to which he was attracted to "Indian" philosophical thought. Perhaps, he believed that it would provide him with the *nourriture spirituelle* that he had earlier sought in vain through science.[79] India provided the philosophical rationale that allowed him to replace God with the satisfactory abstraction of the *néant.*[80]

It is important to note that, although he ostensibly sought to reproduce the "metaphysical and mystical character of Vaiṣṇavite ascetics,"[81] Leconte de Lisle ignored the more speculative texts that were available to him and based his work on the colorful and dramatic episodes of Brahmanical mythology found in Burnouf's translations. In other words, instead of grounding his poetry in philosophical or religious truth, he developed an aesthetic based primarily on an exotic and sumptuous *mise en scène.* The poet read Burnouf's *Bhāgavata Purāṇa* in 1850, and two years later the *Poèmes antiques* appeared containing two Indian poems—the first, "Surya," a derivative hymn to the sun, and the second, "Bhagavat."[82]

According to the preface of the *Poèmes antiques,* Leconte de Lisle intended with "Bhagavat" (1859) to show a bond that he believed existed between Buddhism and the worship of Viṣṇu. This poem examines the human inability to emerge from the prison of earthly existence. Depicted in the poem are three characters incarnating the three cardinal passions thwarting deliverance. The first character, Maitreya, suffers from the illusion of desire. The second, Narada, grieving over his beloved mother's death, beseeches God to reveal himself and assuage his sorrow.[83] The third, the poet Angira,[84] suffers from a specific *mal interieur* more terrible than that of desire or love—religious doubt.[85] On a fundamental level, each of these characters is tormented by their recognition of the illusory nature of reality. In response, the sages seek inaction and redemption from illusory gods. Leconte de Lisle presents emancipation as a mechanical consequence of seeing illusory incarnations of a material God ("L'unique, l'éternelle et Sainte illusion"). In fact, the poem offers homage to *māyā,* which is anomalous from an Indian point of view because Indian ascetics customarily seek to escape from the bonds of illusion. Unlike the beneficial and salutary reunion with Bhagavat found in the *Bhāgavata Purāṇa,* Leconte de Lisle's version concludes with absorption into a void:

> The principle and the end, error and truth,
> Abyss of nothingness and of reality.[86]

The poet's aesthetic project reveals itself in the extent to which he strays from his source material:[87] The ardent desire for *anéantissement* expressed in the poem is nowhere present in the *Bhāgavata Purāṇa.*[88] Furthermore, in the cosmic and individual quest for *nirvāṇa*[89] of "Bhagavat," the poet never disengages himself from images and forms, but wallows in the idea of nature as a mirage and life as a deception. Yet, the poet consistently depicts nature and life clothed in color and full of movement. In fact, Leconte de Lisle's ascetics are saved only upon experiencing "form", witnessing god as a corporeal image. Their desire for immobility contrasts uneasily with the movement of nature around them. If true to the Indian context, they would seek to escape the bonds of illusion. However, in "Bhagavat," no one seeks to uproot illusion. Here, as well as in his other Indian poems, Leconte de Lisle absolutizes illusion. The poet transforms *māyā* from its general meaning, where it denotes illusion, to a modern, almost existential, *ennui* characterized as the anguishing disquiet attending the varied problems for which humanity seeks solutions. From his extensive reading of source material, Leconte de Lisle seems to have focused only on the transcendent unreality of the phenomenal world—in other words, what was most negative. Moreover, for Leconte de Lisle, the *néant* does not begin with death but exists on earth in the reality that the poet expressed in "La Maya:"

> Maya, invisible and open in your heart,
> Contains man and the gods, life and nothingness.[90]

Similarly, Leconte de Lisle has also retained the "negative" threads of Indian morality: A radical undermining of phenomenal existence that fosters a response of indifference.[91] Humankind is as insignificant as the phenomenal world:

> But what is then the heart of ephemeral men,
> O Maya! If not you, the immortal mirage.[92]

This *néant* even engulfs the world of the gods in the "Vision de Brahma," where Leconte de Lisle's divergence from orthodoxy is most extreme. Hindu doctrine demands the recognition of the individual soul's (*Ātman*'s) true status of oneness with the Universal Soul (*Brahman*). Through discipline, individuals detach themselves from illusion and recognize this identity. At issue is the concerted effort to free oneself from the fetters of egotism. Leconte de Lisle, however, equated the suppression of the ego with destruction of the individual self, the *moi haïssable.* In this poem, Leconte de Lisle further transformed *māyā*. No longer the veil of illusion to be drawn aside by a concerted effort, *māyā,* in fact, becomes cosmic nothingness (*néant divin*) from which there is no escape. The poet thus posits nothingness as the underlying structure of the phenomenal world.[93]

Life is not good, since its joys pass with time and are illusory. Like Leopardi, Leconte de Lisle acknowledged the good and beautiful and posited them in the past.[94] In "Illusion suprème,"[95] the poet looks back on the "rose clarté de son heureux matin" in which he recognizes the force of desire. His vision then darkens into a "monde lugubre, où nul ne voudrait redescendre." Humans either are "consumés d'une impossible envie" ("Dies Irae," 1852) or can never restrain their "impossible désir" ("Bhagavat," 1852). Leconte de Lisle's emphasis on the theme of desire, while it distinguishes him from the traditional concerns of a pessimistic poet such as Leopardi, is not unique to French nineteenth-century poetry and should not necessarily be interpreted as exhibiting any legitimate indebtedness to Indian thought.

More significant, for the purposes of our inquiry, is the fact that, throughout these Indian poems, Leconte de Lisle repeatedly presented characters embracing the abyss or establishing some aesthetic ideal.[96] In the poem "Çunacepa," the poet undertakes to deny the reality of this world while describing it in the most exalted terms. He uses particularly colorful language to express the illusory nature of love. The original story of "Çunacepa," found in the *Rāmāyaṇa*,[97] deals with the sacrifice of a son by his father and respect for a sermon. A king offers a sacrifice that is interrupted. As a consequence, he needs another victim. Searching far and wide, the king comes to a poor brahmin's hut, where he purchases the middle son. While returning to the sacrificial site, the prospective victim encounters the sage Viśvamitra and begs for his help. The holy man gives him a prayer that will save his life.

Leconte de Lisle's poem alters this story considerably. While there is no mention of *māyā* or the *néant* in the Sanskrit original, Leconte de Lisle has Viśvamitra preach the merits of entering nothingness, dying to the world of passions, and escaping the bonds of *māyā*.[98] There is no mention of beauty or love in the epic, but Leconte de Lisle has the boy discover beauty in the form of a young woman and opt for a life of suffering rather than the sage's "logical" alternative of nothingness. By choosing life over death, Leconte de Lisle's Çunacepa shows himself to be a true Parnassian, worshiping beauty at all costs. In this poem, the ideal of beauty wins out over *nirvāṇa*.

Leconte de Lisle's expropriation of "Indian" fatalism in the service of a specific aesthetic agenda found its clearest expression in "La mort de Valmiki" (1881). The Sanskrit epic source material[99] relates how a beautiful woman spies two lights shining from an anthill. Not knowing that they are Vālmīki's eyes, she pierces them, inadvertently blinding the poet. Horrified by her act, she marries him, although the anthill still covers him while he meditates. Since he is quite repulsive, her love, needless to say, is selfless. She remains faithful to him, and the Sanskrit epic stresses her wifely virtue.

In adapting this moralistic tale, Leconte de Lisle was interested only in its macabre beginning, when the sage allows himself to be buried alive and even transformed into a termite nest. In his poem, Leconte de Lisle presents the legendary author of the *Rāmāyaṇa* as a world-weary poet who seeks a voluntary death as an escape from *ennui*. Moreover, while the sage of the Sanskrit original has been absorbed in contemplating God for so many years that he has allowed the termites to bury him alive (a common fictitious demise for Hindu saints), Leconte de Lisle's sage-turned-poet has brought destruction upon himself through the contemplation of his literary masterpiece.

> Unceasingly, millions [of ants] contrive,
> To assault the man absorbed in his dream,
> Standing against the throne of an old mossy tree,

He reduces himself to nothing in what he conceived,
His spirit no longer experiences his senses or itself.[100]

Leconte de Lisle transforms the epic Vālmīki from an absorbed ascetic into an artist of passion who is destroyed by his creative dreams. Not only does the mythic poet become a Parnassian but also a martyr of art for art's sake. This poem, the last of the Indian corpus, can be seen to present Leconte de Lisle's definitive statement. The poet attains the *néant* through the only true path, artistic creation.

In "La mort de Valmiki," Leconte de Lisle constructs an exotic episode to advance both the personal sentiment of fatality and the modern aesthetic notions of his time. Valmiki, no longer absorbed in a formless Absolute, is enthralled by his own art, rendered as fetish. Furthermore, as elsewhere in the Indian corpus, Leconte de Lisle employs the exotic to express total destruction in a particularly gruesome form. In the Sanskrit original, the ascetic is covered by the termites. Leconte de Lisle, however, has these insects eat the poet alive. That the poet used the exotic to depict death is less important than that these representations of death differ significantly from those of his contemporaries. Unlike the depictions of death found in the works of Baudelaire or Flaubert, Leconte de Lisle does not evoke emotional or sensual horror. His stylized representaitons of death fail to move the reader. They are, for lack of a better term, cosmic, something into which the characters sink.[101]

Leconte de Lisle, like the other *néantiste* poets, primarily culled from Buddhism or Hinduism a vision of apathy. They all confused a desire for death with a longing for *nirvāṇa*. Contrary to Buddhist thought, there is no attempt in these poems to nullify desire or accept suffering; there is no Buddhist compassion. As Leconte de Lisle expressed it in "Illusion suprême":

So be it! human dust, prey to rapid time,
Its pleasures, tears, battles and remorse,
The Gods which it conceived and the stupid universe
Are not worth the impassive peace of the dead.[102]

Here again, esoteric belief masks a contempt for humanity.

How then can we judge the presence of Indian exoticism in French nineteenth-century poetry? Did a poet such as Leconte de Lisle find the serenity that the Parnassians (at least in the preface of the *Poèmes antiques* and the manifestoes of Catulle Mendès) ostensibly sought in art? Obviously, Indian religious thought offered little consolation in the imagined *anéantissement* of a phenomenal world.

These artistic manipulations of exotic symbols reveal the difficulties encountered by these poets in orienting their message amid myth and philosophical speculation. Whether through error or through literary artifice, the adoption of a radically pessimistic worldview and its masquerade in a rich and sensuous idiom established an unsettling tension. The notions that a resigned suicide in the service of art can resolve problems of existence or that style denotes substance were themes that more clearly echoed Romantic beliefs than the theses of the Vedānta, which holds that nature is deceptive and suicide inoperant. One problem with these Indian poems is that the arduous Hindu or Buddhist quest for self-recognition quite simply cannot be equated with the self-conscious disenchantment worthy of Jean-Jacques or René. India teaches that, for salvation, one must close one's eyes to sensual seduction, whereas the Parnassians call for us to revel in it.

How could poets who lived primarily in a world of images successfully seek inspiration and imagery from India, whose philosophy denied the reality of the phenomenal world? From the Indian point of view, art achieved a completely different aim. Art in ancient Indian culture emphasized tangible reality in order to suggest a superior reality.[103] Art for art's sake, however, inaugurated a sort of idolatry: It absolutized the relative (art) or replaced the Absoltue with Art, believed to be its concrete evocation. For the Parnassians, the work had no other purpose than itself. They did not seem to grasp the fundamental absurdity of their appropriating Indian imagery to support their aesthetic project. This is the ultimate paradox, and indeed the failure of the *néantist* poetry, which embedded themes of nothingness and illusion in a self-consciously stylized art form. When poets choose a thematic that cannot be contained within their aesthetic framework, and this contradiction remains glaringly unresolved, it makes for bad poetry, as in much of the poetry we have examined in this chapter. However, Leconte de Lisle was not a bad poet. In fact, he was a rather good poet who was at pains to address a thematic that was influencing the poetry of his time. Moreover, I would like to suggest that in choosing the subject of the *néant* as the grounding of his poetry, Leconte de Lisle (and to a lesser degree the other poets) made a clear aesthetic decision.

Although an interest in the exotic was often symptomatic of a crisis of faith, in nineteenth-century French poetry such spiritual malaise was foreclosed by a perverse delectation of fatalism and despair. Indian exoticism provided images and overfamiliar clichés with which these poets experimented, entertained, and gratified themselves. Hence, we find, even in discussions treating sober issues such as the death of God or the meaninglessness of existence, a certain ephemerality and bourgeois affectation. In other words, the exotic in French poetry became a fashionable pose to be intermittently adopted and had no deeper reality. Oriental roses were transplanted on the banks of the Seine but did not find the nourishment there to take root. For nineteenth-century French poets, the exotic provided yet another format in which to express the concerns of the time, and these concerns often had to do with eroticism and ennui. It offered a rich opportunity to masquerade and play-act. In France, it was possible to approach the exotic as a *flâneur* for the fundamental political reason that I postulated in the Introduction. Exotic quests presuppose a belief that culture provides its citizens with a right to spiritual and aesthetic compensation. The French sense of a cultural identity and nationhood allowed the nineteenth-century *flâneur* to stroll through exotic locales without compromising any principles.

However, the German metaphorical traveler's fascination with India was no simple, superficial masquerade, and the Indian exotic answered deep emotional issues of racial and national identity. Granted, there was an element of play-acting involved in the Germans' search for origins, but, as we shall see, in the very seriousness of these narratives no one intended to have fun.

7

Indian Thought and the Formation of Aryan Ideology: Aryans, Tschandalen, *and the Lunatic Fringe*

Land of the Aryans, where all particulars are shared, where loyalty resides, purity, sincerity, sense of duty, generosity, honor, and honesty reside in the land of the Aryans. Where falsehood and deception rule where faithlessness, lewdness, and selfishness is allowed to flourish, there begins Klingsor's realm, the empire of the Negative.[1]

Aryans
I

Whereas we began our discussion with examples of the type of discourse Orientalism has engendered with respect to the purported racist and hegemonic designs of early Indology, it is now appropriate to question a natural conclusion: the seeming collusion of scholarship, philosophy, and literature in the formation of Nazi mythmaking. As we have seen, the arguments of Orientalist criticism draw a causal relationship between early Sanskrit philology, imperialism, and racism. The claim that nineteenth-century exoticism was precursor of twentieth-century nationalist totalitarianism is neither unique nor radical. The suggestion that the whole of German history contributed to the formation of the Third Reich is a common theme in historical discourse.[2]

This historical orientation found its most popular expression in the work of Léon Poliakov. In *Le mythe aryen,* Poliakov directly associates the Romantic reception of India with anti-Semitism. Poliakov cites Friedrich Schlegel as the author of the Aryan myth.[3] Herder's enthusiasm for Indian poetry expressed his deep need to dissociate Germany from a Semitic heritage. Schopenhauer's love for the *Upanishads* was a ploy to mask his anti-Jewish ideology.[4] Given Poliakov's identification of anti-Semitism and the myth of the Aryan, he is able to view European philology, philosophy, and history as contributing in a linear fashion to the ultimate destruction of European Jewry.

Even such a sober encyclopedist as Raymond Schwab has made similar claims for the influence of the reception of India upon National Socialism. In *La renaissance orientale* (written in 1950 and recently reedited),[5] one finds a similar refrain with a similar cast of villains. A causal relationship between early philology, F. Schlegel, Schopenhauer, and subsequent racist ideology and policy is proposed.

The cause-and-effect theme also finds expression in journalistic works romanticizing India for a popular audience. In *The Soul of India,* Amaury de Riencourt points out that the Oriental Renaissance indeed did bear bitter fruits[6] and that nineteenth-century European philology and Romanticism were directly responsible for Adolf Hitler's assumption of power. A few degrees distant from such assertions are the claims made by mythologists of Nazism. In *The Occult Reich* (1974), one learns about the influence exerted upon Hitler by Tibetan Buddhists. In *The Morning of the Magicians,* Gurdjieff is shown to have influenced proto-Nazi groups, and the Nazis themselves are purported to have been privy to occult powers. It is in such studies[7] that the reader learns that Himmler really did believe that he was the reincarnation of Henry the Fowler.

One can, therefore, recognize that the spectrum in this thematic ranges from the sensationalist claims of mythologists of Nazism to the sober yet still preposterous and irresponsible claims of contemporary critics of Orientalism and certain historians. As Jürgen Lütt has shown,[8] the recent reprints in English of both Schwab and Riencourt and the publication of other works suggesting a deep connection between Indology and National Socialism indicate that this trend in scholarship is flourishing. Furthermore, it is not surprising that some more-recent works can call upon Orientalist criticism to justify claims to an *apriori* racist/imperialist agenda at work in all East-West literary and philosophical relations. In the following pages, I would like to examine how specific Indian symbols found their way into Nazi ideology and iconography, in the hope of deciphering the role such influences play. Our understanding of the dynamics of exoticism would be incomplete without this investigation. Insight into the irrational and destructive aspect of exotic dualism would remain vague, a torso highlighting dramatic moments but leaving unexplored the deeper, more lasting implications. Exoticism did not provide the impetus for racism and totalitarian revolution, but certain exotic themes and images, in their appeal to superordinate power and valorization of the irrational in human nature, were perfectly positioned to provide suitable decor for political and racial violence. My discussion is not intended as an exclusive explanation of the sources of Nazi ideology, but only as an explanation of aspects of the discourses *chosen* by that movement.

Historians trace the rise of National Socialism to the influences of nationalism, anti-liberalism, cultural pessimism, and racism.[9] The vision of the *Volk,* a national collectivity inspired by a common creative energy, was promulgated as the unique essence of the German people. Mosse has speculated that this ideological preoccupation resulted from Germany's delayed political unification and the Romantic reaction to modernity.[10] When Germans began to conceive of their national unity, they did so in cultural terms. *Sturm und Drang,* the idealization of the medieval period and folk culture, characterized by an emotional appeal that supercedes rationality, asserted a spiritual unity when no political unity existed. Racism, too, had a place in *völkisch* ideology. By exploiting racial differences, Germans lent validity to the claims of national distinctions and superiority. In this direction, they were aided and abetted by Darwinism's claim that the superior would prevail over inferior races. How, then, did Germans identify the *Volk*? Where did the notion of the Aryan race enter into their understanding of their cultural identity?

In the *Petersburger Sanskrit Wörterbuch,* the term *ārya* is defined as *treu, ergeben,* and *fromm. Ārya* can signify "ein Mann des eigenen Stammes." The Petersburg dictionary cites the term's etymology from *areioi,* it cites Herodotos's reference to a people named *arioi* and Diodorus's mention of the *areianoi).* In 1763, the French translator of the *Zend Avesta,* Anquetil Duperron translates Herodotus's and Diodorus's Aryans as *ariens,* and in 1776, his German translator Johann Friedrich Kleuker renders their name as *Arier.*

As a consequence of Sir William Jones's monumental discovery, in the eighteenth century, of the relationship between Sanskrit, Classical, and modern European languages, nineteenth-century scholars such as Friedrich Schlegel, Franz Bopp, Jacob Grimm, and August Friedrich Pott developed their own theories concerning the genealogy of languages and populations. Identifying an *Urvolk, Ursprache,* and *Urheimat* became a pressing issue.[11] The clearest criterion for distinguishing peoples was thought to be found in the relationship between languages. Julius von Klaproth envisioned a migration of a "Indisch-Medisch-Sclavisch-Germanischen Völkerkette" from the Ganges to the British Isles. Grimm and Pott maintained that the Aryans in India and Persia were the *Urvolk*, Sanskrit, the *Ursprache*, and the Central Asian Highlands, the *Urheimat*. It was believed that these Aryans moved south and west, differentiating and isolating themselves. Theodor Benfey in 1868 postulated that they had migrated in the opposite direction, from Europe to Asia

Linguists then sought names for the newly discovered linguistic family, names such as *Japhetisch* (*Japhetitisch* or *Japetisch*) *Sarmatisch, Kaukasisch, Indisch-Teutsch, Mittelländisch, Sanskritisch, Indogermanisch, Indokeltisch, Indoeuropäisch,* and *Arisch*. *Indogermanisch* became the most popular designation, although among non-German speakers *Indoeuropean* was standard. When *Indoeuropäisch* gained parlance in A. F. Pott's article "Indogermanischer Sprachstudium" in the *Allegmeine Encyclopädie der Wissenschaften und Künste,* the author spoke specifically of an "Indogermanischer Sanskritsprachstamm" lest there be any doubt as to which European language stemmed from this branch. By 1833, Sanskrit was generally taken to be the oldest language. In terms of the association between race and language, it is significant to note that in the Brockhaus of 1820, there is no rubric for *Indogermanen*. However, by the edition of 1845, we find mention of "indogermanischen Sprachen" and by 1866, reference to the "Indogermanen."[12]

German linguists identified the *Ursprecher* of this language as the Teutarier, Arioteuten, or Viros. Their descendants included, among others, the Germans.[13] Schlegel in 1819 used *Arier* in the sense of "our Germanic ancestors while they were still in Asia."[14] Thus, Sanskrit became the language of the prediaspora Aryans. These Aryans were the equivalent of the *Urvolk* from which the collected linguistic and *Volk* family descended. To support his argument, Schlegel developed his linguistic theories as well as what we know to be false etymologies.[15] As we have seen, Schlegel's knowledge of Sanskrit was incomplete and nonobjective. His study of language was influenced by a crisis of faith.[16]

Christian Lassen also held that the old Germans were named "*Arier*," although he personally preferred the alternative term *Indogermanen*.[17] *Indische Alterthumskunde* consists, for the most part, of a paean to the Aryan. Lassen takes pains to identify the Aryan as Caucasian. To this end, he posits the racial etymology of *Arier* from *arjuna* (white) in opposition to *kṛṣṇa* (black), although he admits that some Aryan Indians are black. Among these Aryans, the *Indogermanen* were the most talented.[18]

Gobineau also used the term *Aryan* in a racial sense. He judged the Aryan to be culturally superior to other races. Indeed, Gobineau went so far as to maintain that Aryans provided the brute material out of which culture was formed. According to Gobineau, Aryans originated in Asia and subsequently wandered into India.[19] There they mixed with indigenous blacks, and through this intermingling the Aryan race declined. Gobineau maintained that the system of caste came into being due to the Indian lawgiver's gradual recognition of the effect of intermingling upon Aryan culture. But the damage had already been done. Buddhism and Islam, with their wanton disregard for caste, struck the death blow. Gobineau saw India as both a model and a warning. The Aryans' capacity for spirituality[20] enabled them to withstand some of the ravages of racial mixture. Alone among the highly civilized cultures, India had sought remedies to the danger of intermixing. But more significantly, India provided a warning to Europe, especially as it was careening toward bastardization through the overthrow of the class structure. Such was the pessimism of a French aristocrat in the nineteenth century, a Frenchman so disillusioned with his own culture that he sought fictive ancestors among the Vikings.

This identification of India as *Gegenbild* to Europe (and, specifically, to Germany) would reappear in subsequent comments of Nazi ideologues as well as Hitler himself. Thus, Gobineau's remarks concerning the Aryans have a particular interest in retrospect. However, it should be noted that Gobineau's theories concerning the Aryans were hardly circulated in his time and were virtually ignored by his contemporaries. In fact, they never gained wide readership, unlike the work of subsequent race theorists or the principal panegyrist of Aryans in the nineteenth century, Friedrich Max Müller. Many came into contact with Müller's distinctive and authoritative portrayal of the Aryan. Although very few Westerners were capable of reading the Sanskrit text of Müller's *editio princeps* of the *Rig Veda*, many became acquainted with his theories in the form of public lectures and books on India directed toward a popular audience, through which Müller codified and spread to a worldwide audience a specific ideology concerning the Vedic Aryan.

II

Müller's edition, which was begun in 1849 and completed in 1874, is noteworthy for several reasons, not the least of which was his inclusion of the whole of Sāyana's commentary in his edition. The inclusion of this medieval commentary generated a debate concerning the feasibility and accessibility of reading and interpreting the Veda. Could the Veda be read? And, ideally, by whom?

The American Sanskritist W. D. Whitney saw in the Veda the "history of our race which has been transacted within the limits of India."[21] The German Rudolph Roth found in the *Rig Veda* "the high spiritual endowments that belong of right to the Indo-European family of nations, which have placed it foremost in the world's history."[22] Such statements suggest the extent to which the use or rejection of Sāyana's commentary reflected not only issues of translation technique, but, more interestingly, ideological concerns. In its editing and partial translation from Sanskrit into German, the Veda engendered discussions on race and ethnicity and exhibited a European attempt to both appropriate the text and distance it from anything Indian. The claim that the conscientious Anglo-Saxon understood the Veda better than Sāyana did presuppose a common German cultural heritage with the Vedic people. The tradition was subsequently lost to the Indians, but not to the Anglo-Saxon European, who, no matter how far removed from the tradition, was never far removed from its vision. The German Romantics had set the stage for readers to believe that, through the science of language, the modern European had access to knowledge that was denied to modern Hindus.

The *Rig Veda* supplied Müller with the material by which he could discover the true nature of the Aryan *Volk*. The Veda offered "solutions to some of the greatest problems of life, and the needed corrective for the inner life of Europe."[23] While many of the hymns sound "childish and absurd,"[24] the Veda still remains the most important document of "Aryan humanity"[25] and the first book of the "Aryan nations."[26] In fact, it was precisely what was childish, what harkened back to the childhood of humanity, that made the Veda particularly instructive.[27]

As we have noted, the question as to who comprised this Aryan humanity and what their characteristics were had been articulated before Müller. These issues, however, gained legitimacy when asked and answered by the scholarly authority on the Veda. Müller identified the Aryan as "our nearest intellectual relatives."[28] Müller understood these ancestors (his term was *Arier*) to be the northern branch of the *Indogermanen,*[29] who became the Germans, Celts, Greeks, Persians, Hindus, and Romans. At one time they lived "together beneath the same roof, separate from the ancestors of the Semitic and Turanian races."[30]

> They [*Arier*] have been the prominent actors in the great drama of history, and have carried to their fullest growth all the elements of active life with which our nature is endowed.

> They have perfected society and morals; and we learn from their literature and works of art the elements of science, the laws of art and the principles of philosophy . . . In the continual struggle with each other and with Semitic and Turanian races, these Aryan nations have become the rulers of history, and it seems to be their mission to link all parts of the world together by the chains of civilization, commerce and religion. In a word, they represent the Aryan man in the historical character.[31]

Until Müller's translation, "our own" history was only gleaned through guesswork and endless, baseless speculations. Now it was available through Vedic references.

> Those men were the true ancestors of our race; and the Veda is the oldest book we have in which to study the first beginnings of our language, and of all that is embodied in language. We are by nature Aryan, Indo-European, not Semitic: our spiritual kith and kin are to be found in India, Persia, Greece, Italy, Germany; not in Mesopotamia, Egypt, or Palestine.[32]

Müller also noted:

> The fathers of the Aryan race, the fathers of our own race, gathered together in the great temple of nature, like brothers of the same house, and looking up in adoration to the sky as the emblem of what they yearned for, a father and a god.[33]

The American Sanskritist Whitney, not one to dismiss Müller's flights of poetic fancy, mocks such passages where Müller seems to depict the Aryan "perched for a couple of thousand years upon some exalted post of observation, watching thence the successive departure from their ancient home of the various European tribes."[34] Whitney then questions whether Müller wrote these descriptions under the influence of paintings such as the Kaulbach in Berlin, depicting people at the foot of the ruined tower of Babel. Although his assessment is not kind, Whitney touches upon a significant argument: Müller's emplotment of the Vedic Aryan evokes German Romantic painting. In fact, Müller's entire discussion of the Veda elaborated Romantic aesthetic and philosophical concerns.

The Romantics held to the idea that the simplicity of religious dogmas defined their original state, and to the corollaries that monotheism was anterior to polytheism and that primitive revelation had progressively degenerated. Once a people has unfolded its spirit to its fullest expression—from the Romantic point of view—it has fulfilled its role in history and only "repetition" (revivals), stagnation, and decay could follow.

Müller's conclusions concerning Vedic religion corresponded with this Romantic thesis. Furthermore, on an aesthetic plane, the Veda fulfilled many of the requirements established by F. Schlegel and others for Romantic poetry. The Veda presented the "sharp edges of primitive thought, the delicate features of a young language, the fresh hue of unconscious poetry." These have been "washed away by the successive waves of what we call tradition, whether we look upon it as a principle of growth or decay."[35] The Veda, through its simplicity and naturalness,[36] brings us closer to our origins in religious thought and language: "Our Aryan mythology . . . our Aryan religion also, took its origin from a poetical interpretation of the great phenomena of nature."[37]

What we see still growing in the Veda we have only encountered full-grown or fast-decaying elsewhere,[38] where mythology has become a "disease" because "its poetical intention has been forgotten."[39] It was the modern Hindu who misunderstood and perverted the spontaneous and truthful revelation of Vedic poetry.

Müller's constant concern was to distinguish between the idealized Vedic Aryan and the modern Hindu, whose

> mind was like the lotus leaf after a shower of rain has passed over it; his character remained the same—passive, meditative, quiet, and thoughtful. A people of this peculiar stamp was never destined to act a prominent part in the history of the world."[40]

The Vedic forbears, however, were so destined and did fulfill this role. Müller characterized the Teutonic race as the most vigorous and enterprising of all the members of the Aryan family who ruled new states in the West and regenerated the effete kingdoms of the East. By natural law, Müller noted, they were destined to rule the entire world.[41]

Müller was also intent to distinguish these Aryans from "really barbarian" races such as Africans or American Indians.[42] The hymns of the *Rig Veda* were spontaneous expressions of a pure and simple race.[43] Their method of transmission was natural, unlike that of the Semites of the Old Testament.[44] For Müller, the very fact that the Vedic hymns were essentially oral texts supported their spontaneous and natural quality.

Until the deciphering of the Veda, there had been "but one oasis in that vast desert of ancient Asiatic history, the history of the Jews." The Veda now offers another such oasis[45] as well as another instance of revelation.[46] the wisdom of One who is "not the God of the Jews alone."[47]

It was only with the passage of time that Müller distanced himself from the misuse of his formulations by racial theorists,[48] most notably in his *Antrittsrede* at the University of Strasbourg in 1872. Here, Müller articulated the distinction between linguistic and racial classification. He noted that there were only Aryan and Semitic linguistic families, but no Aryan race, blood, or skulls. In other words, he firmly stated that you cannot base ethnological classification on linguistic principles and warned against the mixing of linguistic and anthropological terms.[49] Müller had nothing against a race theory *per se*. On the contrary, he was a member of the Gobineau Vereinigung. He merely asserted that the routine mixing of linguistic classifications with race classifications was faulty scientific method.

Müller eventually became defensive. He no longer spoke of races and *Völkern,* but rather of "the Aryan family," "the Aryan man, whom we know in his various characters as Greek, Roman, German, Celt and Slavs," "Northern Aryan," and "Aryan humanity," "the civilization of the Aryan race, that race to which we and all the greatest nations of the world . . . belong."[50]

The discovery that there existed in India a tradition older than, or at least as old as, the biblical tradition was regarded as an event of the first magnitude, to be compared in its consequences only to the rediscovery of classical antiquity in the Renaissance. Through testimony from Vedic India, in the form of Müller's edition of the *Rig Veda,* scholars could begin to reconstruct the history of humanity's past and origin, the development of religions and philosophies. The Veda provided essential information concerning the European past. Thought to be the oldest available literature of an "Indo-Germanic" language, the *Rig Veda* promised to reveal the state of civilization that was closest to the supposed common ancestors of all Indo-German peoples. Specifically, armed with Müller's voluminous commentary on Vedic India, historically minded Germans, as well as Pan-Germanists and the occult lunatic fringe, believed that the study of the old Aryans could elucidate the history and fate of the Germans as a whole. One can distinguish, therefore, two motives for the beginnings of Vedic scholarship. First, there entailed the search for the oldest forms of religion and language. Second, it set the stage for the inquiry into the origin and past of the German people through information drawn from ancient Sanskrit sources. Thus, in Germany, the beginnings of Vedic scholarship as well as philology offered a cultural attempt to restore one's own tradition.

Müller's promoting the myth of the Aryan throughout his thirty-odd years of editing the *Rig Veda* entailed the very type of categorical mixing that he condemned in the Strasbourg lecture. How do we explain this paradox? I think that it was far less an issue of Müller's blindness toward his methodology than of his adherence to a Romantic emplotment of India. His need to construct the Vedic Aryan from the text and identify with this Aryan stemmed from religious and aesthetic concerns far more akin to the aims of Romanticism than to nineteenth-century race theory. However, as a worthy heir to his father, the renowned German Romantic poet Wilhelm Müller, and as the final avatar of Romanticism in service to linguistics, Müller popularized concepts concerning the Aryan that would have serious repercussions. In hindsight, it is difficult to keep in focus Müller's historical reality as a product of Romantic views of India rather than portray him as an ideological precursor of National Socialist race theory. We must keep in mind that he did not directly influence Nazi race theorists—they did not quote him. However, we must also acknowledge that he created a portrait of pure and cultivated Aryan ancestors and their fictive descendants that found its way into National Socialist mythology.

III

The categorical mixing of linguistic and racial classifications that was problematized in the work of Max Müller was fully systematized in twentieth-century racial theory. Theodor Poesche, Karl Penka, and George Vacher de Lapouge[51] maintained that there existed a linguistic classification of Indo-European languages, necessitating an Indo-European community of speakers, a *Volk* family. These theorists routinely combined linguistic classifications with race classifications. For Poesche and Penka, the *Urtype* was dolichocephalic (German-Scandanavian) and bracycephalic (Celt, Slav). As *Urherrn* (Anglo-Saxons, Germans), they subjugated various *Urknechte* (Celts, Italians, Iberians, and Slavs). In India, these Aryans comprised the brahmin caste: They were strong, blond, and blue-eyed in the North, due to the light and climate. Penka supported this thesis with the etymology of Aryan—from ἀργής (radiant, *strahlend*)—ἀργεστής (bright, *aufhellend*). Poesche situated the *Urheimat* of the Aryan in Lithuania, Penka, in Scandinavia, and Lapouge, in the North Sea. In early times, this *Urvolk* wandered to India but found the climate unamenable. They eventually left, but those who had ties with the dark indigenous population remained. Thus, these Aryans effected a selection of the fittest when the colonizers were decimated and forced to mix for survival. Whereas for Gobineau, India represented the last Aryan bastion, which had valiantly fought bastardization, Poesche, Penka and de Lapouge were strictly Darwinian. Environment had effected the demise of the Indian Aryan. They believed racial mixture to be inevitable. In order to retain their culture, the Aryans in India were forced to sacrifice race. Thus, the present-day inhabitants of India have only a small percentage of Aryan blood coursing through their veins. Poesche held that while modern Indian languages were mostly Aryan, the *Volk* physically could no longer make such a claim. To these Aryan theorists, the Indians were

> Negroes and Mulattoes, who knew how to retain the noble language of some paternal ancestors. Subtropical nature has physically and spiritually overrun the Aryan species in India and stifled it in its fullness.[52]

The downward spiral of the Aryans paralleled the general devaluation of India in nineteenth-century European consciousness. By the end of the century, Romantic enthusiasm with India and her inhabitants had considerably ebbed. Although the Romantics admired and sought inspirational models from the Aryan, with Nietzsche we begin to see the portrayal of the Aryan as a moral and racial failure. Just as India was no longer the cradle of civilization and had become, as Enrico de Michaelis maintained, the grave of the Aryans,[53] so too had the Aryans in India degenerated from their forebears. The Indians were not excluded from the Aryan race category as was stipulated in the *Arierparagraph* in the *Gesetz zur Wiederherstellung des Berufsbeamtentums* of 7 April, 1933.[54] However, by the time of the National Socialist *Nürnberger Gesetze* of 15 September, 1935, it could no longer be a question of Aryan and not-Aryan, but only of "German blood ties." A definite shift had occurred in the German adoption of Aryan parentage. The initial race theorists differed significantly from the National Socialists in that their mechanical race selection theory left little room for factors such as will or self-discipline. As the scholarship and popular emplotment of India had clearly shown, Indian philosophy at an early stage of its reception was characterized in terms of its alleged quietism. In a parallel process, the racial fate of the Indian Aryan was believed to be determined by endemic passivity and fatalism. Lest the same fate befall him as befell his Indian brethren, the destiny of the German Aryan necessitated a will to power. The National Socialist state would embody this will through its preservation of Aryan blood[55] and identity.[56]

> The "völkish" worldview recognizes the meaning of mankind in terms of its racial original elements. It sees the state principally as a means to this end and conceives as its purpose the maintenance of the racial being of mankind. In no way does it believe in the equality of the races, rather it recognizes in their difference their higher or lower worth and feels itself, through this knowledge, bound, in accordance with the eternal will which rules this universe, to promote victory for the better and the stronger and to demand the subordination of the lesser and the weak . . . it can also not allow the existential right of an ethical idea, in so far as this idea represents danger for the racial life of an ethically superior bearer, for, in a bastardized and "niggerized" world, ideas of human beauty and sublimity as well as all conceptions of an idealized future of our humanity are also forever lost. On this earth, human culture and civilization are inseparably bound to the survival (also: "presence") of the Aryan.[57]

Tschandalen *and the Lunatic Fringe*

In actuality, the Nazi link with the Orient has less to do with the migrations of Aryan warlords than with National Socialism's complex pedigree of Theosophy and occult racial theory. Mme. Blavatsky founded the Theosophical Society in New York City in 1875. By presenting a tirade against contemporary Western agnosticism, rationalism, and materialism, Mme. Blavatsky encouraged her readers to seek truth through ancient religion. She first directed them to ancient Egypt in *Isis Revealed* (1877). With her emigration to India in 1879, she shifted her base of operations, as well as the locus of truth, to India. No doubt sensitive to the popularity of translations from Sanskrit scripture, Theosophy received in India its systematic formulation.

The *Secret Doctrine* (1888), describes the activities of God from the beginning of creation. History as a cyclical process was a fundamental concept of Theosophy, with the present universe viewed as an emanation and subsequent progression. Hindu concepts of *karma* and reincarnation were incorporated within Theosophy to provide a definition of the nature of humanity. The individual ego was regarded as a small fragment of the Divine Being. Through reincarnation, individual consciousness negotiated the various stages of enlightenment, culminating in reunion with this Divine Being. One is reborn countless times according to the principle of *karma,* where a virtuous life enjoys rebirth on a high level and ignoble acts ensure rebirth on a low level. The first volume of *The Secret Doctrine* describes cosmogenesis. Here, the primal unity of the Divine Being is sundered, initiating the emanation which fills the entire universe. All subsequent creation then passes through seven evolutionary cycles. Blavatsky illustrated cosmic cycles with a variety of esoteric symbols, of which the swastika, an Indian symbol of luck, was the most popular. In fact, it became the seal of the Theosophical Society.

In the second volume of *The Secret Doctrine,* Blavatsky described anthropogenesis. During each cycle, seven consecutive root races, descending on a scale of spiritual development, come into being and pass away. One of these root races, the Aryan, had as its first underrace the ancient Indians. The fifth Aryan underrace, the Teutonic, currently reigned, possessing such qualities as scientific understanding, which is especially prevalent, we are told, in Germany. These Aryans were in the process of ascent; their process of spiritual advancement lay before them. Agglutinated speech existing in other races became inflected in the Aryan race.

The Jews belong to the second Aryan underrace, the so-called Ario-Semites, a mixture of those Aryans who wandered from India to Egypt. Blavatsky revealed that the Jews stemmed from the fourth root race, the Atlantans, and she identified them with the pariahs (*caṇḍāla*) of ancient India.

> They can just as well be the expelled chandala of Ancient India who are mentioned as the "Brick wall" by Veda-Vyasa and Manu . . . The Semitic languages are the bastard descendants of the first corruption of the eldest children of early Sanskrit . . . The Semites, especially the Arabs, are later Aryans, materially degenerate in intellect and perfection in materiality. To these belong all the Jews and Arabs. The first belong to a branch which descends from the Indian chandalas.[58]

Thus, the concept of the pariah that had in the eighteenth and nineteenth centuries been emplotted as the noble savage, an Enlightenment symbol for social equality, reappears in this inverted form, a polarity of diametrically opposed significations that we have come to expect from the exotic. A third metaphorization of the pariah, distinct still from those of the Enlightenment and Theosophy, is to be found in the fulminations of Nietzsche. Whereas the Enlightenment pariah rebelled against fate, Nietzsche's *caṇḍāla* (*Tschandala*) symbolized fatalistic resignation and passivity in the guise of charity. He was a product of the shift that had occurred in the general reception of things Indian; the pariah as model for inspiration had become a symbol of the despair with the European present, and a threat.

Nietzsche had popularized the figure of the *caṇḍāla* in his discussion of Christianity and Buddhism, which he characterized as the world's two great nihilistic movements, "decadent" and rooted in the monstrous disease of the will.[59] In Buddhism, however, Nietzsche recognized a more consistent type of pessimism.[60] It provided a "nihilism that was freer, more aristocratic, and more cultivated than in Christianity, it was a *Tschandala* religion."[61]

Nietzsche merged his vision of the *Untermensch* with the *caṇḍāla* who, in turn, became identified with the Christian, the man who, ruled by love and pity for humanity, rendered himself an *Untermensch*. Opposed to Christianity, Nietzsche saw in the *Laws of Manu* a realistic acceptance of life and a "jasagende arische Religion"[62] that was skilled in the exercise of power. Led by an elite comprised of noble classes, warriors and philosophers, Indians dominated the rabble. Nietzsche understood Indian morality (as promulgated in *Manu*) in the following manner:

> Here is the task presented, to breed not less than four races at once: a priestly, warrior, merchant peasant, and finally a servant race, the sudras . . . But also it is necessary for this organization to be formidable, not in battle with a brute, but with its opposite idea, the hybrid man, the mishmash man, the chandala.[63]

The *Übermensch* shared with the ancient Hindu a feeling of perfection, a life-affirming sense and a triumphant worldview.[64] The ancient Hindu had been successful in the world because of his ability to segregate himself from the "excrement of society."[65] The *Tschandala* and his religion, on the other hand, reaffirmed the need for Nietzsche's alternative vision.

> These orders are instructive enough—in them we have on the one hand Aryan humanity, completely pure, completely original—we learn that the idea of "pure blood" is the opposite of a harmless concept. On the other hand, it becomes clear which people perpetuated hatred, *chandala* hatred, against this humanity, where it became a religion and a genius . . . From this point of view the Gospels, a document of the first order, more so, the Book of Enoch. Christianity, from a Jewish root and only understandable as a plant from this soil, represents the counter movement to every moral of breeding, race and privilege—it is the anti-Aryan religion par excellence: Christianity overhauls all Aryan values, the victory of the *chandala* values—the Gospel preached to the poor and low, the collected revolt of all the down-trodden, the miserable, failed, those who have come off poorly against the "race"—the immortal *chandala* revenge as a religion of love."[66]

Nietzsche's *Tschandala* represented the individual who has been rendered weak in will by a weak religion. At no time did Nietzsche identify the *Tchandala* with the Jew. This association, when it was made, became an important development in the representation of the *caṇḍāla*.[67] As we have noted, an initial association of the *caṇḍala* and the Jew was effected by Mme. Blavatsky and it can be traced to her unique brand of Slavic anti-Semitism. Perhaps in imitation of the Theosophists, occultists such as List and Lanz von Liebenfels reworked this identification of the Jew and the *caṇḍāla* into their racial ideology.[68]

A theosophical provenance for their association of these two figures is not far-fetched. Theosophy flourished in the last quarter of the nineteenth century, providing "philosophical" justification for various *Lebensreform* groups of Wilhelmian Germany. Under the leadership of Franz Hartmann, a German who had spent twenty years in the United States studying Theosophy, the German theosophical movement flourished and, in addition to providing translations of Mme. Blavatsky's works, published several translations from Sanskrit. German theosophists also published *völkisch* journals dealing with esotericism and sporting exotic titles such as *Lotusblüthen, Prana, Aryavarta* and *Ostara*.

As Goodrick-Clarke has shown, not only was the German occult subculture well developed prior to the First World War, but with the appearance of such publications a definite evolution took place in occult ideology. The earliest Austrian Theosophy was coupled with mystical Christianity; its later Viennese manifestation dealt more with myth, folklore, and comparative religions. Theosophy's eclecticism with respect to esoteric lore and its non-Christian perspective on the cosmos and human origins were well suited to *völkisch* speculation.

Guido von List provided a synthesis of Theosophy and German mythology.[69] In Wotanism, List introduced the Hindu concept of reincarnation, as well as the doctrine of emanation. The unity of man and nature was the hallmark of this cosmic vision. By nature, List meant an identification of *Volk* and race. In *Die Gnosis* (1903), List developed his theories concerning racial purity, eugenics, the immortality of soul, and karmic determination. A Pan-German empire envisioned by List consisted of a hierarchical state with Aryans exercising total control. Access to the professions was restricted solely to Aryans. Menial tasks were the province of non-Aryans in order that Aryans rule unencumbered over all lesser groups.

In List's last work, *Die Ursprache der Ario-Germanen* (1914), the ancient German national past corresponds to a Hindu *kalpa,* or world cycle. His conflation of Theosophy with a suspect reading of Hindu religious concepts formed the basis for an occult vision of the millenium. List's apocalyptic hopes for the end of the present cycle and the dawning of new age struck responsive chords. Vienna at that time was suffering from over-population,[70] epidemics and a general breakdown of social institutions. Hitler described Vienna in the first decade of the twentieth century as the embodiment of a "disgrace of blood."[71] List's faith in the purifying power of the coming apocalypse was such that he claimed that ten thousand war victims would be reborn to fight the coming national revolution.[72]

In the face of growing Slavic nationalism, Pan-Germanism was succeeded by the rise of Ariosophy. Gobineau and Darwin influenced the virulently racist worldview of Ariosophy but ultimately it was a vision of salvation through racial purity that became its essential framework. The maintenance of racial purity was presented as the means to abolish contamination and deterioration.[73]

Ariosophy provided the occult features of German nationalism, combining racist theories with the Hindu concept of *karma.*[74] Hindu religious philosophy which supported Indian caste restrictions also formed the basis for the identification of Germanic Aryans as a superior people gifted with panpsychic energy, rendering them equal to god.[75]

The Ariosophist Lanz von Liebenfels viewed human history as a conflict between a quasi-divine Aryan humanity and *Untermenschen,* referred to as the "*Tschandalen.*" The fall of man resulted from the Aryans racial compromise. Ariosophists were determined to counter what they perceived as the dominant position held by "inferior" races in Europe. Lanz called for extreme measures including the extermination of "inferior" races.[76]

Lanz founded the Pan-German periodical *Ostara*. This journal was devoted to the examination of race in all its ramifications. Special issues examined such concerns as the Manichaean conflict between fair and dark races, antiparliamentarianism and social sexual differences. For a Germanic population suffering from post-war economic and social chaos, the second *Ostara*[77] series provided a vision of a heroic Aryan race ruling over the ancient Western world and the Orient. The modern world was said to be based on evil principles rendering the current social order obsolete. Some historians believe that Hitler was a regular reader of Von Liebenfels's *Ostara*[78] and derived his Manichaean vision of the Aryan versus the Jew from its discussions of "racial somatology." There is also some evidence that Hitler was influenced by a disciple of Lanz, the politician Dr. Karl Lueger.[79]

What is of interest to us particularly is the manner in which this periodical reflected aspects of the racist ideology of the time. It posited an ideal world as a response to disenchantment with contemporary existence. It fabricated this world out of racist ideas culled from German *völkisch* ideology and legitimized this vision with "Hindu" occult conceptions borrowed from Theosophy and supported by creative adaptations of Indological scholarship. An ideal case in point was the 1908 issues of *Ostara* which were devoted to the examination of the *Laws of Manu*.[80] Lanz undertook an analysis of the ancient Sanskrit treatise in response to critics of race research. Lanz maintained that *Manu* presented a scientifically constructed law and that, given its total lack of racial bias, it should serve as a model for modern German law, which he judged to be lie-ridden, foundationless, and ungrounded in biology, anthropology, or racial science.[81] Lanz pretended that the racially grounded law that he and his cohorts advocated represented historical laws, especially since Manu, the "father of Mankind," was in actuality Tacitus's Mannus, the "father of all Germans."

The need for a new system of law was especially urgent because Germans were being ruled by *Tschandala-Rechten* rather than true racial law imposed by ancient Aryan "scripture." Beginning with the Rig Vedic adage, "Ich (Indra) gab den Arya die Erde,"[82] Lanz set out to build his case for racial law, basing his argument on liberal excerpts from *Manu*. As his source material, Lanz used the Christoph Hüttner translation,[83] which he quotes faithfully. To these excerpts, Lanz added his own commentary, which quite often bore no relation to the text and to which he gave a modern racist bent. Although elsewhere Lanz identified the *Tschandala* with the Jew,[84] in these pages the term specifically referred to the lower classes and the "mongrelized inferiors."[85]

Before undertaking an analysis of *Manu,* however, Lanz raised certain theoretical issues that would bear upon his more general thesis. How, for instance, can a lower race judge a higher race?[86] Should not purer races have more rights than those less pure? By demanding order and segregation, Lanz aspired to impose "menschenfreundlich" racial laws that would reinstate a hierarchy of will. Such innovations were necessary because the *Tschandalen* were always in the majority,[87] and the current *Tschandalen-Gesetze* only served a *Tschandala-Menschheit.*[88]

To support his argument, Lanz drew caste-exclusionary concepts from *Manu*. His commentary, given the hindsight of history, bears chilling testimony to the modern appropriation of ancient intolerance. Lanz cites *Manu* as establishing the following regulations:

> One should cleanse oneself from contact with *Tschandalen.*[89]
>
> Brahmins are justified in seizing the property of *Tschandalen.*
>
> The defilement of caste (footnoted by Lanz as "blood") through sexual relations requires seven generations to cleanse itself.[90]
>
> Rich *Tschandalen* can have their own goods confiscated because their possessions are either stolen or swindled from the higher races in times of duress.[91]

Lanz made good use of *Manu* for his specific racist agenda. Since Aryans created culture and graciously allow lower races to participate in it, they should be paid tribute.[92] Aryans possess a unique bond with the land; the city is their grave.[93] Urban culture is intimately bound to the increase of racial mixing.

> Now, however, the ruling caste is no longer an Asian caste, the beautiful outer shell of the ancient Aryan race remains, but its inner core has been eaten out by the *Tschandala*-worms. And so today's India offers a picture that racially no longer corresponds to *Manu's Law Book.*[94]

Lanz opened his discussion with a photograph of an ancient statue depicting the broad brow, sharp round eyes, long nose, and small mouth of the perfect Aryan. He ends with a photograph of a modern Indian who has degenerated through "female lack of discipline" (*Weiberzuchtlosigkeit*).

Hitler was certainly receptive to the comic-book Manichaean vision of the conflict between blonds and the dark races. It is generally believed that he was more influenced by the conflict between Aryans and *Tschandalen* of *Ostara* and similar pamphlets than by Gobineau and Nietzsche. Furthermore, as Lanz's analysis of *Manu* proves, one can find echoes of Lanz's theories as they were articulated in *Ostara* in the Third Reich's decrees banning interrace marriages, destruction of inferior races, and polygamy.

To what degree did occult-nationalistic groups influence Hitler? *Mein Kampf,* contains contemptuous attacks on the "völkisch wandering scholars" of these lodges and asserted that Germany's salvation demanded a mass political party that could be effectual in battle, and not the antiquarianism and ceremonial antics so prevalent in these organizations.[95] In this sense, Hitler acknowledged Ariosophy as a symptom rather than a significant influence. Although a direct line of symbolic succession can be seen in their mutual symbol, the swastika, the NSDAP differed considerably from such organizations in terms of militancy and ideology.

These various occult groups, however, all conformed to a certain stereotype and, as such, reflect the ideological climate of their day. Their doctrines cited exalted ancestors, whose ancient gnostic rule had brought the Aryans wisdom and power until being supplanted by an alien and hostile culture. They contributed to the mythological mood of the subsequent Nazi era by the fact that the NSDAP originated from their ranks. To suggest that they directly influenced people in positions of political power exaggerates their importance.[96] During the Third Reich, such organizations were officially dissolved; the general Nazi policy was to suppress lodge organizations and esoteric groups. However, Nazis traditionally outlawed those tendencies they most suspected in their ranks.

Nevertheless, these groups appropriated elements of Indian provenance and thereby formed a bridge between the nineteenth-century occult Orientalism and Nazism.[97] Indian clichés such as the terms *Aryan* and *caṇḍāla* as well as the symbol of the swastika were transformed into objects of militancy and bore fruit in such groups as the Germanen Orden,[98] founded in 1912, and later the Thule Society. Unlike Theosophists, who viewed humanity as an all-inclusive fraternity, such occult racist groups conceived of Aryans in a biological sense. They imitated Theosophy's use of the swastika, which became the German wheel of the sun.[99]

Rudolf von Sebottendorf, who revived the Germanen Orden in 1917, appropriated the term *Tschandalen* from Lanz von Liebenfels and used it in the *Münchner Beobachter,* soon to become the *Völkischer Beobachter,* whose motto was *Nieder mit den Tschandalen*. The subsequent National Socialist use of the term *Tschandala* derived from this implementation by Lanz and not from Nietzsche (*Götzendämmerung* and *Antichrist*),[100] although Nietzsche's concepts can readily be appropriated by racists.

I am not claiming, therefore, a direct causal connection between Theosophy, Ariosophy, the Thule, and Nazism, but only certain ideological similarities. The anti-Semitism of Theosophy's founder supplied a religious rationalization for occult anti-Semitism and a strong racist substructure. Ariosophy would take the vision of god-men and make them German-Aryans; the Thule Society would take the Ariosophist ideas of racial supremacy and seek to implement them. The entire spectrum borrowed the occult interpretation of human history as apocalypse and was fully grounded in the idea of spiritual superiority.

As I noted in an earlier chapter, the discovery of Indian culture in the eighteenth century, along with such forces as the French Enlightenment, effected the destruction of biblical myth regarding the origin of man. This rejection of the biblical worldview did not establish the *sine qua non* equivalent to anti-Semitism but, rather, established the beginning of the scholarly writing on history.[101] India, among other countries, became an object of study. However, when India entered into discussions of the Nationalist camp of the Weimar Republic, it did so in an interestingly incestuous fashion: Germany had been sacrificed by imperialistic Western powers, who had, by means of the Versailles Treaty, given Germany a colonial status. Oswald Spengler (1924) would typify Germany as "ein europäisches Indien."[102]

As Sieferle has shown, the revolutionary group of the National Socialists broke with Hitler in 1930 with this anti-imperialistic orientation as one of their points of division. They articulated their purpose in the *Gründungsmanifest* of the Schwarzen Front:

> For us, approval of the Indian fight for freedom from English domination and capitalist exploitation has been and is a necessity, as much from the fact that for a German liberation politics every weakening of a Versailles signatory is favorable, as from the emotional support of every battle which subjugated peoples enjoin against their exploitative usurpers, since

> it is a compelling consequence of our concept of nationalism that the right to fulfill a *völkisch* identity, that we claim for ourselves also applies to other peoples and nations.[103]

In contradistinction to this ideology of solidarity, Hitler's position was, however, perfectly clear. He advocated the supremacy of one race of high value over the world.

> An alliance of the down-trodden nations is a dumb slogan. . . . When today the Indian lives under the rule of England . . . or the Black under the rule of any European people, this is grounded in their inferiority . . . The freedom fight of the Blacks, Indians and so forth is an attempt to break the natural order . . . The admiration of Gandhi is, in my estimation, a racial perversity.[104]

In this respect, Hitler repudiated *völkisch* politics in favor of a capitalistic race-imperialism based on the European model.[105]

Many of the same themes that have animated this entire study of the Western expropriation of Indian religious thought are pulled together (if the idea of coherence can be used in this context) in the utterances of the official National Socialist party ideologue, Alfred Rosenberg. Most significantly, the tension between the desire for new inspirational models and the justification of darker irrational impulses, which characterize the Western need for and utilization of an Indian exotic, coalesce in National Socialist ideology promulgated by Rosenberg. The ancient Indians lived their lives not for love, but for the sake of duty and honor.[106] They constituted the first racial cultural wave that, originating in Atlantis, had crossed the mountains of India, pushed back and surpassed the inferior races, and prevailed over non-Aryan superstitions and magical cultic practices. The Aryan Indians kept apart from the dark inhabitants by instituting a policy of separation. Thus, racial purity was responsible for the great achievements of these Indians. Non-Aryan magic disappeared when Aryan spirituality, based on aristocratic self-consciousness, overcame the non-Aryan magical sacrifice-based religion.

> After this separation of blood and blood, the Aryans constructed for themselves a picture of the world, which, in its depth and breadth, even today can be surpassed by no philosophy.[107]

However, this supremacy was eventually overturned as the Aryans lost their sense of color and blood. In other words, the Aryans died in their quest for the individual self.[108] Aryan blood was diluted through infelicitous mixing of the races, "after long-lasting proximity with the ever-more-penetrating representation of the low-caste indigenous population."[109]

With their supremacy thus overturned, Indian Aryans became less creative as bastard art (such as phallic worship) took over. Although traces of Aryan genius occasionally blossomed in the lyrics of Kālidāsa and the philosophy of Śaṅkara, it could not stem the tide. It was not simply the issue of blood that precipitated the Aryans' downfall, but rather their spiritual values. In a party speech of 12 September, 1923, apropos the pacifists' deleterious effect upon Germany, Hitler noted: "Yes, they want to make an India out of Germany, a dreamy people who turn away from reality. . . ."[110]

When he spoke these words, Hitler was not thinking back to his reading of Hegel. However, others more popular and easier to read than Hegel recycled the emplotment of India that scholarship had legitimized and Hegel had ratified.

Is it an issue, then, of scholarly collusion and cause-and-effect processes? I do not suggest anything so simple. The scholarship coming out of the tradition of nineteenth-century philology was still eminently dedicated to certain Enlightenment and Romantic presuppositions. This scholarship drew some naive and, in hindsight, irresponsible conclusions. At the same time, spurred by the publication of Darwin, race theorists fed nationalist concerns. Theosophy effectively packaged anti-Semitism, *völkisch* ideology, and occult, superficial exoticism. The lunatic fringe proselytized an amalgamation of race theory, Theosophy, anti-Semitism, and *völkisch* nationalism. It supported its agenda with a selective reading of Indological scholarship (*Rig Veda, Manu's Gesetzbuch*).

The stage was set for a National Socialist "philosopher" to explain that the concepts of *Ātman/Brahman* had also destroyed the Indians' sense of race, just as it had once destroyed their personality.[111] In the misguided quest for the individual Self, the Aryan oversoul perished.[112] With the loss of personality and racial consciousness, the loss of honor followed suit. In terms reminiscent of Nietzsche, (but not necessarily originating in him), Alfred Rosenberg could claim that India had fallen prey to influences that had sapped its spiritual strength.[113]

Buddhist and Christian compassion effected the apotheosis of the Aryan *Untermensch,* as did the lure of *nirvāṇa.*[114] Compassion, longing for *nirvāṇa,* loss of individual racial Self, and inaction and its ultimate consequence, fatalism, characterized the destiny of the Aryan in India.[115] The land of German dreams and hopes for cultural invigoration perished due to its spiritual flaw. Those advocating this spirituality in the West, those indulging in the fatuous quest for *nirvāṇa,* might well take notice of where their flirtation was leading them. It has been a function of this volume to show that although Nazi race theorists echoed warnings against the same Indian predestination that underpinned the fatalism earlier condemned by Friedrich Schlegel, Hegel, French Catholic philosophers, and Nietzsche alike,[116] they were motivated by different concerns.

For the National Socialists, India's tragedy consisted in the disappearance of the Indian Aryan. The society that had given us the genius of Sanskrit epic and the sophistication of speculative philosophy had now degenerated into race chaos. India was used up (*verbraucht*) and weak. It needed a *Herrenhand* to rule over it.[117] Among other things, National Socialism provided a response to the *nirvāṇa* seeker's and "Indian" philosophy's implicit call for inaction and fatalism. Literally, National Socialist ideology provided a response to Indian "irrationalism" in its condemnation of Gandhi. The Indian situation was bad enough: Its rejection of the world led to the Aryans' mixing with indigenous populations, which led to spiritual weakness and loss of a racial "will to self-assertion" (*Selbstbehauptungswille*).[118] Gandhi, with his pacifism, struck the death blow.

Rosenberg took particular issue with the Gandhi-rapture (*Gandhi-Verzückung*) that was raging in the *völkisch*-nationalist camp. Just as many European thinkers rejected the deleterious effects of Indian philosophy, so did Rosenberg recognize in Gandhi's politics the modern historical praxis of this philosophy, an instrument for the destruction of nature and the myth of race.[119] Either there would be a universal reawakening, or Germany would follow India's course and redescend into chaos.[120] Within this narrative, myths of filiation were sustained. Although Germany's contributions to myth ranked above those of all other nations, like India it too would fall prey to mongrelization. Germany was fortunate in that, having observed the racial decline of its Aryan forbears, it could attempt to avoid their destiny.[121]

> First, race must be denationalized. First it must unlearn that its strength lies in its blood, and when it has done that and possesses no more pride, then the product arises, a second race, which is more profound than its predecessor and needs to be so, since what the Jew needs, in order to organize, build and maintain his definitive world dominion, is the sinking of

> the level of race of other peoples, so that he alone can be racially pure and finally rule over all the others, that is the sinking of race, of which we can see the effects in a whole series of peoples in the world today. We know that the Hindus are a people in India who have been mixed out of the high-ranking Aryan immigrants and the dark-black original inhabitants and that this people today bears the consequences; for they are also the slaves of a race which appears to us in many respects almost like a second form of Jew.[122]

As did Nietzsche, however, Rosenberg attributed this mulattoization of the world to Christianity. Like Buddhist compassion, Jesuitical-Roman spineless pity was un-Germanic and degenerate. Humanitarianism as advocated in the eighteenth and nineteenth centuries presented a fatal error that only compounded Oriental abstract fantasy.[123] The vision of man's equality, articulated in the early-nineteenth-century pariah literature, is subverted in the later image of the *caṇḍāla*. The enlightened project of *Humanität* with all its presuppositions, must be repudiated lest it justify the enfranchisement of Negroes, the incurably sick, and the insane.[124]

Thus, in place of the Nordic "desire for the enhancement of life" (*Lust an der Steigerung des Lebens*), Rosenberg found the "world conquest of the decrepit Aryan Indian" (*Weltüberwindung des gealterten arischen Inders*), and Buddhism represented the total ruin of the Nordic Aryan racial spirit in the tropical Indian environment.[125] Buddhism struck the final blow to Aryanhood. By breaking all remaining bonds to family, *Volk,* and State, Buddhism led to the destruction of race. India had moved from being an ideal projection of Enlightenment and Romantic ideals. Both Rosenberg and Günther present India as a projection of the European racial situation. The decline of the Indian Aryan provided a paradigm for the kind of degradation that civilization could undergo: vanity of the individual, racial self-destruction and the disfunctional family unit. In the beginning of the nineteenth century, India metaphorically represented the cradle of German civilization, at the end of the century, it had come to represent its grave. While India had traditionally functioned as a model to Germans, now it also served as an admonishment to modern German Aryans. In this manner, but for the grace of God, they too would perish, if inexorable fate were not reversed.

Gobineau viewed the Indian caste system as a successful method of conserving racial purity. The duration of Indian culture was based on conservation of Aryan master elements, and the gradual decline of the Indian Aryans through racial admixture was an unavoidable natural process.

The decline of the Indian Aryan convinced Darwinian race theorists that certain races, due to physical characteristics alone, could not survive in unsuitable environments. It was from this judgement that a Darwinian anticolonialism developed. Rosenberg saw in the fall of the Indian Aryans a parable for the fall of race through the lack of the will to self-assertion. Indian Aryans did not understand the myth of race sufficiently and, therefore, did not sufficiently fulfill caste rules. They mixed with indigenous populations, lost their moral identity, made cities, disappeared in race chaos, and finally died. They represented "a racial disgrace, whose products today as miserable bastards plead for a cure for their crippled existence in the waters of the Ganges."[126] Rosenberg did not accept Gobineau's view that dimunition of racial purity was historically inevitable. On the contrary, he believed that through the exercise of a will to self-discipline a race could revitalize itself. Race was not, as in Darwin, a unidirectional and passive movement determined by environment, but rather a process legitimizing the mastery of the Nordic races over lesser races, the British over the Indians, the Germans over everyone else.

Concluding Remarks

Certain books can capture the spirit of their time. Literature has the capacity to prefigure political ideologizing. In this study, I have attempted to focus on individual motivation as manifested in texts. As the history of the reception of the exotic makes clear, this locus became increasingly politicized. Charles Péguy held that a "mystique" transformed into a "politique" engenders decadence.[1] In *A German Identity, 1770–1990,* Harold James cites Harry Graf Kessler quoting Hermann Graf Keyserling in July 1933:

> The Germans desire purposeless death in the shape of self-sacrifice. And they sense that [Hitler] . . . is emphatically the suicidal type, one who, in seeking death, embodies a fundamental trait of the German nation, which has always been in love with death, and for whom *Nibelungennot* is a constantly recurring fundamental experience. Only in this situation do the Germans feel entirely German: they admire and desire death without a purpose, self-sacrificing. And they sense that through Hitler they are once more being led toward grandiose destruction, toward another *Nibelungennot;* that is what fascinates them about him. He is fulfilling their deepest longing. The French or the English want victory, all the Germans ever want is to die.[2]

This quote does not strike me as necessarily true. In fact, if Keyserling was not mythologizing Hitler, he was certainly romanticizing Nazism. However, according to James, this quote does suggest a deep truth concerning the crucial issue of the unstable borderline between literature and politics. It describes a behavior pattern that was first articulated in literature. The tale of the Nibelungs founded a literary tradition whose power was demonstrated when it became a paradigm for behavior outside literature, in social and historical situations that were themselves partly formed by a literary tradition. For Keyserling's concept of *Nibelungennot,* we could easily have substituted that of *nirvāṇa* or *Tschandalen*. The essential view is that the relationship between *māyā* and pessimism, pariah and Enlightenment, Aryan and National Socialism, is not one of cause and effect. It is to highlight the intertextuality of artistic, scholarly, spiritual, and social paradigms that the essays have been collected in this volume.

Initially, India represents doctrinal and spiritual superiority. As Jules Michelet noted in *La Bible de l'humanité:* "De l'Inde . . . descend un torrent de lumière, un fleuve de Droit et de Raison."[3] Concomitant with the stimulating expropriation of Indian models, one can recognize the theme of historical corruption and degeneration articulated in a return to Indian sources. The Enlightenment provided nineteenth-century exoticism with much of its conceptual apparatus by initiating the doubling in the emplotment of India. Bhartṛhari's poetic vision of the return to *Brahman* legitimized Günderrode's will to autodestruction. F. Schlegel's search for a perfect language was thwarted when he discovered a language and philosophy that had degenerated through a mixture of alien (albeit non-Aryan, proto-Indian) elements. Lord Krishna's teaching, viewed in light of Hegel's historical consciousness, became a death sentence for modern man. The bliss of *nirvāṇa* metamorphosed into an abyss into which we are all inexorably drawn. In short, the new faith sought in the exotic offered neither consolation nor salvation. The exotic remedy was much more a symptom than a cure.

Thus, an important element of the metaphorical journey to the Aryan India of our origins, the escape to the Ideal, is its necessary failure, or rather, the negation of the quest for meaning. Disappointment with India's failure to fulfill all our vague longings has been seen as the source of a modern rejection of India[4] and symptomatic of the Western imperialist mind-set.[5] Or, indeed, the European rejection of India is attributable to the European discovery of Buddhism.[6] Although it is true that the Oriental Renaissance developed from the discovery of Brahmanical texts and that Europe's initial vision was of a comparatively rational and quasi-Western India, we have shown that the West was often unable to distinguish Buddhism from Brahmanism (for such mundane reasons as the unavailability of, and the inability to decipher, source material). The tension between the search for inspirational models and the escape into despair circumscribed much of the Western emplotment of India from the beginning and throughout the process of reception. At the risk of trapping myself in an emplotment of my own, I have chosen to see this tension in the reception of India as integral to the dynamic of exoticism and its failed hermeneutic.

I began by questioning how the exotic functioned hermeneutically. I sought to show how linguistic, poetic, and philosophical discourse assimilated Indian notions and symbols to a Greek or Christian worldview and what ruses (such as good or bad morality, and the search for origins and perversions thereof) were formulated in the appropriation of India for various ideological and aesthetic European agendas. It has also been an aim of this study to question whether the working of the exotic functions as a paradigm for the hermeneutical process in general. Such would appear to be the case, if we glance at the self-conscious posture of exotic endeavors in light of Gadamer's vision of *Bildung*.

> In going to the East . . . everyone who has enjoyed the advantages of a liberal . . . education, ought to feel that he is going to his 'old home,' full of memories, if only he can read them.[7]

However, these essays have shown instances where making the "alien one's own" has failed, or, rather, the attempt to encounter the Other reveals itself as both an anthropological and a hermeneutical illusion. Clearly, the development (or disintegration) of exoticism through the nineteenth century reveals a crucial change in the "excursion into the alien." India is encountered less as a real place in this world and acquires an exclusively psychical reality. This reality is not one of seriously considered texts or concepts but merely a collection of words like *nirvāṇa, māyā,* or *saṃsāra*. These words are increasingly drained of denotative meanings while they come to connote through vague associations whatever accords with the needs and prejudices of the Western subject. This process culminated in National Socialism, which rendered all reception of India meaningless.

Either exoticism effects an incomplete hermeneutics or it necessitates the privileging of hermeneutical investigations of exotic representation. The hermeneutical epiphany gained through art is not attained but rather subverted in the exotic quest itself. Perhaps the hermeneutical process of "going home" is detoured by the exotic's very love of flight and the abyss. Hugo von Hofmannsthal expressed this hermeneutical lapse succinctly in the *Tagesbuch eines Willenskranken:*

> The Christian heart, the will to life clings to each beloved heritage, each venerable word, wants to wish, hope and believe. The pagan spirit, the perception, pushed toward Pessimism, Quietism, and Nirvana. They wrestle with each other and all strength and talent, sharpness of sight and strength of dialectic, German philosophy and universal Knowledge strive together to make this conflict more torturous. A hundred times the will begins an impotent demonstration to force itself back to lost naivete, prejudice, Nation and Individuality. A hundred times the waves of an omniscient, comfortless knowledge crash over the sinking edifice of dead ideas, sounding in unison: "Nada," "Nirvana," "Nothing," and "Emptiness." The heart desires to draw conclusions from judgments in which the head no longer believes: From this can only arise disease, as from a physical maladjustment.[8]

What is significant here is the tension between a longing that springs from a crisis of exoteric spirituality and a longing that seeks fulfillment in the esoteric. Hofmannsthal makes the point that the will is rendered impotent in this fight and is forced to revivify itself either through cultural clichés or through escape and defeat in vague nothingness. The desire to draw truths from judgments is mitigated then by the overwhelming feeling that these judgments can no longer deliver truth. We recognize this process, with its strongly self-defeating aspect, among artists and writers dealing with the exotic.

Animated by the lure of the abyss, the exotic quest necessarily fails because its impetus is flawed. The exotic quest does not seek understanding, the hallmark of the hermeneutical venture, but rather seeks an escape from quotidian reality. If hermeneutics implies the workings of intellect to strive for understanding, then in the exotic such a meeting of horizons cannot be attained. We have seen in these exotic episodes how it was not a question of using prejudice to open understanding; rather, authors sought to validate their prejudices and give themselves totally over to these prejudices, particularly those that mirrored demonic and pagan impulses. A figure such as Hegel poses an interesting alternative to the abortive exotic quest, though one that is equally sterile from a hermeneutical point of view. By attempting to demolish the lure of the exotic, Hegel does no more than close India off to dialogue. By denying India any vision of universality, Hegel squandered a unique opportunity to define Indian thought as anything but a Greek appendage. His determination to establish his own system and "save" the intelligibility of history precluded a true interpretation of Indian metaphysics.

Finally, in addition to showing how the same clichés have a different fate in different psychological climates, we have examined how the model for inspiration becomes the alibi of despair, the cradle of humanity becomes its grave, and elements of supportive faith speak ultimately to the darker purlieus of being. Thus, the exotic seems to function as the legitimization of an ongoing irrationalism.

What is consistent in Europe's reception of India is the negation of the quest for meaning. Once the desire for inspiration has been thwarted, we are left with an admonition about our own human limitations and a deterrent example. There, but for the grace of God, go we. Barthélemy Saint-Hilaire, a friend and disciple of Victor Cousin with a chair of Greek philosophy at the Collège de France, only saw the abyss and *anéantissement* in Buddhist India. Indians lack identity and liberty; their limitless submission reveals the horror and inhumanity of the human condition. In contemplating Buddhism, Barthélemy Saint-Hilaire saw what we as Westerners should escape,[9] else we risk contamination. Europe was in danger of being perverted as Asia had been. He sought a defense not from Buddhism itself, but rather from the crypto-Buddhists he saw around him in the fatalism of Ballanche or the godless humanity of Comte or Quinet. Penultimately, the theme of corruption acts itself out in biological terms (Christian Lassen, *Indische Alterthumskunde*) or in the biological/ideological concerns of the race theorists. From Gobineau's treatise of despair, we receive a diagnostic for the ineluctable death of civilization. For subsequent National Socialists, decay is intimately bound with the will. F. Schlegel posited that, the West being in decline, India was the Romantic haven from modernity. *Ex Oriente lux*. In each instance, however, the East provides light for but a short time.[10]

How then shall we understand the hermeneutical illusion of encountering the Other? It has been said, apropos Romanticism, that the quest was what mattered, with success being secondary or even unwanted. Exoticism, which reached its literary acme during the Romantic period, also asserts the primacy of the doomed quest. Quests, etymologically grounded in the act of seeking, are never geared to success. The hermeneutical dilemma of exoticism is this: It foregrounds the modern individual as a subject desirous of experience through the agency of the Other. Above the ruins of quotidian existence, an exotic dream is erected. It holds forth a lure, offering a promise of fulfilment that it can never totally satisfy. Therein lies its attraction to which those who choose to be seduced respond with an apocalyptic Nietzschean "yea." Exoticism is thus an experience the structure of which is predicated upon the impossibility of fulfilment. Nevertheless, the nihilistic gesture which foregrounds the exotic quest is not abandoned. The subject continues to seek reification in an endeavor whose ephemerality stands revealed and, in a capitulation of reason, is embraced. The fanaticism of the abyss and the perversity of the subject who freely chooses evil tempt humanity to embrace *nirvāṇa* rather than God.

Notes

Introduction

1. Théophile Gautier, "Les papillons:"

Savez-vous, ô belle des belles,
Ma Bayadère aux yeux de jais,
S'ils pouvaient me prêter leurs ailes,
Dites, savez-vous où j'irais?

Sans prendre un seul baiser aux roses
À travers vallons et forêts,
J'irais à vos lèvres mi-closes,
Fleur de mon âme, et j'y mourrais.

All translations, not otherwise specified, are my own.

2. Henry H. H. Remak, "Exoticism in Romanticism," *Comparative Literature Studies* 15, no. 1 (1978): 53.

3. *The Viṣṇu Purāṇa,* trans. H. H. Wilson (London: John Murray, 1840), lxxv.

4. F. Max Müller, *The Sacred Books of the East,* vol. 1 (Oxford: Clarendon Press, 1879), xxxvii.

5. E. W. Said, "Kim, the Pleasures of Imperialism," *Raritan* 7, no. 2 (1987): 61.

6. Henry H. H. Remak, "Exoticism in Romanticism," 56.

7. Roger-Pol Droit, *L'Oubli de l'Inde, une amnésie philosophique* (Paris: Presses Universitaires de France, 1989), 145.

8. Ronald B. Inden, "Orientalist Constructions of India," *Modern Asian Studies* 20, no. 3 (1986): 416.

9. Aijaz Ahmad, *In Theory: Classes, Nations, Literatures* (Bombay, Oxford University Press, 1993), 166.

10. Ibid., 178.

11. Ibid., 172.

12. Ibid., 167.

13. Ibid., 181.

14. Homi K. Bhabha, "The Other Question: Difference, Discrimination, and the Discourse of Colonialism," in *Out There: Marginalization and Contemporary Cultures,* eds. Russell Ferguson et al. (Cambridge: MIT Press, 1990), 73.

15. Henry Louis Gates, Jr., "Critical Fanonism," *Critical Inquiry* 17 (Spring 1991): 466: "My claim is that what Jacques Derrida calls writing, Spivak, in a brilliant reversal, has renamed colonial discourse. The Derridean *mot,* that there is nothing outside the text, is reprised as the argument that there is nothing outside the discourse of colonialism . . . Indeed, I think Spivak's argument put in its strongest form, entails the corollary that all discourse is colonial discourse."

16. Gayatri Chakravorty Spivak, "The Rani of Sirmur," in *Europe and Its Others,* vol 1, *Proceedings of the Essex Conference on the Sociology of Literature, July 1984,* eds. Francis Barker et al. (Colchester: University of Essex, 1985), 131.

17. Benita Parry, "Problems in Current Theories of Colonial Discourse," *Oxford Literary Review* 9, nos. 1–2 (1987): 39.

18. Ibid., 35.

19. A recent case in point is Lata Mani's ubiquitous article on the *satī* where an analysis of representations of *satī* are based upon fragmentary English-language texts in published accounts which are read in isolation from the socio-historical context and the indigenous exegetical

traditions. An examination of documentation from a "real" archive, rather than a metaphorical archive of literary criticism, belies such a constriction of the silent and unproblematized *satī*. I have benefitted from the insights of Anne B. Water's work in the Peshwa Daftar (Poona).

20. Ahmad, *In Theory,* 171.

21. Ibid., 197.

22. Aijaz Ahmad, "Jameson's Rhetoric of Otherness and the 'National Allegory,' " *Social Text* 5, no. 17 (1986): 7–12.

23. Fredric Jameson, "Third World Literature in the Era of Multinational Capitalism," *Social Text* 5, no. 15 (1986): 66–88.

24. Ahmad, "Jameson's Rhetoric," 9–11.

25. Ashis Nandy, *The Intimate Enemy: Loss and Recovery of Self under Colonialism* (Delhi: Oxford University Press, 1983), xv.

26. Ranajit Guha, "On Some Aspects of the Historiography of Colonial India," *Subaltern Studies: Writings on South Asian History and Society,* vol. 1 (Delhi: Oxford University Press, 1982), 1–8.

27. Partha Chatterjee, "More on Modes of Power and the Peasantry," in *Selected Subaltern Studies,* eds. Ranajit Guha and Gayatri Chakravorty Spivak (New York: Oxford University Press, 1988), 351–90.

28. Parry, "Current Theories," 40.

29. Gates, "Critical Fanonism," 463.

30. For a summary of this literature, see my *Translating the Orient* (Albany: State University of New York Press, 1991), introduction.

31. Maurice Olender, *The Languages of Paradise: Race, Religion, and Philology in the Nineteenth Century,* trans. Arthur Goldhammer (Cambridge: Harvard University Press, 1992), 18.

32. However, by positioning my study on the reception of India in France and Germany, I do not venture to suppose that India poses a more

legitimate paradigm for a study of Orientalism than does Said's Middle East. Throughout this study, I posit Indian exoticism as one among a multiplicity of Orientalisms.

33. Ahmad, *In Theory,* 69–71.

34. Parry, "Current Theories," 29.

35. Ahmad, *In Theory,* 207.

36. Nandy, *The Intimate Enemy,* xii. Nandy disparagingly speaks of such critics as "circus-tamed opponents" and "tragic counterplayers performing their last gladiator-like acts of courage in front of appreciative Caesars." See ibid., xiv.

37. As an Hispanic female, I have learned to tread warily, realizing how an accession to the pose of *Magister Implicatus* is not my particular birthright. For an interesting discussion of the role of this figure in contemporary academe, see James J. Sosnoski, *Token Professionals and Master Critics: A Critique of Orthodoxy in Literary Studies* (Albany: State University of New York Press, 1994).

38. E. W. Said, *Orientalism* (New York: Pantheon, 1978), 24.

39. Sharon Lowen, "An American Sanskrit Scholar," *Span* 31, no. 4 (April 1990): 18.

40. Nandy, *The Intimate Enemy,* xiv.

41. Apropos reading the *Rāmāyaṇa,* Sheldon Pollack remarks: "So the text should not be read as a naive Indian might, but read critically with the clear awareness that culture recapitulates or interacts with or carries on a dialogue with power. This is a different way of looking at the *Rāmāyaṇa* that builds on the Indian tradition but goes beyond it." See Lowen, "An American Sanskrit Scholar," 18.

42. For a discussion of the psychoanalytic conception of the lack, see Jacques Lacan, *The Four Fundamental Concepts of Psychoanalysis,* trans. Alan Sheridan (New York: Norton, 1978), 203–29.

43. My use of the concept of the "dominant fiction" borrows from the insights of Kaja Silverman, *Male Subjectivity at the Margins* (New York: Routledge, 1992), 15–46.

44. Even a cursory reading of Orientalist and post-Colonialist literature brings to light the fact that the same authors and texts are repeatedly subject to analysis. In this respect, Orientalist and post-Colonialist critical methods resemble Deconstructive readings, which tend to deconstruct works of a limited group of authors.

45. Chris Bongie, *Exotic Memories: Literature, Colonialism, and the Fin de Siècle* (Stanford: Stanford University Press, 1991), 5.

46. I use the term *spokesmen* deliberately, as it denotes a relation between gender, critical dogmatism, and esotericism that enters into my discussion.

47. Nandy, *The Intimate Enemy,* 73.

48. Nandy, *The Intimate Enemy,* 80.

49. Ibid.

50. V. S. Naipaul, *India: A Million Mutinies Now* (London: Minerva, 1991), 427.

51. Nandy, *The Intimate Enemy,* 86–87.

52. F. de Saussure, *Cours de la linguistique générale* (Paris: Payot, 1985), 16.

53. Bongie, *Exotic Memories,* 5.

54. Here I disagree with Bongie's thesis that exoticism is an "idea without a future" and a "posthumous project" (ibid., 17).

55. Hans-Georg Gadamer, *Wahrheit und Methode* (Tübingen: J. C. B. Mohr, 1960), 11.

56. Paul Ricoeur, *Le conflit des interprétations: Essais herméneutiques* (Paris: Seuil, 1969), 16–17.

57. Joel C. Weinsheimer, *Gadamer's Hermeneutics: A Reading of Truth and Method* (New Haven, CT: Yale University Press, 1985), 70.

58. For these insights, I thank an anonymous reader.

59. Homi Bhabha, "Sly Civility," *October* 31 (1985): 74. In addition to this doubling at the source, Colonialist discourse is also subverted by the object of its address.

60. Bongie, *Exotic Memories,* 16–17.

61. For a reasoned study of the external influence on Eliade's theory of myth, see Ivan Strenski, *Four Theories of Myth in the Twentieth Century* (Iowa City: University of Iowa Press, 1987).

62. For an examination of this scholarship, see my *Translating the Orient,* chap. 1.

63. Ronald B. Inden, "Orientalist Constructions of India," 402.

64. The Sanskrit phrase denoting the identity of the Self with the Absolute translates literally as "That Thou Art."

65. Hugo von Hofmannsthal, *Das Tagesbuch eines Willenskranken: Prosa,* ed. Herbert Steiner, 4 vols. (Frankfurt: S. Fischer, 1950), 1:22: "Die einzelnen sind es, welche die Leiden der Zeit leiden und die Gedanken der Zeit denken. Und Bücher, aus denen solch ein Schmerz der Zeit spricht, sind die traurigsten und werden sehr berühmt, weil es die einzigen sind, die wir beinahe ganz verstehen können. Was in uns ist von vagem Schmerz, von verborgener Qual und verwischtem Sehnen, jedes erstickte Anderswollen und alle Disharmonien, die der Wille zur Erhaltung übertäubt hat, sie erwachen zu einem unbestimmten Leben und leben auf im Mitleid des Tat Tvam asi. In Qualen wird das 'gute Europäertum,' die vaterlandlose Klarheit von morgen errungen; den Geschlechtern von gestern und heute, zwei Generationen von Schwankenden und Halben, war der Weg zu rauh. Nach rückwärts zieht die Verführung, die nervenbezwingende Nostalgie, die Sehnsucht nach der

Heimat . . . Zurück zur Kindheit, zum Vaterland, zum Glaubenkönnen, zum Liebenkönnen, zur verlorenen Naivetät: Rückkehr zum Unwiederbringlichen."

66. Friedrich Nietzsche, *The Will to Power,* trans. Walter Kaufmann and R. J. Hollingdale, ed. Walter Kaufmann (New York: Random House, 1968), § 27.

67. For this definition, I have borrowed significantly from Bongie, *Exotic Memories,* 27.

68. Richard Gilman, *Decadence: The Strange Life of an Epithet* (New York: Farrar, Straus & Giroux, 1978), 103.

69. Ibid., 157.

70. Giorgio Agamben, *Infanzia e storia: Distruzione dell'esperienze e origine della storia* (Turin: Einaudi, 1978), 23–24, cited in Bongie, *Exotic Memories,* 22.

71. Hofmannsthal, *Das Tagesbuch*, 1:149: "Heute scheinen zwei Dingen modern zu sein: die Analyse des Lebens und die Flucht aus dem Leben, man treibt Anatomie des eigenen Seelenlebens, oder man träumt. Reflexion oder Phantasie, Spiegelbild oder Traumbild . . . Modern ist . . . Buddha."

72. A. Schopenhauer, *Fragments sur l'histoire de la philosophie* (Paris: Alcan, 1912), 174.

Chapter 1. The Dynamics of Eroticism

1. Bhartṛhari is thought to have lived in the fourth or fifth century. For a chronology, see George Cardona, *Pāṇini: A Survey of Research* (The Hague: Mouton, 1976), 298–99.

2. Abraham Rogerius, *Offne Thür zu dem verborgenen Heydenthum* (Nuremberg: J. Schipper, 1663).

3. These appear under the title "Gedanken einiger Bramanen" in the fourth collection of Herder's *Zerstreute Blätter* (1792).

4. Bhartṛhari, *The Epigrams Attributed to Bhartṛhari,* ed. D. D. Kosambi (Cambridge: Harvard University Press, 1950), no. 301.

5. In fact, they were retained in a later German translation of the epigrams written by Peter von Bohlen (1796–1840) under the title *Die Sprache des Bhartṛharis* (Hamburg: A. Campe, 1835).

6. J. G. Herder, *Sämtliche Werke*, ed. B. Suphan, 33 vols. (Berlin: Weidmannsche Buchhandlung, 1877–1913), 13:222, 225–26.

7. Ibid., 13:222.

8. Ibid., 14:32, 73–74.

9. Ibid., 5:50.

10. Ibid., 1:32.

11. Ibid., 16:74. It was primarily with the appearance of Forster's translation of Kālidāsa's *Śākuntala* that Herder was forced to reevaluate an earlier negative judgment on Indian poetry.

12. Ibid., 16:74.

13. A. Rogerius, *Offne Thür,* 501:

O Mutter die Erde!
O Vater der Wind!
O Freund das Feuer!
O Verwandschaft das Wasser!
O Himmel der Bruder!
Auf dar aller Freundlichste bezeige ich
euch alle Ehrerbietung;
Denn weil mit euch wol gelebt hab'ich
Erhalte ich nun die Seeligkeit:
Ich will euch aber gern alle verlassen
Und nach dem Himmel zugehen.

14. Herder, *Sämtliche Werke,* 19:416:

Erde, du meine Mutter, und du mein
Vater, der Lufthauch, und du Feuer,
Mein Freund, du mein Verwandter, der Strom,
Und mein Bruder, der Himmel, ich sag' euch
Allen mit Ehrfurcht freundlichen Dank.
Mit euch hab'ich nieden gelebt,
Und geh jetzt zur andern Welt, euch gerne verlassend;
Lebt wohl, Bruder und Freund,
Vater und Mutter, lebt wohl.

15. The Sanskrit text is not at issue here, as it was not at Herder's disposal. However, an excellent translation of the poem in question can be found in a review of this volume by D. H. H. Ingalls in the *Harvard Journal of Asiatic Studies* 13 (1950): 257–8. Ingalls translates the poem in the following manner:

My father wind and you my mother earth,
Fire, my friend, water, my near relation
And you my brother sky; in this last breath
Of mortal life I send you salutation.
From living ever with you comes this birth
Of uncontaminated wisdom with increase
Of goodness that all darkness and all folly cease
As now I live in Brahma in my death.

16. Herder, *Sämtliche Werke,* 16:341–59. Herder's views on transmigration are found in early writings such as "Journal meiner Reise" (1769), as well as later works such as "Palingenesie: Vom Wiederkommen menschlicher Seelen" (1797). Over the years, his ideas were expressed under various rubrics and titles, including "Seelenwanderung," "Metempsychose," "Unsterblichkeitsglaube," and "Analogie." The development of the concept involved many struggles and contradictions, as well as a clear evolution in his thought. His first reference to transmigration can be found in a fragment from 1768 ("Ein Gesprüch zu Mendelssohns Phädon", in *Sämtliche Werke,* 32:200–201), where he stated that no such thing existed. In his essay on palingenesis, he argued that souls are in a constant process of refinement. By 1785, he argued not only that there was a refinement of the human soul, but that this was the "wahre Palingenesie dieses Lebens" ("Über die Seelenwanderung", in *Sämtliche Werke,* 15:303). It must be noted that Herder falsely uses the term *palingenesis* interchangeably with *metempsychosis.* Palingenesis is primarily a

Buddhist notion. Buddhists accept the existence neither of an individual soul (*Ātman*) nor of a world-soul (*Brahman*). They do, however, account for existing differences among individuals that are justified in terms of past sins and projected into future lives.

17. Herder, *Sämtliche Werke,* 15:248.

18. "Über die Seelenwanderung" was written in 1785. *Zerstreute Blätter,* which contains Bhartṛhari's poem, was written between 1785 and 1787. Although his rewriting of Bhartṛhari's poem coincides with his fully refined thoughts on palingenesis, Herder chose to omit this theme from the very Sanskrit poem in which it has the most significance.

19. Herder, *Sämtliche Werke,* 16:351.

20. Ibid., 15:248. Forms such as Petrarch, Montaigne, and Luther existed before in time.

21. The premature death of the father in 1786 left the family in financial straits and led to their move to Hanau, where Karoline spent most of her youth. Three of her sisters died as children, and a sister and brother survived.

22. "Liebe," "Hochroth," "Ein Kuss im Traume," "Ist alles stumm und leer," and, most notably, "Lethe."

23. His bizarre letters sufficiently alarmed Karoline, and she, having lost all confidence in Clemens, retreated from close involvement. For one such letter, see Karoline von Günderrode, *Karoline von Günderrode und ihre Freunde,* ed. Ludwig Geiger (Stuttgart: Deutscher Verlag, 1895), 108–11: "Gute Nacht! Du lieber Engel! Ach, bist Du es, bist Du es nicht, so öffne alle Adern Deines weissen Leibes, dass das heisse, schäumende Blut aus tausend wonnigen Springbrunnen spritze, so will ich Dich sehen und trinken aus den tausend Quellen, trinken, bis ich berauscht bin . . ." He was, for a time, banished from the "paradise of confidence" that existed between Karoline and Bettina. Nevertheless, Karoline and Clemens reconciled in 1804. He married Sophie Moreau and remained Karoline's faithful friend. In addition to the short poem "An Clemens," it is quite possible that the "Geschichte eines Brahminen" also refers to him.

24. He was thirty-three years old and she was twenty-four.

25. J. W. Goethe, *Goethes Briefwechsel mit einem Kinde,* ed. Jonas Fränkel, 2 vols. (Jena: E. Diederichs, 1906), 1:78.

26. She was his perfect disciple, and he was her often-pedantic intellectual master. Creuzer's wife was a considerably older woman whose wealth enabled him to pursue the life of a scholar and whose expertise as a homemaker insured his comfort. Not only did he recognize his debt to his wife, but he was painfully aware of his social responsibilities as a professor; he felt bound by this marriage and his responsibilities to the State. Creuzer wrote to Karoline of his role as a moral educator of youth, noting that although he was to teach poetry in public, he could have no poetry in his life. These lofty notions did not deter their liaison. Encouraged by promises of a possible future divorce and escape to Russia, Karoline resigned herself to being his mistress with the hope of eventually becoming his wife.

27. As one might expect, Creuzer never left his wife. His inability as an intellectual to manage day-to-day existence without his spouse's help and to serve "Poetry" without the free conditions that her wealth provided ultimately decided the issue. In 1806, Creuzer severed relations with Karoline through his intermediaries. At sunset on the day that Karoline received his letter (26 July), she tied a scarf filled with stones around her neck and stabbed herself to death on the banks of the Rhine. (For an account of Günderrode's last hours, see the letter from Susanne von Heyden to Hektor von Günderrode of 29 July 1806 [Günderrode, *Der Schatten eines Traumes,* 254–55].) As for Creuzer, he went on living. Perhaps it was merely discretion that led him to omit any mention of Karoline in his autobiography. After the death of his wife, he remarried.

28. Liselotte E. Kurth-Voigt, "Existence after Death in Eighteenth-Century Literature," *South Atlantic Review* 52, no. 2 (1987): 3–14.

29. Günderrode, "An Eusebio," *Der Schatten eines Traumes,* 110–11. Further evidence of Karoline's growing despair can be seen in Bettina's letters encouraging her to maintain the will to live, in Richard Wilhelm, *Die Günderrode, Dichtung und Schicksal,* 2 vols. (Frankfurt: Societäts Verlag, 1938), 2:173, 184, 234–35.

30. Günderrode, "Fragment aus Eusebios Antwort," in *Der Schatten eines Traumes,* 112–13.

31. Günderrode, "Ein apokaliptisches Fragment," in *Der Schatten eines Traumes,* 108. "Die Vergangenheit war mir dahin! Ich gehörte nur der Gegenwart. Aber eine Sehnsucht war in mir, die ihren Gegenstand nicht kannte, ich suchte immer, aber jedes Gefundene war nicht das Gesuchte, und sehnend trieb ich mich umher im Unendlichen."

32. Karl Preisendanz, *Die Liebe der Günderrode* (Munich: K. Piper, 1912), 34. Preisendanz cites a letter to Karoline in which Creuzer writes: "Der Gedanke, sich durch Vernichtung des Leibes früher zu nähen dem Ewigen, der Sie beherrscht, ist unrichtig selbst nach den Grundsätzen der Philosophie, die Ihnen so lieb ist."

33. Günderrode, "Ein apokaliptisches Fragment," 107–9.

34. This theme is also found in Günderrode's poems "Udohla," "Magie und Schicksal," and "Mahomets Traum in der Wüste."

35. See "Wandel und Treue" and "Melete."

36. Günderrode, "Ein apokaliptisches Fragment," 107–8.

37. Günderrode, "Geschichte eines Brahminen," in *Der Schatten eines Traumes,* 121: "Ich wählte mir einem Palmenwald am persischen Meerbusen zum Aufenthalt. Dieser stille Ort diente mir zum Hafen gegen die Untiefen und Klippen der Welt; aber es ist nicht so leicht, sich von ihr zu scheiden. Tausend geheime Bande knüpfen uns an sie, und der Entschluss, der uns von ihr trennt, ist nicht viel kleiner als der Schritt von dem diesseitigen Leben in das jenseitige."

38. Ibid., 122: "Hier in dieser stillen Einsamkeit habe ich meine Eigenheit, meinen Frieden, meinen Gott gefunden, und tausend Geisterstimmen reden Offenbarungen zu mir, die ich im Getümmel des Lebens nicht vernehmen konnte."

39. Ibid., 118–27. See also "Ein apokaliptisches Fragment," 108: "Drum, wer Ohren hat zu hören, der höre! Es ist nicht zwei, nicht drei, nicht tausende, es ist Eins und alles; es ist nicht Körper und Geist geschieden, dass das eine der Zeit, das andere der Ewigkeit angehöre, es ist

Eins, gehört sich selbst, und ist Zeit und Ewigkeit zugleich, und sichtbar, und unsichtbar, bleibend im Wandel, ein unendliches Leben."

40. Günderrode, "Geschichte eines Brahminen," 124: "Es ist zugleich der Grund aller Dinge, und die Dinge selbst, die Bedingung und das Bedingte, der Schöpfer und das Geschöpf, und es theilt und sondert sich in mancherley Gestalten, wird Sonne, Mond, Gestirne, Pflanzen, Thier und Mensch zugleich, und durchfliesst sich selber in frischen Lebenströmen und betrachtet sich selber im Menschen in heiliger Demuth."

41. Günderrode, "Briefe zweier Freunde," in *Der Schatten eines Traumes,* 116–17; "Die Manen," in *Der Schatten eines Traumes,* 102–7.

42. Günderrode, "Geschichte eines Brahminen," 126: "Er lehrte mich, wie in jedem Theile des unendlichen Naturgeistes die Anlage zu ewiger Vervollkommenung läge, wie die Kräfte wanderten durch alle Formen hindurch, bis sich Bewusstseyn und Gedanke im Menschen entwickelten; wie von dem Menschen an, eine unendliche Reihe von Wanderungen, die immer zu höherer Vollkommenheit führten, der Seelen warteten; wie sie endlich auf geheimnissvolle Weise sich alle vereinigten mit der Urkraft, von der sie ausgegangen, und Eins mit ihr würden, und doch zugleich sie selbst bleiben, und so die Göttlichkeit und Universitalität des Schöpfers mit der Individualität des Geschöpfes vereinigten."

43. Günderrode, "Briefe zweier Freunde," 117: "So wird die Allheit lebendig durch den Untergang der Einzelheit, und die Einzelheit lebt unsterblich fort in der Allheit, deren Leben sie lebend entwickelte, und nach dem Tode selbst erhöht und mehrt, und so durch Leben und Sterben die Idee der Erde realisieren hilft."

44. Günderrode, "Briefe zweier Freunde," 113: "[A]lles was jetzt Sonne und Mond ist, und Blume und Edelstein, und Äther und Meer, ein Einziges ist, ein Heiliges, das in seinen Tiefen ruht ohne Aufhören, selig in sich selbst, sich selbst ewig umpfangend, ohne Wunsch nach dem Thun und Leiden der Zweiheit, die seine Oberfläche bewegt."

45. Günderrode, "Briefe zweier Freunde," 115: "Welche Thaten warten noch meiner, oder, welche bessere Erkenntnis auf Erden dass ich länger leben müsste?"

46. Wilkins's translation of 1785 was subsequently rendered into German in 1801.

47. Günderrode, *Karoline von Günderrode,* 66ff.

48. She was introduced to Schelling by Creuzer with notes from his lectures (unedited letters of June 1805); see letter from Creuzer to Karoline, 21 July 1805, in *Der Schatten eines Traumes,* 227–28.

49. F. W. von Schelling, *Sämtliche Werke,* ed. K. F. A. Schelling, 6 vols. (Stuttgart and Augsburg: J. G. Cotta, 1856–61), 1:162–244.

50. Indian philosopher (ca. A.D. 800), commentator to the *Upanishads, Brahmasūtra,* and *Bhagavad Gītā.*

51. The "nondualist" (*advaita*) school of Indian philosophy founded by Śaṅkara. This philosophy held that the Self (*Ātman*) is the sole reality, and all other phenomena are phantasmagoric products of ignorance. This Self is none other than *Brahman,* the Eternal Reality.

52. The *Upanishads* under the title *Oupnek'hat* were translated by Anquetil Duperron in 1801.

53. Schelling, *Sämtliche Werke,* 1:43–83. For a discussion of Schelling's reception of Indian philosophy, see René Gérard, *L'Orient et la pensée romantique allemande* (Paris: Didier, 1963), 210.

54. Schelling, *Die Philosophie der Kunst,* in *Sämtliche Werke,* 5:423, cites the *Gītagovinda* and the *Śākuntala.*

55. Schelling, *Die Philosophie in ihrem Übergang zur Nichtphilosophie,* in *Sämtliche Werke,* 6:12, 18.

56. Schelling, *Sämtliche Werke,* 6:44–47, 69.

57. See chapter 4.

Chapter 2. Rationalist Heroes and Irrational Victims

1. Hayden White, *Tropics of Discourse* (Baltimore, MD: Johns Hopkins University Press, 1978), 181, 194.

2. *Satī* refers to the widow who immolates herself on her husband's funeral pyre. In English, the term *suttee* incorrectly came to denote the act of immolation itself and not the victim.

3. The term *bayadera* (from the Portuguese term *baiadeira,* "dancer") refers to the *devadāsī* (Sanskrit for "servants of the god(s)"), who were ritual dancers and temple prostitutes.

4. Günderrode, *Der Schatten eines Traumes,* 88:

Zum Flammentode gehen an Indusstranden
Mit dem Gemahl, in Jugendlichkeit,
Die Frauen, ohne Zagen, ohne Lied
Geschmücket festlich, wie in Brautgewanden.

Die Sitte hat der Liebe Sinn verstanden,
Sie von der Trennung harter Schmach befreit,
Zu ihrem Priester selbst den Tod geweiht,
Unsterblichkeit gegeben ihren Banden.

Nicht Trennung ferner solchem Bunde droht,
Denn die vorhin entzweiten Liebesflammen
In einer schlagen brünstig sie zusammen.

Zur süssen Liebesfeyer wird der Tod,
Vereinet die getrennten Elemente,
Zum Lebensgipfel wird des Daseins Ende.

5. R. H. Major, ed. *India in the Fifteenth Century* (New York: Burt Franklin, 1957), pt. 4, 4–5.

6. Ludovico di Varthema, *The Travels of Ludovico di Varthema,* trans. J. Jones (New York: Burt Franklin, 1963), 207.

7. Poggio Bracciolini and Ludovico di Varthema, *Travelers in Disguise: Narratives of Eastern Travel,* trans. J. W. Jones (Cambridge: Harvard University Press, 1963), 28.

8. Tomé Pires, *The Suma Oriental* (Liechtenstein: Kraus, 1967), 39, 52, 59.

9. Duarte Barbosa, *A Description of the Coasts of East Africa and Malabar,* trans. Henry E. J. Stanley (New York: Johnson, 1970), 92.

10. Pierre Sonnerat, *Voyage aux Indes orientales et la Chine,* 2 vols. (Paris: n.p., 1782), 1:71–73.

11. One of the earliest comments on the bayaderas was made by Marco Polo (1254–1324) in *Il Milone* (bk. 151):

> Qui ha molti, ministeri d'idoli, e havvi molte donzelle et fanciulli offerti da loro padri e da loro madri per alcuna cagione. E il signore del ministero quando vuole fare alcuna sollazza agli idoli, si richeggiono questi offerti; ed egli sono tenuti d'andarvi, e quivi ballano e trescono ed fano gran festa. Sono le baiadere sacre o devadasis "le serve del dio" di caste bramina, il cui officio è di danzare e cantare nei templi in onore delle divinità.

The Venetian gives the significance of their Sanskrit name (*devadāsī*) and describes their role as ritual dancers. He does not, as does his compatriot Pietro della Valle, mention that they act also as temple prostitutes (see Angelo de Gubernatis, *Storia dei viaggiatori italiani nelle Indie orientali* [Livorno: F. Vigo, 1875], 228–38).

12. Abraham Rogerius, *Le théâtre de l'idolatrie ou la porte ouverte,* trans. Thomas La Grue (Amsterdam: J. Schipper, 1670), 220–21. Rogerius relates the following account of the tale. Dewendre comes to earth as a man and visits a whore. He wishes to find out whether she can be faithful. He pays her well, and they make love the entire night. In the morning, Dewendre pretends to be dead. The whore wants to be burned with him. In vain, her parents try to dissuade her by saying that she was not his legitimate wife. When the pyre is ready, Dewendre awakes and admits the ruse. As a reward, he takes her to Dewendre-locan. In his commentary, Rogerius suggests that if a society has such a high opinion of whores, it is no wonder that it allows them to serve gods.

13. André Guillaume Dontant Dorville, *Histoire des differens peuples du monde, contenant les cérémonies religieuses, l'origine des religions, leurs sectes, leur superstitions, et les moeurs et usages de chaque nation,* 6 vols. (Paris: n.p., 1770).

14. This terminology coincides with the most widely read account on suttee, written by the Abbé Dubois. His *Description of the Character, Manners, and Customs of the People of India* was written in the late eighteenth century and published in French and English in the early nineteenth century and postdates most of the texts in question here. Dubois refers to the bayadera as a strumpet who is open to the embraces of all. Like prostitutes in the West, she resorts to artifice. However, unlike her European counterparts, the bayadera is generally attractive, charming, and gracious rather than indecent, imprudent, and shameless. See Abbé Jean Antoine Dubois, *Description of the Character, Manners, Customs of the People of India* (London: Largman, Hurst, Rees, Orme & Brown, 1817), 387–89.

15. Herder, *Sämtliche Werke,* 11:382f.

16. Goethe, "Der Gott und die Bajadere":

Schmeichelnd zieht sie ihn zur Schwelle
Lebhaft ihn ins Haus hinein.

17. Goethe, "Der Gott und die Bajadere":

Und er kusst die bunten Wangen,
Und sie fühlt der Liebe Qual,
  Und das Mädchen steht gefangen,
Und sie weint zum ersten mal,
  Sinkt zum seinen Füssen nieder,
Nicht um Wollust noch Gewinst,
  Ach! und die gelenken Glieder,
Sie versagen allen Dienst.

18. Sonnerat, *Reise nach Ostindien und China,* (Frankfurt: A. G. Schneider, 1784).

19. Elements in the poem suggest that Goethe was also familiar with Rogerius's *Offne Thür* (1663) and Dopper's *Asia oder ausführliche Beschreibung des Reiches des grossen Mogols und eines grossen Teils von Indien* (1681).

20. This opera enjoyed considerable success. Translated into German by J. F. Castelli with the title *Die Bayaderen,* it was presented in Vi-

enna in 1813. Contemporary reviews criticized the modest staging (*Allgemeine Musikalische Zeitung* 15 (1813): 760) and the "absurdly comic" plot (770). The opera was subsequently presented again in Berlin (1814) without much success (Ibid., 16 (1814): 210, 301), in Munich (1818), and again in Vienna (1821).

21. *La Presse,* 27 November 1838, reprinted in Théophile Gautier, *Histoire de l'art dramatique en France depuis vingt-cinq ans,* 6 vols. (Paris: Edition Hetzel, 1858–59), 1:72–74.

22. *La Presse,* 10 June 1844, reprinted in Gautier, *L'art dramatique,* 3: 215–18. See also Charles Victor Maximilien Albert Vicomte de Spoelberch de Lovenjoul, *Histoire des oeuvres de Théophile Gautier,* 2 vols. (Paris: Charpentier, 1887), 1:686.

23. *La Presse,* 20 August 1838, reprinted in Gautier, *Caprices et zigzags* (Paris: Hachette, 1855), 357–69; *La Presse,* 27 August 1838, reprinted in Gautier, *L'art dramatique,* 1:162–65.

24. Gautier, *Caprices et zigzags,* 357: "Le seul mot de bayadère éveille dans les cerveaux les plus prosaïques et les plus bourgeois une idée de soleil, de parfum, et de beauté: à ce nom doux comme une musique, les philistins eux-mêmes commencent à sauter sur un pied et à chanter *Tirely,* comme le Berlinois de Henri Heine; l'imagination se met en travail, l'on rêve de pagodes decoupées à jour, d'idoles monstreuses de jade ou de porphyre, de viviers transparents aux rampes de marbre, de chauderies au toit de bambou, de palanquins enveloppés de moustiquaires et d'éléphants blancs chargés de tours vermeilles; l'on sent comme une espèce d'éblouissement lumineux, et l'on voit passer à travers la blonde fumée des cassoulettes les étranges silhouettes de l'Orient."

25. Gautier, "Les bayadères," in *Caprices et zigzags,* p. 364.

26. Gautier, *Caprices et zigzags,* 358–59: "Cette poésie parfumée, qui n'existait pour nous qu'à l'état de rêve, comme toutes les poésies, on nous l'a apportée, à nous autres paresseux Parisiens qui ne pouvons quitter le ruisseau de la Rue St. Honoré, et pour qui le monde finit à la banlieue . . . L'Inde, toute sauvage, toute lointaine qu'elle soit, ne peut se passer de l'opinion de Paris . . . À défaut de l'Hoogly ou du Gange, le fleuve sacré, les devadasis ont établis leur bungalow à quelques pas de la Seine, allée des Veuves . . . C'est là, une invalide, de garde à la porte, vous fera aisement reconnaître la maison mystérieuse . . . L'invalide

n'est pas une précaution inutile, car il parait que l'on a déjà tenté d'enlever ces beautés exotiques."

27. *La Presse,* 31 January 1844; see Spoelberch de Lovenjoul, *Gautier,* 1:659. *La Presse,* 10 June 1844; see Spoelberch de Lovenjoul, *Gautier,* 1:686; Gautier, *L'art dramatique,* 3:215–19.

28. His reminscences of Amani and her troupe are found in almost everything Gautier was to subsequently write. In 1842, he cites her in *Mille et deuxième nuit* (published in the *Musée des familles* in April 1842; Spoelberch de Lovenjoul, *Gautier,* 1:576). In 1843, an Indian in London reminds Gautier of one of Amani's musicians (*La Presse,* 31 January 1844). In 1845, when some moorish (mauresque) dancers have an unsuccessful run at the Cirque Olympique, Gautier notes that the French can only understand what is familiar to them, that is, genuine Indian dancers. *Dieu et la bayadère* had made them unjust toward Amani (*La Presse,* 22 September 1845). While traveling in Greece in 1852, he notes that some Indians there remind him of Amani. She inspired the character of the heroine in Gautier's novel *La partie carrée* (1851). Inspired by Indian dance, he even wrote his own "Indian" ballet, *Sacontala* (1858), based on Kālidāsa's drama. Amani remained in Gautier's memory for the remainder of his life; he evoked her memory thirty-three years later (1871) when describing a performance of acrobats at the Cirque d'Hiver. See Gautier, *L'Orient,* 2 vols. (Paris: Charpentier, 1877), 2:21–22.

29. Spoelberch de Lovenjoul, *Gautier,* 1:686.

30. Jean Richer, *Études et recherches sur Théophile Gautier, prosateur* (Paris: A. G. Nizet, 1981), 117.

31. Gérard de Nerval, "Les danseuses de l'Inde," in *Le Monde dramatique* (1835): 161ff.

32. An adaptation by Nerval and Joseph Méry of the Sanskrit drama the *Mrichchhakaṭikā* of Śūdraka.

33. Gérard de Nerval, *Oeuvres complémentaires de Gérard de Nerval: La vie du théâtre,* ed. J. Richard (Paris: M. J. Minard, 1959), 444.

34. Nerval, *La vie du théâtre,* 443: "Oui; nous avons vu les Bayadères, nous avons même *touché* les Bayadères; mais dans le sens le plus convenable du mot, et pour nous convaincre seulement que leur peau

était bien d'un *noir doré* véritable et non pas enduite d'une décoction de jus de réglisse . . . Oui, ce sont bien là des beautés de l'Orient, et leur visage porte le type irrécusable d'une race primitive et non mélangée. Vous les aviez rêvées plus blanches peut-être, mais non pas mieux faites, plus vives et plus séduisantes."

35. Charles Bernheimer, *Figures of Ill-Repute* (Cambridge: Harvard University Press, 1989), chaps. 2, 5, 6.

36. Bernheimer, *Figures of Ill-Repute,* 219–20.

37. Gérard de Nerval, *Oeuvres complémentaires de Gérard de Nerval: La vie des lettres,* ed. J. Richard (Paris: M. J. Minard, 1959), 216–66.

38. Gustave Flaubert, *Dictionnaire des idées reçues,* "Bayadère:" "Mot qui entraîne l'imagination fort loin. Toutes les femmes de l'Orient sont des bayadères (v. odalisques)."

39. Gustave Flaubert, *Correspondence* (Paris: Conard, 1926), 2:304: "Je rêve bayadères, danses frénétiques et tous les tintamarres de la couleur."

40. Ibid., 3:136: "On a compris jusqu'à présent comme quelque chose de miroitant, de hurlant, de passionné, de heurté. On n'y a vu que des bayadères et des sabres recourbés, le fanatisme, la volupté, etc."

41. Gustave Flaubert, *Smarh,* in *Oeuvres complètes,* 2 vols. (Paris: Seuil, 1964), 1:211: "Un jour que j'aurai de l'imagination, que j'aurai été penser . . . aux bayadères sur les bords du Gange j'intercalerai la plus belle page qu'on ait faite; mais je vous avertis d'avance qu'elle sera superbe, monstrueuse, épouvantablement impudique . . ."

42. Flaubert, *Novembre,* in *Oeuvres complètes* (Paris: Seuil, 1964), 1:272: "Danse, danse, bayadère, fille du Gange, tournoie bien tes pieds dans ma tête! Comme une couleuvre, elle se replie, dénoue ses bras, sa tête remue, ses hanches se balancent, ses narines s'enflent, ses cheveux se dénouent . . ."

43. Gustave Flaubert, *Madame Bovary,* in *Oeuvres complètes de Gustave Flaubert* (Paris: Conard, 1930), 53: "Et vous y étiez aussi, sultans à longues pipes, pâmés sous des tonnelles, aux bras des bayadères."

44. Flaubert, *Madame Bovary,* 90–91. "Des sarabandes à n'en plus finir se déroulaient dans sa tête, et, comme une bayadère sur les fleurs d'un tapis, sa pensée bondissait avec les notes."

45. Written by Baron Gebler, 1779. Other musical scores under the title *Lanassa* were composed by André (Berlin, 1782), B. A. Weber (Berlin, 1797), Ebell (Breslau, 1802), Lindpainter (Munich, 1816), and Lachner (Vienna, 1832). Operas with that title were composed by Kalkbrenner (Rheinsberg, 1792), Tuczek (Pest, 1813), and Spohr (Kassel, 1823).

46. Libretto by Delacour and Cremieux.

47. Composer Doche, librettists E. R. Basset and Sirandin.

48. Anke Schmitt, *Der Exotismus in der deutschen Oper zwischen Mozart und Spohr* (Hamburg: Karl Dieter Wagner, 1988), 206.

49. In 1792, Gaveau adapted *La chaumière indienne* (under the title *Le paria ou la chaumière indienne,* libretto by Dumoustier) with a peculiar apologetic bent. The opera differs considerably from Bernardin de Saint-Pierre's novel. The wife, rather than accepting her husband's pariah status, is horrified and flees. He kills himself in despair but is resuscitated by St. Francis Xavier. Upon witnessing this miracle, the Indian "savages" convert *en masse.* The priests, however, are not pleased. They try to immolate the pariah, his wife, and St. Francis, only to have the funeral pyre, which had been erected on a beach, wash away in a sudden tempest. Fortunately, the pyre serves as a raft and the Indian couple and the saint are eventually saved by a Portuguese ship.

50. The implicit critique of organized religion, which plays a role in all these pariah stories, is also present in M. Beer, *Der Paria* (Leipzig: Reclam, n.d.), 39:

> Dein Gott des Fluches ist ein Gott des Abscheus.
> Ich glaub' an seine Lieb'; von seinem Hass
> Spricht Blödsinn, Habgier oder Frevel nur.
> Wer sich's von seinen Priestern überliefern,
> Von ihren Ammenmärchen lehren lässt,
> Was Glaube sei und Gott, der schmäht sich selbst.
> Er ist unläugbar, wie sein himmlisch Licht;

Des eignen Busens flammende Erkenntniss
Macht seine Welt zum Spiegel seines Wesens.

51. Ibid., 7:

Mein Leben ist ein elendes Gewimmer,
Der leise Seufzer des getretnen Wurms,
Den vor dem Dasein schon ein ew'ger Fluch
Verdammt, im Staub sich ächzend hinzuwenden,
Indess vor seinem Blick in Sonnenhöhe
Die Mitgeschöpfe, reich beflugelt, schwinden.

See also p. 25: "Verflucht ist mein Geschlecht . . ."

52. Goethe's source, as with "Der Gott und die Bayadère," was Sonnerat's travel account (*Voyage aux Indes orientales,* 2: 92–5). The French traveler presents the tale of Mariatale, a brahmin heroine possessing the magical ability to carry water. She was also defiled by lustful thoughts, and her head was decapitated and transposed on a pariah's body.

53. Goethe, "Paria Legende," lines 95–102:

Mich nun hast du ihrem Körper
Eingeimpft auf ewige Tage;
Weisen Wollens, wilden Handelns
Werd' ich unter Göttern sein.
Ja, des Himmelsknaben Bildnis
Webt so schön vor Stirn und Auge—
Senkt sich's in das Herz herunter,
Regt es tolle Wutbegier.

54. Goethe, "Dank des Paria":

Grosser Brahma! nun erkenn' ich,
Dass du Schöpfer bist der Welten!
Dich als meinen Herrscher nenn' ich,
Denn du lässest alle gelten.

Und verschliessest auch dem Letzten
Keines von den tausend Ohren;
Uns, die tief Herabgesetzten,

Alle hast du neu geboren.

Wendet euch zu dieser Frauen,
Die der Schmerz zur Göttin wandelt!
Nun beharr' ich anzuschauen
Den, der einzig wirkt und handelt.

55. Nineteenth-century Europeans had knowledge of Orphism, secret religious rites growing out of Dionysian mysteries in the sixth century B.C., which held that humans were subject to transmigration, reincarnation in animal or plant form, and a wheel of rebirth. They were familiar as well with the teaching of Pythagoras (c.582–507 B.C.), and Empedocles (c.495–c.435 B.C.), who dealt with the theme of palingenesis.

56. The teleological aspects of metemphychosis are mentioned by Rogerius, *Offne Thür,* 447. Mandelslo notes how metempsychosis was connected with works of a person; see Adam Olearius, *The Voyages and Travels of the Ambassadors,* trans. John Davies, 3 vols. (London: Thomas Dring & John Starkey, 1662), 3:68. Mandelslo draws the conclusion that they kill not out of humanity or sympathy but from religious conviction (Olearius, *Travels,* 3: 33–35, 43).

57. Kurth-Voigt, "Existence after Death," 3–11. This author cites Goethe's *Die Braut von Korinth* (1798), Lessing's *Erziehung des Menschengeschlechts* (1780), Wieland's *Sympathien,* and Schiller's "Das Geheimnis des Reminiszenz—An Laura" (1782).

58. Schopenhauer saw it as a transcendental truth that was accessible to the common man through mythical representation. He chided his fellow Europeans for sending English clergymen and Moravian linen weavers to teach the brahmins a better doctrine and convince them that they were formed out of nothing. (Arthur Schopenhauer, *The World as Will and Representation,* trans. E. F. Payne, 2 vols. [New York: Dover, 1969), 1:356]). Novalis asks, apropos metempsychosis, whether earthly birth might not be the result of death in the beyond. See Novalis, *Schriften,* ed. Paul Kluckhohn, 4 vols. (Leipzig: Bibliographisches Institut, 1929), 3:33: "Wer hier nicht zur Vollendung gelangt, gelangt vielleicht drüben-oder muss eine abermalige irdische Laufbahn beginnen. Sollte es nicht auch drüben einen Tod geben, dessen Resultat irdische Geburt wäre." See also Novalis, *Heinrich von Ofterdingen,* in *Schriften,*

1:101–2), where Heinrich dreams of metempsychosis. In the cavern of the hermit, he looks through a book with illustrations seemingly depicting him in former existences (1:168–69). Discussion of metempsychosis by Saint Simonians, such as Ballanche (*Essais de palingénésie sociale*), were animated by an evolutionist, positivist spirit. Charles Nodier saw in metempsychosis a possibility for infinite perfectability as well as a link between mineral and spiritual domains. See also *Adèle* and *De la palingénésie humaine*. Baudelaire commented on metempsychosis in "La vie intérieure," and Rimbaud evoked it in *La saison en enfer.* "Vite! est-il d'autres vies . . ."; (in "Mauvais sang"): "À chaque être, plusieurs 'autres' vies me semblaient dues. Ce monsieur ne sait ce qu'il fait: il est ange. Cette famille est une nichée de chiens. Devant plusieurs hommes, je causai tout haut avec eux un moment d'une de leurs autres vies. Ainsi, j'ai aimé un porc" (in "Faım").

59. In three dialogues, the characters Charikles and Theages debate on its value. Theages speculates that incarnation as an animal would never result in spiritual or moral improvement, because in animals that very attribute that could improve the soul has been taken away (Herder, *Sämtliche Werke,* 15:299). Moreover, God would not ordain that humans be given an opportunity to recover the dignity and perfection of the soul once it had been lost through neglect. Theages prefers other depictions of the afterlife, such as Elysium and Valhalla—they are more attractive than the notion of a cow waiting for the soul of a moribund human (15: 299–300). Charikles offers an adaptation of the theory of metempsychosis, elevating it to a metaphysical idea with a more sublime, though unknown, goal.

60. Herder, *Sämliche Werke,* 16:363; see also 16:349: "Hinweg . . . mit der Seelenwanderung als einer Büssungshypothese."

61. Most notably "Über die Seelenwanderung" (Herder, *Sämtliche Werke,* 16:341–59). See also *Journal meiner Reise* (1769) and "Palingenesie: Vom Wiederkommen menschlicher Seelen" (1797).

62. Herder, *Sämtliche Werke,* 14:30. Herder notes that this doctrine has other unpleasant consequences. It arouses false sympathy for animals (16:345–46), which lessens true empathy for humans; that is, humans are believed to be sinners in a past life and deserve what happens to them. (14:30–31).

63. Ibid., 16:367.

64. Flaubert, *Correspondence,* ed. Jean Bruneau, 2 vols. (Paris: Pléiade, 1973, 1980), 1:832.

65. A twentieth-century *satī* opera, Roussel's *Padmâvati,* exemplifies this tension between desire and death when the heroine, in her lust for an incendiary coupling, condemns her people to subjugation, torture, and death.

66. In this regard, see Alphonse Esquiros, *Les vierges folles,* 2d ed. (Paris: Auguste le Gallois, 1841), 183; also Sue's *Les mystères de Paris.*

67. This theme was certainly not new to Goethe. In *Die Leiden des jungen Werthers,* Goethe has Werther write on 15 May of the first year: "Ich weiss wohl, dass wir nicht gleich sind, noch sein können; aber ich halte dafür, dass der, der nötig zu haben glaubt, vom sogenannten Pöbel sich zu entfernen, um den Respekt zu erhalten, ebenso tadelhaft ist als ein Feiger, der sich vor seinem Feinde verbirgt, weil er zu unterliegen fürchtet." See also the entry on 4 September of the second year.

68. Hans-Georg Gadamer, *The Relevance of the Beautiful and Other Essays,* trans. Nicholas Walker and Robert Bernasconi (Cambridge: Cambridge University Press, 1986), 7.

Part II. Introduction

1. Herder attacked those who sought to classify races by geological origin or color (*Sämtliche Werke,* 13:257) or rank peoples (ibid., 5:511, 527ff.; 14:289, 294). However, as Olender points out (*The Languages of Paradise,* 48), numerous instances occur where Herder falls prey to an urge to compare.

2. Olender, *The Languages of Paradise,* 8.

3. Foucault has commented on how the birth of philology, though less critiqued than the births of biology and political science, had a comparable effect on Western visions of history. See *Les mots et les choses* (Paris: Gallimard, 1966), 294.

4. Paul Feyerabend, *Wissenschaft als Kunst* (Frankfurt: Suhrkamp, 1984), 8–11, 136–37.

5. Jürgen Habermas, *Der philosophische Diskurs der Moderne,* 3d ed. (Frankfurt: Suhrkamp, 1986), 348–49, 372–73, 376–77.

6. Sir William Jones, "The Third Anniversary Discourse on the Hindus" (1786). Reprinted in *A Reader in Nineteenth-Century Historical Indo-European Linguistics,* ed. W. Lehmann (Austin: University of Texas Press, 1967), 15.

7. Filippo Sassetti, *Lettere edite e inedite,* ed. Ettore Marcucci (Florence: F. le Monnier, 1855), 415.

8. G. W. Leibniz, *Nouveaux essais sur l'entendement humain* (Amsterdam and Leipzig: Raspe, 1765).

9. E. B. de Condillac, *Essai sur l'origine des connaissances humaines* (Paris: Le Roy, 1947), 98, 103.

10. Johann David Michaelis, *De l'influence des opinions sur le langage,* (Bremen: G. L.Forstieri, 1762), 187.

11. Herder, *Sämtliche Werke,* 19:4.

12. Ibid., 14:236, 7:370.

13. Ibid., 5:116: "Kein einzelner Mensch ist für sich da; er ist das Ganze des Geschichtes eingeschoben, er ist nur Eins für die fortgehende Folge. Was dies auf die ganze Kette für Wirkung thue, sehen wir später; hier schränken wir uns auf die Bildung einer Familiendenkart durch den Unterricht der Erziehung und da der Unterricht der eigenen Seele, der Ideenkreis der Eltern Sprache ist: so wird die Fortbildung des menschlichen Unterrichts durch den Geist der Familie durch den die Natur das ganze Geschlecht verknüpft hat, auch Fortbildung der Sprache."

14. Gadamer, *Wahrheit und Methode,* 167ff.

15. See Herder, *Über den Fleiss in mehreren gelehrten Sprache* (1764).

16. Herder, *Sämtliche Werke,* 2:12.

17. Ibid., 2:26–28.

18. Friedrich de la Motte Fouqué, *Etwas über den deutschen Adel über Rittersinn und Militärehre* (Hamburg: Perthes & Besser, 1819), 9.

Chapter 3. The Politics of Exoticism

1. Friedrich Justin Bertuch and Johann Severin Vater, *Allgemeines Archiv für Ethnographie und Linguistik* (Weimar: Industrie-Comptoir, 1806), 6: "Der Geist der Nationen spricht sich in ihrer Sprache aus, und die Abstammung der Nationen von einander wird, wo nicht die Physiognomie schon entschieden hat, fast allein aus der Ähnlichkeit ihrer Sprachen gefolgert."

2. Friedrich Schlegel, *Seine prosaischen Jugendschriften, 1792–1802,* ed. Jakob Minor, 2d ed., 2 vols. (Vienna: C. Konegan, 1906), 2:362.

3. E. W. Said, *The World, the Text, and the Critic* (Cambridge: Harvard University Press, 1983), 264.

4. Martin Bernal, *Black Athena: The Afroasiatic Roots of Classical Civilization,* vol. 1 (London: Free Association Books, 1987), 230: "Although he did not spell it out, the concept of an Aryan race can also be traced to Schlegel."

5. Introductory article by Sebastiano Timpararo to Friedrich Schlegel, in Schlegel, *Über die Sprache und Weisheit der Indier,* Amsterdam Studies in the Theory and History of Linguistic Science (Amsterdam: Benjamins, 1977), xiii.

6. E. W. Said, *World, Text, and Critic,* 267.

7. Said, *Orientalism,* 11.

8. Aijaz Ahmad, *In Theory,* 178.

9. E. W. Said, *Orientalism,* 25.

10. Ahmad, *In Theory,* 171.

11. E.W. Said, *Orientalism,* 98.

12. Ibid., 150. Said asserts that Orientalism's "restructurings of inequality grew out of the fluctuation between enthusiasm and disenchantment." Schlegel's disenchantment with India led to a "underhumanized, antidemocratic . . . barbaric Orient."

13. Martin Bernal, *Black Athena,* 232.

14. The oldest of the three brothers was an officer in the British East India Company. He died on 9 September 1789 in Madras. In the introduction to *Über die Sprache* (xii), Schlegel wrote of him: "Auch bemerke ich, dass mein älterer Brüder Carl August . . . in den letzten Jahren seines Lebens durch Reisen und durch Umgang mit den Eingeborenen ein Studium des Landes, der Verfassung und des indischen Geistes begonnen hatte, das nur zu früh durch seinen Tod unterbrochen ward."

15. Friedrich Schlegel, *Friedrich Schlegels Briefe an dem Bruder August Wilhelm,* ed. O. Walzel, (Berlin: Speyer & Peters, 1890), 631: "Was sagst Du zu Goethes Diwan? Wirst Du es ihm so ausgehen lassen, dass er draussen unverständig und wie ein Rohrsperling auf alles Indische schimpft?"

16. Jakob Körner, *Krisenjahre der Frühromantik: Briefe aus dem Schlegelkreis* (Berlin: R. M. Rohrer, 1936–1958), 129, 521ff.; Schlegel, *Über die Sprache,* vii ff.

17. Friedrich Schlegel, *Gespräche über die Mythologie und symbolische Anschauung,* in *Sämtliche Werke,* 15 vols. (Vienna: I. Klang, 1846), 4:174.

18. Schlegel, *Sämtliche Werke,* 4:197.

19. Schlegel, *Seine prosaischen Jugendschriften,* 2:362.

20. Ibid., 2:357ff.

21. Ibid., 2:362: ". . . eine Nation, die immer stumpfer und brutaler wird."

22. Friedrich Schlegel, *Kritische-Friedrich-Schlegel-Ausgabe,* ed. Ernst Behler, 24 vols. (Munich: Ferdinand Schöningh, 1966), 7:74.

23. These consist of the lectures given at Cologne on Universal History, collected and edited by C. J. H. Windischmann, in Friedrich Schlegel's *Philosophische Vorlesungen aus den Jahren 1804–1806,* 2 vols. (Bonn: Edward Weber, 1836–37).

24. René Gérard, *L'Orient et la pensée romantique allemande,* 104.

25. By the term *emanation,* Schlegel refers to the cosmogonic doctrine where there occurs the splitting of divine power, with creation emanating from it and returning to it.

26. The belief that the universe of individuals consists of the outpourings of the Ultimate Divine Essence that is absolutely perfect. Schlegel held that emanated beings are degenerate in proportion to their distance from this Essence. He believed that, as opposed to Judeo-Christian belief, emanation denied the personality of both God and man.

27. Schlegel, *Philosophische Vorlesungen,* 1:110.

28. Ibid., 2:149ff.

29. Ibid., 2:173.

30. Ibid., 1:204.

31. Ibid., 2:155–56.

32. Ibid., 2:123.

33. That is to say, absent from the works he knew, namely the *Mānava Dharma Śāstra, Bhagavad Gītā,* and Kālidāsa's *Śākuntala.*

34. René Gérard, *L'Orient et la pensée romantique allemande,* 105.

35. Körner, *Krisenjahre der Frühromantik,* 494, 509, 519.

36. Helmina von Chézy, *Unvergessene Denkwürdigkeiten aus dem Leben von Helmina von Chézy* (Leipzig: F. A. Brockhaus, 1858), 264ff.

37. Heinrich Heine, *Romantische Schule, Sämtliche Werke,* ed. Ernst Elster, 7 vols. (Leipzig and Vienna: Bibliographisches Institut, 1893), 5:

270ff: "Zu tadeln habe ich nur den Hintergedanken des Buches. Es ist im Interesse des Katholizismus geschrieben. Nicht bloss die Mysterien desselben, sondern auch die ganze katholische Hierarchie und ihre Kämpfe mit der weltlichen Macht hatten diese Leute in den indischen Gedichten wiedergefunden . . . Friedrich Schlegel übersieht hier die ganze Literatur von einem hohen Standpunkte aus, aber dieser hohe Standpunkt ist doch immer der Glockenturm einer katholischen Kirche. Und bei allem, was Schlegel sagt, hört man diese Glocken läuten; manchmal hört man sogar die Turmraben krächzen, die ihn umflattern. Mir ist, als dufte der Weihrauch des Hochamts aus diesem Buche, und als sähe ich aus den schönsten Stellen desselben lauter tonsurierte Gedanken hervorlauschen. Indessen trotz dieser Gebrechen wüsste ich kein besseres Buch dieses Fachs."

38. Letter from Goethe to Reinhard, cited in Gerhard Hopfner, *Die indischen Studien Fr. Schlegels im Zusammenhang seines Denkens,* Ph.D., University of Breslau (1921), 205: "Die Absichtlichkeit von jeder Zeile wurde klar, meine Ansicht aber ward vollkommen, als ich Seite 97 des indischen Büchleins den leidigen Teufel und seine Grossmutter mit allem ewigen Gestanksgefolge hineingeschwärzt sah. Eben habe ich erst heute Seite 201 die alleinseeligmachende Kirche entdeckt."

39. Alfred von Martin, "Romantischen Konversionen," *Logos* 17 (1928): 146ff.

40. Noteworthy in this sense are the mythological and religious errors found in the Śakuntalā episode. In the *Bhagavad Gītā* translation, Schlegel resolves the seemingly contradictory description of the Divine Principle by emphasizing the unity of the Godhead (vs. 19). In his translation from the *Rāmāyaṇa,* Schlegel renders the term *devaṛsi* (divine seer) as "*Altvater,*" and the context suggests that he meant it in an Old Testament sense of "Patriarch." For an analysis of Schlegel's translations, see Ursula Oppenberg, *Quellenstudien zu Friedrich Schlegels Übersetzungen aus dem Sanskrit* (Marberg: N. G. Elwert, 1965).

41. Schlegel, *Sämtliche Werke,* 7:39, 40.

42. Schlegel, *Über die Sprache,* 41–59.

43. Ibid., xxii–xxiii, 65–70.

44. Schlegel did not see that inflection was made up of suffixes and desinences; he wanted to show these as sprouting from the root itself.

45. Schlegel, *Über die Sprache,* 41ff, 50ff.

46. Ibid., 3, 35–36, 71, 62, 66.

47. Ibid., 33, 44ff, 48, 50ff.

48. Ibid., 68–69.

49. Ibid., 51. Timpararo sees the problem of monogenesis and polygenesis of languages as having consequences for the debate on monogenesis and polygenesis of the human species and its racist beliefs.

50. Ibid., xxiii.

51. Ibid., xxxv.

52. Ibid., 55.

53. Schlegel had married the daughter of Moses Mendelssohn and had advocated Jewish emancipation.

54. Schlegel, *Über die Sprache,* 55.

55. Schlegel, *Briefe,* 636.

56. Oppenberg, *Quellenstudien,* 121–22.

57. Jakob Körner, *Krisenjahre der Frühromantik,* 129, 521ff.; Schlegel, *Über die Sprache,* viii ff.

Chapter 4. Scholarly Collusion and the Ethos of Despair

1. See, for instance, the French Hellenist Jean-Pierre Vernant's introduction to M. Olender's *The Languages of Paradise,* xi.

2. Wilhelm Halbfass, *India and Europe* (Albany: State University of New York Press, 1988), 2.

3. Halbfass, *India and Europe,* chaps. 4–9.

4. Halbfass, *India and Europe,* chap. 9. For an interesting discussion of Cousin and Hegel, see Roger-Pol Droit, "Victor Cousin, la Bhagavad Gītā et l'ombre de Hegel," in *L'Inde et l'imaginaire,* ed. Catherine Weinberger-Thomas (Paris: Editions de l'École des Hautes Études en Sciences Sociales, 1989), 175–96. See Michel Hulin, *Hegel et l'Orient* (Paris: Vrin, 1979), for a specific discussion of Hegel's essay.

5. Friedrich Maier translated Wilkins's translation into German in 1802. This rendition appeared in Klaproth's *Asiatisches Magazin.*

6. E. Windisch, *Geschichte der Sanskrit-Philologie und indischen Alterthumskunde,* 2 vols. (Strasbourg: K. J. Trübner, 1917–20), 1: 24.

7. A. W. Schlegel, *Bhagavad Gītā, id est THESPESION MELOS sive Almi Chrishnae et Arjunae Colloquium de rebus divinis. Textum recensuit, Adnotationes criticas et interpretationem Latinam adiecit* (Bonn: Eduard Weber, in Academia Borusska Rhenana, 1823).

8. Henry Thomas Colebrooke, "On the Philosophy of the Hindus," parts 1 and 2, *Transactions of the Royal Asiatic Society* 1 (1824): 19–43, 93–118. Part 1 was first read on 21 June 1823, and part 2 on 21 February 1824.

9. Henry Thomas Colebrooke, *Essays on the Religion and Philosophy of the Hindus* (London and Edinburgh: Williams & Norgate, 1858), 76–142.

10. Ever prescient, Schopenhauer maintained that, aside from A. W. Schlegel's translation of the *Bhagavad Gītā* and Colebrooke's work, most translations offer a view of Indian philosophy where both the general and the abstract meanings are imprecise and weak, expressing only the contours of the original. The tone is strange, modern, empty, pale, flat, poor in meaning, and Western. See Schopenhauer, *Fragments,* 174.

11. Colebrooke, *Essays,* 143–48. For a discussion of Hegel's reading of Colebrooke, see Ignatius Viyagappa, *G. W. F. Hegel's Concept of Indian Philosophy* (Rome: Università Gregoriana, 1980), 42. Viyagappa notes that Hegel presented Mīmāṃsā as the system that teaches the art of

reasoning with the expressed view of aiding the interpretation of the Vedas. The Vedānta deduces from the sacred books a refined psychology. Nyāya "furnishes a philosophical arrangement with strict rules of reasoning." Vaiśeṣika, like Nyāya, has a method of reasoning and teaches the doctrine of atomism. Sāṃkhya proposes a means to acquire salvific knowledge by way of right discrimination. Yoga promises final liberation through contemplation.

12. A. S. Langlois, "Bhagavad Gītā id est thespesion melos . . . traduit par M.A.G. de Schlegel," *Journal Asiatique* 4 (1824): 105–16, 236–52. Langlois criticized Schlegel's translation up to the twelfth canto.

13. W. von Humboldt, "Über die Bhagavad Gītā. Mit Bezug auf die Beurtheilung der Schlegelschen Ausgabe im Pariser Asiatischen Journal," in *Gesammelte Werke,* 7 vols. (Berlin: G. Reimer, 1841), 1:110–84.

14. W. von Humboldt, "Über die unter dem Namen Bhagavad-Gītā bekannte Episode des Mahâ-Bhârata," in *Gesammelte Werke,* 1: 26–109.

15. G. W. F. Hegel, "Über die unter dem Namen Bhagavad-Gītā bekannte Episode des Mahabharata von Wilhelm von Humboldt," *Werke in zwanzig Bänden,* vol. 11, *Berliner Schriften* (Frankfurt: Suhrkamp, 1970), 131–204; hereafter cited as *Berliner Schriften.* With the exception of the *Berliner Schriften,* in all other citations the edition used is the *Sämtliche Werke, Neue kritische Ausgabe,* ed. G. Lasson and d. Hoffmeister, 2nd ed. (Leipzig: F. Meiner, 1944).

16. Victor Cousin, *Cours de l'histoire de la philosophie* (Paris: Pichon & Didier, 1829), vol. 1, lessons 5 and 6.

17. Helmut Gipper, "Understanding as a Process of Linguistic Approximation: The Discussion between August Wilhelm Schlegel, S. A. Langlois, Wilhelm von Humboldt, and G. W. F. Hegel on the Translation of the *Bhagavad Gītā* and the concept of Yoga," in *Studies in the History of Western Linguistics in Honor of R. H. Robins,* eds. Theodora Bynam and F. R. Palmer (Cambridge: Cambridge University Press, 1986), 109–28.

18. Humboldt, *Gesammelte Werke* 1:110–84.

19. Ibid., 1:136.

20. Ibid., 1:137.

21. For an examination of how early German translations of Sanskrit differed from the European language translation conventions of the nineteenth century, see my *Translating the Orient.*

22. Humboldt, "Über die Verschiedenheiten des Menschlichen Sprachbaues und ihren Einfluss auf die geistige Entwicklung des Menschengeschlechts." in *Gesammelte Werke,* 6:2.

23. Ibid., 6:6.

24. Humboldt, "Über das vergleichende Sprachstudium in Beziehung auf die verschiedenen Epochen der Sprachentwicklung," in *Gesammelte Werke,* 3:241–268.

25. Humboldt, "Über die Verschiedenheiten," 6:42.

26. Humboldt's letter first appeared in the *Indische Bibliotek,* where Schlegel followed it with his own response to Langlois's review. See August Wilhelm Schlegel, *Indische Bibliothek,* vol. 2, part 2 (Bonn: Weber, 1826), 218–58; part 3 (1828), 328–72. Reprinted in W. von Humboldt's, *Gesammelte Werke,* vol. 1.

27. He had initially considered translating the Sanskrit into Greek.

28. This reservation is particularly relevant in translating from Sanskrit, given the importance and role in Sanskrit poetry of *dhvani,* the suggestion or reverberation of words.

29. Humboldt, *Gesammelte Werke,* 1:145.

30. Two parts. The first part was read on 30 June 1825, and the second part on 15 June 1826, at the Royal Academy of Sciences, Berlin. The entire article was first printed in the *Abhandlungen der historisch-philologischen Klasse der preussischen königlichen Akademie der Wissenschaften* (Berlin, 1827).

31. Humboldt, *Gesammelte Werke,* 1:38.

32. Ibid., 1:58–59. Humboldt defines Sāṃkhya as "the spiritual begetting upon nature."

33. Ibid., 1:57–61.

34. Ibid., 1:62–63.

35. Ibid., 1:47.

36. Ibid., 1:66–67.

37. Ibid., 1:67; he cites Colebrooke, *Essays,* 20, 24–26, 37, 38.

38. *Bhagavad Gītā* 2.25; 8.20, 21; 13.27.

39. Humboldt, *Gesammelte Werke,* 1:28: ". . . und dass von dem nach Vollendung strebenden jede Handlung ohne alle Rücksicht auf ihre Folgen, und mit völligem Gleichmuth über dieselben, vorgenommen werden muss."

40. Ibid., 1:28.

41. Ibid., 1:48; he cites the *Bhagavad Gītā* 3.22–24; 4.13–14; 9.10; 13.31–32.

42. Humboldt, *Gesammelte Werke,* 1:77.

43. Ibid., 1:68.

44. Ibid., 1:70.

45. Ibid., 1:73–74.

46. Ibid., 1:79.

47. Ibid., 1:82.

48. Ibid., 1:29–30.

49. Halbfass, *India and Europe,* 85.

50. Olender, *The Languages of Paradise,* 19.

51. G. W. F. Hegel, *Vorlesungen über die Philosophie der Weltgeschichte,* vol. 1, *Die Vernunft in der Geschichte,* ed. J. Hoffmeister, 5th ed. (Hamburg: F. Meiner, 1955), 158ff (hereafter cited as *Philosophie der Weltgeschichte*).

52. Hegel, *Philosophie der Weltgeschichte* 1:138ff.

53. The *Symbolik* of Creuzer and Görres's *Mythengeschichte der asiatischen Welt* (1810) promulgated the origins of Greek and Latin mythology in India. Myths were superior in India and became poorer and degraded in the West, just as Sanskrit was closer to a more primitive language.

54. According to F. Schlegel, humans led by primitive revelation, lived in direct contact with nature presented through sentiment and interiority. After original sin, they were left to themselves, guided by their memory of primitive revelation. Vestiges of the time immediately after the Fall appear in the system of emanation. Left to himself, man creates philosophical systems that are more and more barbaric, dualistic, pantheistic, and polytheistic, eventually culminating in the *Old Testament.* Hegel took umbrage not so much with the particular issues in Schlegel's thought as with his entire approach to the philosophy of history. Schlegel held that the task of the philosopher of history was "to reestablish the divine image in man, the image which is lost" (Schlegel, *Sämtliche Werke,* 9:5). His starting point is fallen man, who is believed to have had in the beginning of history very high powers but, by misusing them, gradually lost them (Ibid., 31ff; 43f). Hegel cannot help but disparage Schlegel [*Vorlesungen über die Geschichte der Philosophie,* ed. J. Hoffmeister, 2d ed. (Leipzig: F. Meiner, 1944), 1:264. Hereafter, cited as *Geschichte der Philosophie*]. He made a snide remark about Schlegel's conversion in a letter to Niethammer (7 May 1809, in *Briefe,* 1:283) and maintained that neither Schlegel brother was capable of laying claim to speculative thinking (*Sämtliche Werke,* 10:81): They "admire matters of mediocre value" and "give universal honor to what is only relatively important" and are "enthusiastic even with cheekiness" about things that are "cheap and secondary" as though they were the most important (*Sämtliche Werke,* 10:81–82).

55. Hegel, *Vorlesungen über die Philosophie der Religion,* ed. G. Lasson (1st ed., Leipzig: 1925–1929; 2d ed., Hamburg: F. Meiner, 1966), I.2:168 (hereafter, cited as *Philosophie der Religion*).

56. Although Hegel's essay contra Humboldt comprised his authoritative response, Hegel's general attack on Indian philosophy is found interspersed throughout his work, notably in his lectures on the history of philosophy, the philosophy of world history, and the philosophy of religion, see Halbfass, *India and Europe,* 86.

57. Hegel, *Geschichte der Philosophie,* 1:14.

58. Ibid., 1:34f.

59. Hegel, *Philosophie der Religion,* I.3:118ff.

60. Hegel, *Geschichte der Philosophie,* 1:227.

61. Hegel, *Berliner Schriften,* 67.

62. Hegel, *Geschichte der Philosophie,* 1:379.

63. Ibid., 1:370.

64. Ibid. See *Werke* (*Theorie Ausgabe*), vol. 13, *Vorlesungen über die Ästhetik,* 1:472. This description of Hinduism as a reduction and disappearance of everything in *Brahman* is repeated in the *Philosophie der Religion* and recapitulated in the *Encyclopädie.*

65. Hegel, *Geschichte der Philosophie,* 1:229, 235.

66. Hegel found in Colebrooke the most reliable and authoritative of all the scholars of his time dealing with Indian materials; Ibid., 1:293. Colebrooke's method differed radically from that of Hegel. He did not proceed from the definition of what is or what ought to be philosophy; nor did he question the relationships between religion and philosophy; nor were art, religion and philosophy of interest to Colebrooke.

67. Colebrooke's essay appeared in 1824. In the winter semester of 1825–26, Hegel integrated "Oriental" philosophy into his history of philosophy. Hegel had begun to study India in 1822. During the culminating years of his academic life, he kept abreast of the Orientalist scholarship of colleagues in Berlin such as Franz Bopp. He used the only sources readily available to him: Wilkins's translation of the *Bhagavad Gītā* (1775); Jones's *Śākuntala* (1789); the *Hitopadeśa* (1787); Jones's rendition of the *Laws of* Manu (1794); the beginning of the *Rāmāyaṇa,* translated by J. Marshman

and W. Carey (1806); fragments of the *Mahābhārata,* translated by Bopp (1819, 1824); Duperron's *Upanishads* (1801–2) and its German translation of 1808 by T. A. Rixner; and Creuzer's *Symbolik* (French translation by J. D. Guignaut). We should note that, for the most part, these sources were only specimens and not coherent wholes.

68. Hegel, *Geschichte der Philosophie,* 1:232.

69. Ibid., 1:293ff. In the *Encyclopädie,* Hegel used the *Gītā* to argue against the shallow idea of rationalist and modern theological pantheism. Indian thought was discussed in a long "exoteric" note to paragraph 573. The note is not included in the Heidelberg edition of 1817, but it is found in the enlarged edition of 1827 and the subsequent edition of 1830. This note, by far the longest of its kind in the *Encyclopädie,* deals primarily with the relationship of philosophy to religion.

70. Halbfass, *India and Europe,* 91.

71. Hegel, *Berliner Schriften,* 142: ". . . das Handeln wird im Erkennen oder vielmehr in der *abstrakten Vertiefung* des Bewusstsein in sich absorbiert." See also ibid., 182.

72. Ibid., 183.

73. Ibid., 151. See also *Philosophie der Weltgeschichte* 2:407: "Die Erhebung zum Brahm wird durch höchste Abgestumpftheit und Bewusstlosigkeit bewirkt," cited in Halbfass, *India and Europe,* 91.

74. Hegel, *Berliner Schriften,* 157–58.

75. Ibid., 161: "Das indische Vereinsamen der Seele in die Leerheit ist vielmehr eine Verstumpfung."

76. Ibid., 145, 148, 151. Hegel perceived that union with *Brahman* was achieved by birth and *yoga* (ibid., 145), with *yoga* as the designated path for nonbrahmins (ibid., 146) and the real focus of Indian philosophy and religion (ibid., 148).

77. Ibid., 146.

78. Ibid., 100–101.

79. Ibid., 151.

80. Ibid.

81. Ibid., 152.

82. Ibid., 157. See also ibid., 152, 165; and *Geschichte der Religion,* 2.1:166.

83. Hegel, *Berliner Schriften,* 163. Hegel defines *yoga* alternately as the absence of thought, vacuity (*Philosophie der Religion* 2.1:116), and a *Verdumpfung* of self-consciousness (*Berliner Schriften,* 185). See also *Philosophie der Weltgeschichte,* 2:378.

84. Hegel, *Berliner Schriften,* 185–90. Hegel defines Brahm (*sic*) as the "abstrakte Einheit ohne Bestimmung," "die Einheit nur als die abstrakte Allgemeinheit, als bestimmungslose Substanz," "Substanz ohne Subjektivität," "das reine Sein, ohne alle konkrete Bestimmung in sich," and "das Nichts alles Endlichen." In *Philosophie der Weltgeschichte,* it is "geistlose Substanz."

85. Hegel, *Berliner Schriften,* 181ff. Nor does Hegel conceive of the undivided unity of *Brahman* and the multiplicity of the world as permeating each other (*Berliner Schriften,* 158, 175, 184f, 190ff). Rather, he maintains that they relate to each other in unreconciled negation and exclusion.

86. Hegel also defined *Brahman* as "das Nichts alles Endlichen" (ibid., 190).

87. Hegel, *Philosophie der Religion* I.1:95ff.

88. Hegel, *Philosphie der Weltgeschichte,* 2:334.

89. Ibid., 2:332, 334.

90. Ibid., 2:399.

91. Ibid., 2:333.

92. He valued European vanity of the subject because of its permanent element of the subjective power of unity.

93. Hegel, *Philosophie der Weltgeschichte,* 2:334. Hegel expresses these thoughts elsewhere in his writings. In *Lectures on Philosophy of Religion,* Hegel identifies Buddhism (the religion of Fo) with *yoga* as he understood it. *Nirvāṇa,* which Hegel uses in the sense of "nothingness," is perceived as their ultimate goal (*Philosphie der Religion* I.2:124–34). Through meditation, one should produce emptiness within oneself (*Philosophie der Weltgeschichte,* 2:334f.). Hegel sees liberation (*mokṣa*) only as something negative.

94. Hegel, *Geschichte der Philosophie,* 1:227.

95. Hegel, *Berliner Schriften,* 163, 181.

96. Hegel, *Philosophie der Weltgeschichte,* 2:334.

97. Although contemptuous of A. W. Schlegel, Hegel made good use of A. W. Schlegel's translation of the *Gītā* in the *Encyclopädie,* the lectures in *Philosophy of Art,* and the review of Humboldt's essay. Hegel recognized Schlegel's possession of a "cultivated, poetical and spirited gift" for translation (*Berliner Schriften,* 150), although he had utter disdain for his supposed lack of depth (Letter to Daub, *Briefe* 3:165, 171). He compared Schlegel's translation to that of Wilkins. Hegel knew Charles Wilkins as "the first translator" of the *Gītā* (*Berliner Schriften,* 134). It is clear from Hegel's review of Humboldt's article on the *Gītā* that he had consulted Wilkins's translation. (*Berliner Schriften* 135, 150, 153, 155, 157).

98. Hegel's exposé is completely tributary to Colebrooke's essay "On the Philosophy of the Hindus."

99. Michel Hulin, *Hegel et l'Orient,* 114. Hulin suggests that Hegel was possibly led by Colebrooke himself, who distinguished Mīmāṃsā and Vedānta as "emphatically orthodox" and Jainism and Buddhism as heretical. Orthodoxy (i.e., agreement with the Veda) would not interest Hegel, since he was convinced that he had finally isolated the fundamental determination of Indian religion (i.e., abstraction of Brahma). Also, Colebrooke's description of the Vedānta ("On the Philosophy of the Hindus," 19)—that it "deduces from the text of the Indian scriptures a refined psychology which goes to a denial of a material world"—masks

its originality and allows Hegel to see it as resorption of all things in *Brahman*. For his examination of Nyāya-Vaiśeṣika, Hegel merely gave a simple analysis without personal commentary.

100. Hegel, *Berliner Schriften,* 143, 144.

101. Hulin, *Hegel et l'Orient,* 119.

102. As Cousin subsequently did, Hegel alters Colebrooke's order. This change might be explained by Colebrooke's having emphasized the affinity of the two doctrines by treating Yoga separately only when it manifests a divergence in reference to Sāṃkhya. Hegel subordonates Yoga to Sāṃkhya, associating it with religious cults (*Berliner Schriften,* 148) and reduces Sāṃkhya more or less to a systematic inventory of phenomenal categories.

103. As Hulin notes (*Hegel et l'Orient,* 121) the fundamental idea of this *kārikā* is that the frontier between nature and spirit passes at the interior of concrete psychological experience. The passive *puruṣa* possesses will and knowledge, although, in its ignorance, it identifies with the products of *prakṛti*. By falling victim to this false identification, the self comes to feel that it experiences pain and suffering. It then develops attachments and becomes entangled in *saṃsāra*. Deliverance consists in breaking these bonds of ignorance and illusion and realizing one's true being as the *puruṣa* rather than some product of *prakṛti*. Thus, in Sāṃkhya, salvation comes from knowledge of the total independence of the self from the nonself as it manifests itself in activity, sensation, or volition.

104. Hulin, *Hegel et l'Orient,* 121.

105. Colebrooke, "On the Philosophy of the Hindus," 42.

106. Colebrooke, "On the Philosophy of the Hindus," 32.

107. Hegel, *Geschichte der Philosophie,* 1:321.

108. Hulin, *Hegel et l'Orient,* 120.

109. Colebrooke, "On the Philosophy of the Hindus," 37.

110. Hulin, *Hegel of l'Orient,* 121.

111. Hegel, *Geschichte der Philosophie,* 1:321.

112. The appendix entitled "The Mongolian Principle" in the Lasson edition of *Philosophie der Weltgeschichte,* 2:332–42, after the chapter on China, deals with the religions of China, Burma, and Sri Lanka. Hegel defines the Mongolian Principle as the principle of "Nichts" (ibid., 334). This appendix is followed by the chapter on India. In Karl Hegel's edition, the India chapter follows that on China, which in turn is followed by six pages on Buddhism, consisting of a lecture given in 1822–23. India is treated more extensively in the Lasson edition than in that of Karl Hegel.

113. The Buddhist draws his mind into himself and comes to bliss (*Philosophie der Weltgeschichte,* 2:335). "The Mongolian Principle" deals mainly with the concept of *nirvāṇa.*

114. Hegel, *Philosophie der Religion,* 2:124.

115. Hegel, *Philosophie der Weltgeschichte,* 2:339.

116. Hegel maintained that, in order to render the state of *yoga* permanent, Indians resort to a long ascetic training consisting of acts such as the practices of fakirs, suttee, the Jaggernath torture, and the like.

117. Hegel, *Philosphie der Weltgeschichte,* 2:378.

118. Hegel, *Vorlesungen über die Philosphie der Weltgeschichte,* II: *Die orientalische Welt,* ed. G. Lasson, 3rd ed. (Hamburg: F Meiner, 1968), 393.

119. Hegel, *Geschichte der Philosphie,* 1:333.

120. Ibid., 1:336. Later civilizations avoid such an impasse. The Greeks, for example, begin directly at level of second syllogism (where finite spirit serves as the middle term between logos and nature), so that the true objective terrain of thought consists in the liberty of the subject.

121. Hegel, *Berliner Schriften,* 188.

122. Ibid., 150–51.

123. Ibid., 149.

124. Gipper, "Linguistic Approximation," 117.

125. Droit, "Victor Cousin," 175.

126. Ibid., 177–78.

127. Lessons 5 and 6 were presented in 1828 and appeared in Cousin, *Cours*.

128. Cousin, *Cours,* 212–14.

129. Droit, "Victor Cousin," 175–96, judges Cousin's positioning of the origin of civilization in the Orient, and his identification of the Orient with India, as reductive. As far as Cousin is concerned, India alone of Asian nations possesses philosophy. Egypt and Persia have only theologies. Cousin virtually ignores China.

130. Cousin, *Cours,* 175.

131. As Droit notes ("Victor Cousin," 180–82), Colebrooke arranges the Indian philosphical schools in the following order: 1) Sāṃkhya; 2) Nyāya-Vaiśeṣika; 3) Mīmāṃsā; 4) Vedānta; and 5) the heterodox sects. This order is maintained in Pauthier's French translation of Colebrooke's essay.

132. Although Cousin recognizes Buddhism's Indian origin, he views it as developmentally Chinese.

133. Cousin, *Cours,* 158.

134. Ibid., 157.

135. Ibid., 213.

136. Ibid., 217. In the *Sāṃkhya Kārikā*, Cousin recognizes absolute nihilism as the final fruit of scepticism (Cousin, *Cours,* 214). India, however, lacks a coherant skeptical school, although Cousin recognizes skepticism in all the otherwise dogmatic Indian schools of philosophy.

137. Droit, "Victor Cousin," 182.

138. Wilhelm von Humboldt had suggested this point in his essay on the *Gītā,* and Cousin feels that he can confirm it.

139. Cousin examines in depth the *Bhagavad Gītā* in the second half of the sixth lesson. He uses the A. W. Schlegel Latin translation of 1823, which Antoine de Chézy reviewed in the *Journal des Savants* (January 1825): 37ff. In addition to Wilkins's rendition (1784), other translations of the time include the French translation by Abbé Parraud (1787) and the German translation by Meier (1802).

140. Cousin, *Cours,* 220.

141. To support such a reading, Cousin (*Cours,* 136–37) cites the *Gītā* 2.46 translated as: "Quot usibus inservit puteus, acquis undique confluentibus, tot usibus praestant universi libri sacri theologo prudenti."

142. Schlegel, *Bhagavad Gītā,* 136: "Rituum varietate abundantem . . . sedem apud superum finem bonorum praedicantes."

143. Cousin, *Cours,* 223–24: "Toute commence toujours bien, et le précepteur d'Ardjouna ne lui recommande pas d'abord l'inaction, ce qui choquerait le sens commun et les mâles habitudes du jeune schatria: mais il lui recommande d'agir avec pureté, c'est à dire sans rechercher les avantages de son action, d'agir par la simple considération du devoir, arrive ensuite que pourra. C'est le désintéressement, la pureté intérieure. Rien de mieux assurément: mais la pente est glissante, car la pureté est modeste, elle doit fuir toutes les occasions de chute; et comme on n'est jamais plus sûr de ne pas mal agir qu'en n'agissant point, bientôt on va du désintéressement à l'abstinence et de l'abstinence à l'inertie."

144. A. W. Schlegel, *Bhagavad Gītā,* 144: "Qui in opere otium cernit et in otio opus, is sapit inter mortales."

145. Ibid., 137: "Mente devotus in hoc aevo utraque dimittit, bene et male facta."

146. Ibid., 136.

147. Cousin, *Cours,* 225.

148. A. W. Schlegel, *Bhagavad Gītā,* 226.

149. Cousin, *Cours,* 227: "Le plus criminel, s'il me sert sans partage, est purifié et sanctifié par là."

150. A. W. Schlegel, *Bhagavad Gītā,* 160: "Si vel admodum facinorosus me colit cultu non aliorsum distracto, is probus est aestimandus, is utique recte compositus."

151. *Bhagavad Gītā* 9:30: "Sādhur eva sa mantavyaḥ samyag vyavasito hi saḥ."

152. See, for example, the *Gītā,* 3:27 (in A. W. Schlegel, *Bhagavad Gītā,* 141): "Naturae qualitatibus peraguntur omni modo opera; sui fiducia qui fallitur, eorum seipsum auctorem esse arbitratur." In Cousin (*Cours,* 227) this becomes: "Le présomptueux se croit l'auteur de ses actions; mais toutes ses actions viennent de la force et de l'enchaînement nécessaire des choses."

153. A. W. Schlegel, *Bhagavad Gītā,* 147: "Cunctis operibus animo dimissis commode sedet temperans mortalis in urbe novem portis instructa, neque ipse agens nes agendi auctor."

154. Cousin, *Cours,* 229: "Délivré de tout souci de l'action, le vrai dévot reste tranquillement assis dans la ville à neuf portes (le corps), sans remuer lui-même et sans remuer les autres."

155. A. W. Schlegel, *Bhagavad Gītā,* 138: "Sicuti testudo undecunque, sensus abstrahit a rebus quae sensibus observantur: tunc apud eum sapientia commoratur."

156. The Sanskrit *yatacitta* refers to one "who performs yoga of the self"—i.e., the *yogī* of controlled thought.

157. Cousin, *Cours,* 229: "Il se recueille en soi, comme une tortue qui se retire en elle-même."

158. Cousin, ibid., translates A. W. Schlegel, *Bhagavad Gītā,* 138–39, "Quae nox est cunctis animantibus, hanc pervigilat abstinens; qua

vigilant animantes, haec est nox verum intuentis anachoretae," as "Ce qui est la nuit pour les autres est la veille du sage, et la veille des autres est sa nuit."

159. *Bhagavad Gītā,* 2:47.

160. G. W. F. Hegel, *Briefe von und an Hegel,* ed. J. Hoffmeister, 4 vols. (Hamburg: F. Meiner, 1954), 3:406 (notes).

161. For example, Captain Samuel Turner's (1749–1802) travel accounts found in *Asiatick Researches,* 1:197ff., cites ascetical exercises and how they stupefy the adept. Hegel does not question the truth of Turner's assertions. They confirm that "the Indian withdrawal of the Soul into the emptiness is rather a benumbing, which perhaps does not deserve even the name of mysticism at all and which cannot lead one to the discovery of truths, because it is without content" (*Berliner Schriften,* 161). H. J. Schoeps ("Die ausserchristlichen Religionen bei Hegel," *Zeitschrift für Religions- und Geistesgeschichte* 7, no. 1 [1955]: 6) believes Hegel's prejudices against the "amoral" character of the Hindu were due to Abbé Jean Antoine Dubois, *Description of the Character, Manners, Customs of the People of India,* author's preface. Hegel makes a specific reference to Dubois when he discusses the amoral character of the Hindus (see *Philosophie der Weltgeschichte,* 2:390–91, cited in Ignatius Viyagappa, *Hegel's Concept of Indian Philosophy,* 29.

162. Viyagappa, *Hegel's Concept of Indian Philosophy,* 60. Viyagappa notes that Hegel praised Creuzer and Bopp because they had searched for an inner rationality or one idea that governed all aspects of Indian life (Ibid.) and that Hegel was influenced by Creuzer's contention that Indian religion exhibited three main features: (1) the naiveté of childhood; (2) religious devotion and reflection; and (3) the element of speculation and philosophy (Ibid., 55). In this regard, see F. Creuzer, *Symbolik und Mythologie der alten Völker, besonders der Griechen,* 3d ed. (Leipzig and Darmstadt: C. W. Leske, 1837–42), 1:391, 401. Hegel found Creuzer's manner of presentation "of immense interest for himself as well as for the world at large" (*Briefe,* 2:218).

163. See specifically Wilhelm von Humboldt's assessment of *bhakti* (*Gesammelte Werke,* 1:31).

164. Schopenhauer saw Hegel as a worthless charleton and a corruptor of minds. He viewed Hegel's philosophy as confused and empty verbiage, as absolute nonsense, claiming that Hegel was unable to see beyond the farce of history (*World as Will and Representation,* vol. 2, chap. 35). Schopenhauer was familiar with Colebrooke's essays, although he himself did not use them. His own sources (J. J. Schmidt, Spence Hardy, E. Burnouf, and C. F. Köppen) informed him enough to assume that he recognized the errors of Hegel's interpretation. One can only guess whether Hegel's misreading of the *Gītā* contributed significantly to Schopenhauer's negative assessment of Hegel.

165. Cousin, *Cours,* 237: "La dévotion ou logisme consiste, nous l'avons vu, à préférer la contemplation à la science, l'inaction à l'action, la foi aux oeuvres, à se fixer dans la prédestination, à ne chercher dans toutes choses que Dieu, et en même temps à voir Dieu en toutes choses, dans les moindres comme dans l'esprit, enfin à tendre à l'union le plus intime avec Dieu par l'extase."

166. Hegel does not even discuss Indian mysticism, the cornerstone of Cousin's thesis. Cousin, on the other hand, ignores Hegel's extensive discussion of the caste system.

167. Hegel, *Berliner Schriften,* 152: "Diese Verzichtleistung auf den Erfolg ist nicht ein Enthalten vom Handeln selbst, setzt dasselbe vielmehr voraus."

168. Halbfass, *India and Europe,* 60.

169. Hegel, *Philosophie der Weltgeschichte,* 2:355; also *Sämtliche Werke,* 9:205. He speaks of the dreaming spirit of the Indians in *Berliner Schriften,* 169–71; *Philosphie der Weltgeschichte,* 2:339.

170. Hegel, *Philosophie der Weltgeschichte,* 2:365.

171. Droit, "Victor Cousin," 187.

172. Cited in Halbfass, *India and Europe,* 167.

173. Olender, *The Languages of Paradise,* 20.

Part III. Introduction

1. George Mosse, *The Crisis of German Ideology* (New York: Grosset & Dunlap, 1964), 74.

Chapter 5. The German Quest for Nirvāṇa

1. Monier Monier-Williams, *A Sanskrit English Dictionary* (Delhi: Motilal Banarsidass, 1990), 557.

2. For a summary of the canonical understanding of *nirvāṇa,* see T. Stcherbatsky, *The Conception of Buddhist Nirvāṇa.*

3. For an examination of the scholarly reception of the concept of *nirvāṇa* in the West, see Guy Richard Welbon, *The Buddhist Nirvāṇa in the West* (Chicago: University of Chicago Press, 1968).

4. Arthur Schopenhauer, *Gespräche und Selbstgespräche,* ed. E. Grisebach (Berlin: E. Hofmann, 1902), 50.

5. Schopenhauer, *World as Will and Representation,* 2:169.

6. A. Schopenhauer, *Handschriftlicher Nachlass,* ed. E. Grisebach, 4 vols. (Leipzig: Reclam, n.d.), 4:350. See also *World as Will and Representation,* 1:393, where suffering is seen as the foundation of all life.

7. A. Schopenhauer, *Parerga und Paralipomena: Kleine philosophische Schriften,* 2 vols. (Leipzig: F. A. Brockhaus, 1877), 2:304.

8. Schopenhauer, *Parerga und Paralipomena,* 2:304: "Unser Daseyn hat keinen Grund, darauf es fusst als die dahin schwindende Gegenwart . . . Also Unruhe ist der Typus des Daseyns . . . Die Glucksäligkeit kann nicht wohnen, wo Platons 'beständiges Werden und nie Seyn' allein statt findet. Zuforderst: Keiner ist glücklich, sondern strebt sein Leben lang einem vermeintlichen Glücke, welches er selten erreicht und auch dann nur, um enttäuscht zu werden." See also 2:429–30.

9. Schopenhauer, *Handschriftlicher Nachlass,* 4:117: "Freilich ist dies (Wort: Wille) ein subjektiv . . . gewählter Ausdruck: aber diese Rücksicht ist . . . wesentlich. Also ist es unendlich besser, als hätt' ich es

genannt etwa Brahm oder Brahma, oder Weltseele." Schopenhauer also identified the will with *prakṛti* (*Parerga und Paralipomena,* para. 187).

10. Schopenhauer, *World as Will and Representation,* 1:410–11.

11. The fourth truth of Buddhism concerns the path leading to deliverance and has no equivalent in Schopenhauer.

12. Schopenhauer, *World as Will and Representation,* 2:628.

13. Ibid., 2:608: "The Buddhists with complete frankness describe the matter negatively as nirvana, which is the negation of this world, or of samsara. If nirvana is defined as nothing, this means only that samsara contains no single element that could serve to define or construct nirvana."

14. Ibid., 1:356.

15. Schopenhauer's life, although austere, was not without its earthly comforts, and he was anything but reclusive. Paul Challemel-Lacour, reporting his visit to Schopenhauer, suggests to what extent the philosopher was confused with his philosophy. Upon seeing the philosopher, Challemel-Lacour affirms having felt pass over him "un souffle glacé à travers la porte entrouverte du néant" ("Un bouddhiste contemporain en Allemagne," *Revue des deux mondes,* 15 March 1870).

16. Schopenhauer, *Handschriftlicher Nachlass,* 4:212.

17. Schopenhauer, *World as Will and Representation,* 2:508.

18. Ibid., 1:411–12.

19. Ibid., 2:640.

20. Ibid., 1:411.

21. Ibid., 1:412.

22. Schopenhauer uses the term *Quietiv* to describe the eternal sleep caused by the definitive extinction of the will to live. He viewed

asceticism as the most powerful sedative (*World as Will and Representation,* supplements to book 4, nos. 65, 68, 69).

23. He did, however, accept Hegel's notion that Indian religion had stagnated while Christianity continued to develop.

24. Karl Robert Eduard von Hartmann, *Philosophische Fragen der Gegenwart* (Leipzig; W. Friedrich, 1885), 171–72: "Nirwana ist das Nichts . . . Das folgt schon aus seiner Bedeutung 'Erlöschen.' Wäre Nirwana nicht das Nichts, sondern das überweltliche reine Sein des nicht mehr erscheinenden reinen Wesens, so wäre der Hauptunterschied zwischen Brahmanismus und Buddhismus aufgehoben . . . Samsara hat also nicht etwa ein wesenhaftes Sein hinter sich, sondern als wesenloser Schein hat es nur das Nichtsein oder Nichts hinter sich."

25. Philipp Mainländer [Philipp Batz], *Die Philosophie der Erlösung* (Berlin: T. Grieben, 1876), 613–20.

26. Schopenhauer, *World as Will and Representation,* 1:411.

27. Ibid., chap. 35.

28. Schopenhauer, *Parerga und Paralipomena,* para. 187.

29. Schopenhauer, *World as Will and Representation,* chap. 28.

30. Ibid., supplement to bk. 4, chap. 48. As a case in point, see Schopenhauer's letter to A. von Doss of 27 February 1856, where he defines *karma* (action) as the individual will without intellect (A. Schopenhauer, *Gesammelte Briefe,* ed. Arthur Hübscher [Bonn: Bouvier Verlag Herbert Grundmann, 1978], 384).

31. Schopenhauer, *World as Will and Representation,* 2:638.

32. Sausendes, brausendes Rad der Zeit,
Messer du der Ewigkeit;
Leuchtende Sphären im weiten All,
Die ihr umringt den Weltenball;
Urewige Schöpfung, halte doch ein,
Genug des Werdens, lass mich sein!

Halte an dich, zeugende Kraft,
Urgedanke, der ewig schafft!
Hemmet den Atem, stillet den Drang,
Schweiget nur eine Sekunde lang!
Schweltende Pulse, fesselt den Schlag;
Ende, des Wollens ew'ger Tag!

. . .

Weit in sehnendem Verlangen
Breitet ihr die Arme aus,
Und umschlinget wahnbefangen
Öde Leere nicht'gen Graus.

33. R. Wagner, *Gesammelte Schriften und Dichtungen,* ed. W. Golther, 10 vols. (Berlin, Vienna, and Stuttgart: Deutsches Verlags Bong, 1913), 6:255–56:

Grane, mein Ross,
Sei mir gegrüsst!
Weisst du, Freund,
wohin ich dich führe?
Im Feuer leuchtend
liegt dort dein Herr,
Siegfried, mein seliger Held.
Dem Freunde zu folgen
wieherst du freudig?
Lockt dich zu ihm die
lachende Lohe?
Fühl meine Brust auch,
wie sie entbrennt;
helles Feuer
fasst mir das Herz:
ihn zu umschlingen,
umschlossen von ihm,
in mächtigster Minne
vermählt zu sein!—
Heiaho! Grane!
Grüsse den Freund!
Siegfried! Siegfried!
Selig gilt dir mein Gruss.

From a musical point of view, it is interesting to note that the curse in F# at the end of Brünnhilde's encounter with Waltraute in the first act will be musically recalled in her final suttee monologue. What in the first act is expressed as a hope is fulfilled at the end of the opera; the gods and the world are redeemed.

34. Wagner, *Gesammelte Schriften und Dichtungen,* 1:234. The first musical sketches for *Tristan* were most likely based on the early outline made in December 1856. Wagner completed the full score of act 1 on 3 April 1858, act 2 in March 1859, and act 3 on 6 August 1859. The score was published in its entirety in January 1860, and the opera premiered on 10 June 1865, at the Munich Hof- und Nationaltheater.

35. Wagner, *Gesammelte Schriften und Dichtungen,* 6:255–56:

Führ' ich nun nicht mehr
nach Walhalls Feste,
wisst ihr, wohin ich fahre?
Aus Wunschheim zieh' ich fort,
Wahnheim flieh' ich auf immer;
des ew'gen Werdens
offene Tore
schliess'ich hinter mir zu:
nach dem wunsch- und wahnlos
heiligsten Wahlland,
der Welt-Wanderung Ziel,
von Wiedergeburt erlöst,
zieht nun die Wissende hin.
Alles Ew'gen
sel'ges Ende,
wisst ihr, wie ich's gewann?
Trauernde Liebe
tiefstes Leiden
schloss die Augen mir auf:
enden sah ich die Welt.

36. R. Wagner, *Sämtliche Schriften und Dichtungen,* edited by H. von Wolzogen and R. Sternfeld (Leipzig: Breitkopf & Härtel, 1911), 6:210–11:

Trauernde Minne
tiefstes Mitleid

schloss die Tore mir auf:
Wer über alles
achtet das Leben,
Wer aus Mitleid
der Scheidenden nachblickt
dem dämmert von fern
die Erlösung, die ich erlangt.
So scheid' ich
grüssend, Welt, von dir!

For a discussion of these variants, see Carl Suneson, *Richard Wagner und die indische Geisteswelt* (Leiden: E. J. Brill, 1989), 63–69.

37. Wagner first became acquainted with Schopenhauer's *Die Welt als Wille und Vorstellung* in 1854. The poet Georg Herwegh introduced him to the work. Of his initial reading, Wagner wrote to Liszt that the book "wie ein Himmelsgeschenk in meine Einsamkeit gekommen ist . . . so habe ich dagegen doch nun ein Quietiv gefunden, das mir endlich in wachen Nächten einzig zu Schlaf verhilft; es ist die herzliche und innige Sehnsucht nach dem Tod: volle Bewusstlosigkeit, gänzliches Nichtsein, Verschwinden aller Träume—einzigste endliche Erlösung." See R. Wagner and F. Liszt, *Briefwechsel zwischen Wagner und Liszt,* 2 vols. (Leipzig: Breitkopf & Härtel, 1887), 2:45–46.

38. Richard Wagner, *Mein Leben,* ed. Martin Gregor-Dellin (Munich: List, 1967), 614.

39. Richard Wagner, *Wagner on Music and Drama,* ed. Albert Goldman and Evert Sprinchorn (New York: E. P. Dutton, 1964), 277–78.

40. Wagner's critique of Judaism within the context of a general critique of religion can be seen in one of his early letters to Liszt concerning Buddhism. Christianity was nothing but a branch of Buddhism that had degenerated under the influence of Judaism, which Wagner viewed as a decadent faith; see Wagner and Liszt, *Briefwechsel zwischen Wagner und Liszt,* 2:80–84. Although Cosima's references to topics relating to Judaism are suspect, we can nevertheless trust them to the extent that they are trustworthy in those cases where she was either too stupid to see the true significance of Wagner's words or she could not fit them into any of her hidden editorial agendas: "Die christliche Lehre aber lehnt sich an die jüdische Religion, und das ist ihr Unheil. Das Leiden Christus' erregt uns tiefer als das Mitleiden Buddhas, durch die Betrachtung.

Christus will leiden, leidet und erlöst uns, Buddha schauet und bemitleidet, lehrt, wie wir zur Erlösung kommen." See Cosima Wagner, *Die Tagebücher, 1878–1883,* 2 vols., ed. M. Gregor-Dellin and D. Mack (Munich and Zurich: Piper, 1977), 1:744.

41. Wagner, *Mein Leben,* 2:603–4.

42. Wagner and Liszt, *Briefwechsel zwischen Wagner und Liszt,* 2:78–82.

43. As did many other thinkers interested in Indian thought, Wagner had his contacts in the realm of scholarship. His sister Ottilie was married to Herman Brockhaus (1806–77), a pioneer in Indology. During Wagner's tenure as *Kapellmeister* in Dresden, he spent much time with his brother-in-law.

44. In a letter to Mathilde Wesendonck, Wagner referred to Köppen's work as "ein unerquickliches Buch"; see R. Wagner, *Richard Wagner an Mathilde Wesendonk: Tagebuchblätter und Briefe 1853–1871,* ed. W. Golther (Leipzig: Breitkopf & Härtel, 1914), 108. In the library at Villa Wahnfried, Wagner possessed translations of the *Rig Veda,* the *Upanishads,* the *Bhagavad Gītā,* the *Bhāgavata Purāṇa,* and the *Suttanipāta.*

45. Wagner and Liszt, *Briefwechsel zwischen Wagner und Liszt,* 2:83: "Die Brahmanen-Lehre stellt . . . den Mythos von einer Entstehung der Welt durch Gott auf; allein sie preist diesen Akt nicht als eine Wohltat, sondern stellt ihn als eine Sünde Bramas dar, die dieser, der sich selbst in diese Welt verwandelte, durch die ungeheuren Leiden eben dieser Welt abbüsst, und sich in denjenigen Heiligen erlöst, die durch vollständige Verneinung des Willens zum Leben in der einzig nur noch die erfüllenden Sympathie für alles Leidende in das Nirwana, d.h. Land des Nicht-mehr-seins, übergehen."

46. Although the source for Wagner's project was the *Śārdūlakarṇavadāna,* retold in Burnouf, the poet-composer may have been acquainted with the legend of the *Tschandala-Mädchen,* translated by Louise Hitz.

47. Wagner and Liszt, *Briefwechsel zwischen Wagner und Liszt,* 2:83: "Alles ist mir fremd, und sehnsüchtig blicke ich oft nach dem Land Nirwana. Doch Nirwana wird mir schnell wieder *Tristan*. Sie kennen die buddhistische Weltentstehungstheorie. Eine Hand trübt die Himmels-

klarheit: das schwillt an, verdichtet sich, und in undurchdringlicher Massenhaftigkeit steht endlich die ganze Welt wieder vor mir. Das ist das alte Los, solange ich noch solche unerlöste Geister um mich habe."

48. Ulrich Weisstein, "The Little Word *und:* Tristan und Isolde as Verbal Construct," in *Wagner in Retrospect: A Centenial Reappraisal,* ed. Leroy R. Shaw, Nancy R. Cirillo, and Marion S. Miller (Amsterdam: Rodopi, 1987), 70–90. Weisstein bases his argument on an examination of the verbal structures of the libretto. My evaluation of *Tristan* borrows generously from his interpretation.

49. R. Wagner, *Gesammelte Schriften,* ed. Julius Kapp, 14 vols. (Leipzig: Hesse & Becker, 1914), 7:50:

Tristan: Du Isolde,
Tristan ich
nicht mehr Tristan!
nicht Isolde!

For a clear exposition of this point, see Weisstein, "The Little Word *und,*" 81.

50. Wagner, *Gesammelte Schriften,* 7:81:

In des Wonnemeeres
wogenden Schwall,
in der Duftwellen
tönenden Schall,
in des Welt-Atems
wehendem All—
ertrinken,—
versinken—
unbewussst—
höchste Lust!

51. R. Wagner, *Gesammelte Schriften,* 7:44–45:

Tristan: Von deinem Zauber
sanft umsponnen
vor deinen Augen
süss zerronnen;

Isolde: Herz an Herze dir,
Mund an Mund;

Tristan: eines Atems
einiger Bund;

Beide: bricht mein Blick sich
Wonn' erblindet,
erbleichet die Welt
mit ihrem Blenden;

Isolde: die uns der Tag
trügend erhellt,

Tristan: zu täuschendem Wahn
entgegenstellt,

Beide: Selbst dann
bin ich die Welt.

52. *Die Sieger* was to have formed a diptych with *Tristan und Isolde*.

53. Wagner and Liszt, *Briefwechsel zwischen Wagner und Liszt*, 2:131: "Ich habe wieder zwei wundervolle Stoffe die ich noch einmal ausführen muss: Tristan und Isolde, (das weisst Du!)—dann aber—der Sieg—das Heiligste, die vollständigste Erlösung: das kann ich Dir aber nicht mittheilen."

54. Ibid., 2:136: "Erst müsstet Ihr auch meinen Tristan verdaut haben, namentlich seinen dritten Act, mit der schwarzen und der weissen Flagge. Dann würden erst die 'Sieger' deutlicher werden."

55. R. Wagner, *Briefe: Richard Wagner's an Otto Wesendonck*, ed. Albert Heintz (Charlottenburg: Verlag der Allgemeinen Musik-Zeitung O. Lessman, 1898), 26.

56. The sketch for this unwritten opera can be found in R. Wagner, *Dichtungen und Schriften: Jubiläumsausgabe in zehn Bänden*, ed. Dieter Borchmeyer (Frankfurt: Insel, 1983), 4:380f. It is dated 16 May 1856. Note that the earliest outline for *Tristan* dated from December 1856. For

references to *Die Sieger,* see the correspondence with Mathilde of 5 October 1858, in *Mein Leben,* 542.

57. Wagner agreed with his guru Schopenhauer in viewing suicide as an false path to transcendence. See Cosima Wagner, *Die Tagebücher,* 1:681 (11 May 1873): "Das ist eigentlich die höchste Affirmation des Willens—sie wollen lieber nicht sein als nicht befriedigt sein—warum sie aber nicht allen Hemmnissen trotzen, das zeigt, dass die Anlage zum Selbstmord etwas Urbestimmtes ist; man könnte es hier als einen tiefen Blick bezeichnen, ungefähr: Was helfe uns das, die Hindernisse zu bewältigen? Dafür sollte es Klöster geben, wie der Buddhismus sie hatte; vollständige Entsagung bei vollständigem sich Angehören war da möglich—aber unsere moderne Zivilization hat nichts!"

58. F. Nietzsche, *Der Fall Wagner: Schriften und Aufzeichnungen über Richard Wagner,* ed. D. Borchmeyer (Frankfurt: Insel, 1983), 121: "Er schmeichelt jedem nihilistischen (-buddhistischen) Instinkte und verkleidet ihn in Musik, er schmeichelt jeder Christlichkeit, jeder religiösen Ausdrucksform der Décadence."

59. K. F. Köppen, *Die Religion des Buddha und ihre Entstehung,* 2 vols. (Berlin: Schneider, 1857–59), 215–16: "Denn z. B. ohne den Glauben an die Wiedergeburt, deren Begründung ihm trotz aller Mühe nie recht gelungen ist, würde er in der Praxis schwerlich zu etwas Anderem geführt haben, als zum Selbstmorde oder zum Morde überhaupt, wohin ja das Dogma von der Verderbtheit der Welt schon so viele brahmanische und civaitische Fanatiker geführt hat; denn eine Religion, welcher das Nichts für das Wesen der Dinge und für das hochste Gut erklärt, hätte ohne die Lehre von der Seelenwanderung und Wiedergeburt ihren Bekennern kaum eine andere Pflicht auferlegen können, als die, sich selbst und Andere so schnell wie möglich ins Nichts zu befördern."

60. See letters to Liszt (7 June 1855) and Mathilde Wesendonck (August 1860).

61. Schopenhauer, *Parerga und Paralipomena,* 2:302.

62. Wagner, *Mein Leben,* 626–27: "Da ich in den Tagen der Krankheit mich höchstens mit Lektüre beschäftigen konnte. Von dieser regte mich am bedeutendsten Burnouf's *Introduction à l'histoire du boud-*

dhisme an; dieser entnahm ich sogar den Stoff zu einer dramatischen Dichtung, welche seitdem, obwohl nur im ungefährsten Entwurfe, stets in mir fortgelebt hat und vielleicht noch einmal ausgeführt werden dürfte. Ich gab ihm den Titel *die Sieger* . . ."

63. The projected heroine of *Die Sieger* is a pariah (*Tschandala-Mädchen*).

64. The sketch is as follows (Wagner, *Mein Leben*, 2: 626–27): "[*Die Sieger*] gründete sich auf die einfache Legende von der Aufnahme eines *Tschandala*-Mädchens in den erhabenen Bettlerorden *Cakyamounis,* wozu sie durch die schmerzlichst gesteigerte und geläuterte Liebe zu *Ananda,* dem Hauptjünger des Buddha, sich würdig macht. Ausser der tiefsinnigen Schönheit des einfachen Stoffes, bestimmte mich zu seiner Wahl alsbald ein eigentümliches Verhältnis desselben zu dem in mir seitdem ausgebildeten musikalischen Verfahren. Vor dem Geiste des *Buddha* liegt nämlich das vergangene Leben in früheren Geburten jedes ihm begegnenden Wesens offen, wie die Gegenwart selbst, da. Die einfache Geschichte erhielt nun ihre Bedeutung dadurch, dass dieses vergangene Leben der leidenden Hauptfiguren als unmittelbare Gegenwart in die neue Lebensphase hineinspielte. Wie nun der stets gegenwärtig miterklingenden musikalischen Reminiszenz dieses Doppellebens vollkommen dem Gefühle vorzuführen möglich werden durfte, erkannte ich sogleich, und dies bestimmte mich, die Aufgabe der Ausführung dieser Dichtung mit besondrer Liebe mir vorzubehalten. . . . So hatte ich denn, neben der immer noch in riesenhaften Dimensionen vor mir liegenden Arbeit des *Nibelungen,* zwei neue Stoffe, den *Tristan* und *die Sieger,* meiner Phantasie eingeprägt, welche von jetzt an neben jener Arbeit mich stets lebhaft beschäftigten."

65. Wagner, *An Mathilde Wesendonk,* 108: "Çakyamuni war anfänglich durchaus gegen die Aufnahme der Frauen in die Gemeinde der Heiligen. Er spricht von ihnen wiederholt die Ansicht aus, die Frauen seien von Natur viel zu sehr der Geschlechtsbestimmung, und somit der Laune, dem Eigensinn und dem Hange an der persönlichen Existenz unterworfen, als dass sie zu der Sammlung und weiten Beschaulichkeit gelangen könnten, durch die der Einzelne von der Naturtendenz sich lossage, um zur Erlösung zu gelangen."

66. Ibid., 109: "Es löst sich nun dadurch, dass er selbst noch eine letzte Entwicklungsstufe erreicht, durch Aufnahme einer neuen Erkennt-

nis, die ihm hier—wie alle Erkenntnisse—eben nicht durch abstracte Begriffsverbindungen, sondern durch anschauliche Gefühlserfahrung, somit auf dem Wege der Erschütterung und Bewegung des eigenen Inneren, zugeführt wird, und die ihn daher in einem letzten Fortschreiten zur höchsten Vollendung zeigt."

67. Ibid., 109–10: "Der dem Leben noch näher stehende, durch die heftige Liebe des jungen Tschandala-Mädchens unmittelbar berührte Ananda, wird zum Vermittler dieser letzten Vollendung. Ananda, tief erschüttert und gerührt, kann diese Liebe nur in seinem, dem höchsten Sinne erwidern, als Verlangen, die Geliebte zu sich heranzuziehen, auch ihr das letzte Heil theilhaft werden zu lassen. Hierin begegnet ihm, nicht schroff, sondern einen Irrthum, eine Unmöglichkeit beklagend, der Meister. Endlich aber, als Ananda schon in tiefster Trauer die Hoffnung aufgeben zu müssen glaubt, fühlt Çakya, durch sein Mitleiden, und wie durch ein letztes, neuestes Problem, dessen Lösung noch sein Verweilen im Dasein aufgehalten hat, angezogen, sich bestimmt, das Mädchen zu prüfen. Dieses kommt nun, in seinem tiefsten Jammer den Meister selbst anzurufen, sie dem Ananda zu vermählen. Nun legt er die Bedingungen vor, der Entsagung der Welt, der Ausscheidung aus allen Banden der Natur: bei dem Hauptgebote ist sie endlich aufrichtig genug, machtlos zusammenzubrechen; worauf sich denn . . . die reiche Szene mit den Brahmanen entspinnt, die ihm den Verkehr mit solchen Mädchen, als Beweis für das Irrige seiner Lehre, vorwerfen."

68. Ibid., 110: "In der Zurückweisung jedes menschlichen Hochmuthes gelangt endlich sein wachsender Anteil an dem Mädchen, deren frühere Existenzen er sich und den Gegnern enthüllt, zu solcher Stärke, dass, als sie—die nun den ganzen ungeheuren Zusammenhang des Welt-Leidens an ihrem eigenen Leiden erkannt hat—zu jedem Gelübde sich bereit erklärt, er, wie zu letzter eigener Verklärung, sie unter die Heiligen aufnimmt, und somit seinen erlösenden, allen Wesen zugewendeten Weltlauf als vollendet ansieht, da er auch dem Weibe—unmittelbar—die Erlösung zusprechen konnte. Glückliche Sawitri! Du darfst nun dem Geliebten überallhin folgen, stets um ihn, mit ihm sein. Glücklicher Ananda! sie ist Dir nah, gewonnen, um nie sie zu verlieren!"

69. The sinful female in need of redemption plays an important role in Wagner's subsequent female characterizations, most specifically, in the character of Kundry. For a discussion of Wagner's alterations on Burnouf's account, see Suneson, *Richard Wagner,* 74.

70. R. Wagner, *Sämtliche Schriften und Dichtungen,* 11:325ff: "Der Buddha auf seiner letzten Wanderung.—Ananda am Brunnen von Prakriti, dem Tschandala-Mädchen, getränkt. Heftige Liebe dieser zu Ananda; dieser erschüttert.—Prakriti, im heftigsten Liebesleiden: ihre Mutter lockt Ananda herbei: grosser Liebeskampf: Ananda bis zu Thränen ergriffen und geängstigt, von Chakya befreit.—Prakriti tritt zu Buddha, am Stadtthore unter dem Baume, um von ihm Vereinigung mit Ananda zu bitten. Dieser fragt sie, ob sie die Bedingungen dieser Vereinigung erfüllen wolle? Doppelsinniges Zwiegespräch, von Prakriti auf eine Vereinigung im Sinne ihrer Leidenschaft gedeutet, sie stürzt erschreckt und schluchzend zu Boden, als sie endlich hört, sie müsse auch Anandas Gelübde der Keuschheit ertragen. Ananda von Brahmanen verfolgt. Vorwürfe wegen der Verfassung Buddhas mit einem Tschandala-Mädchen. Buddhas Angriff des Kastengeistes. Er erzählt dann von Prakritis Dasein in einer früheren Geburt; sie war damals die Tochter eines stolzen Brahmanen; der Tschandala-König, der sich eines ehemaligen Daseins als Brahmane erinnert, begehrt für seinen Sohn des Brahmanen Tochter, zu welcher dieser heftige Liebe gefasst; aus Stolz und Hochmut versagte die Tochter Gegenliebe und höhnte den Unglücklichen. Dies hatten sie zu büssen und ward nun als Tschandala-Mädchen wiedergeboren, um die Qualen hoffnungsloser Liebe zu empfinden; zugleich aber zu entsagen und der vollen Erlösung durch Aufnahme unter Buddhas Gemeinde zugeführt zu werden—Prakriti beantwortet nun Buddhas letzte Frage mit einem freudigen Ja. Ananda begrüsst sie als Schwester. Buddhas letzte Lehren. Alles bekennt sich zu ihm. Er zieht dem Orte seiner Erlösung zu."

71. Prakriti is renamed Sawitri (Savitri) after Wagner read Adolf Holtzmann's *Indische Sagen* (3 vols., Stuttgart, 1845–47) in 1855. In a letter to Mathilde Wesendonck (*An Mathilde Wesendonk,* 7), he praises the divine Savitri, who confronts death to save her husband (see Holtzmann, 1:243–273). A similar motif was familiar to him in Brockhaus's translation of the *Kathāsaritsāgara* (1.7.88–97).

72. Wagner, *An Mathilde Wesendonk,* 110: "Heiliger werden; und als Heiliger dürfte ich Dir sagen: komm verlass alles, was Dich hält, zertrümmere die Banden der Natur: um diesen Preis zeige ich Dir den offenen Weg zum Heile!—Dann wären wir frei; Ananda und Sawitri!"

73. Ibid., 111: "Um nicht unterzugehen, blicke ich auf Dich . . .

hilf mir! sei mir nahe! rufe, desto ferner entschwindest Du; und mir antwortet es: 'In dieser Welt, wo du diese Not dir auflädst, um deine Bilder zu verwirklichen, in dieser Welt—gehört sie dir nicht! . . . Glücklicher Ananda! Glückliche Sawitri!' "

74. C. Wagner, *Die Tagebücher,* 2:36: "R. arbeitet. Gegen Mittag sagt er mir, 'es ginge ihm so gut, dass er gleich nach dem Parsifal die Sieger komponieren wolle, um diesen Zustand nicht aufhören zu sehen.' " See also the notation of 25 November 1873 (1:755): "R. sagt, mit dem 70. Jahre schreibt er Parcival [sic], mit dem 80. die Sieger."

75. Ibid., 2:319: "Noch einmal betont R., dass dies sein letztes Werk sei, im hohen Alter würde er noch 'Die Sieger' dichten, das mag dann Fidi komponieren."

76. Ibid., 2:659: "Noch im Bett sagt er, wenn du mich gut hältst, gut kleidest, gut nährst, dann komponiere ich noch 'Die Sieger.' "

77. Ibid., 2:1007: "Nachts war er ein Mal auf und las im Buche 'Buddha' . . . Wir sprechen jetzt fast immer vom Buddha; neulich bemerkte R., wie unmöglich es ihm gewesen sei würde, ihn zu komponieren, wenn er hätte müssen mit Mango-Bäumen, Lotos-Blumen etc. umgehen."

78. Ibid., 2:1007: "Bei dem Christentum ist die erhabene Simplizität, im Buddhismus ist so viel Bildung—Bildung ist sehr unkünstlerisch."

79. Wagner, *An Mathilde Wesendonk,* 147–48: "Jetzt nun, wo Savitri—Parzival [sic]—meinen Geist ahnungsvoll erfüllen, und zunächst zur dichterischen Idee sich zu gestalten streben—: jetzt, bei meiner künstlerisch vollendeten Arbeit mit plastisch sinnender Ruhe über meinen Tristan mich hinbeugen,—jetzt: wer ahnt es, welches Wunder mich dabei erfüllen muss, und mich so der Welt entrückt, dass sie mich fast schon ganz überwunden dünken kann? Sie ahnen es, Sie wissen es! Ja, und wohl nur Sie!"

80. C. Wagner, *Die Tagebücher,* 2:659: "Wir sprechen davon, dass ungefähr dasselbe Thema (die Erlösung des Weibes) in beiden, Parsifal und Sieger, behandelt würde."

81. Richard Wagner, *Briefe: Die Sammlung,* ed. Burrell, commentary by J. N. Burk (Frankfurt: S. Fischer, 1953), 816: "Seit ich den Parsifal erfasste, gab ich—als in einem schwächern Sinne mit diesem verwandt—das buddhistische Projekt gänzlich auf, und habe seitdem nie davon gedacht, etwas davon auzuführen."

82. The role of the sexually active pariah woman in *Die Sieger* calls to mind the similar images in the *satī*/bayadera/pariah literature. Here, too, the man's redemption is intimately bound up with the female's sexuality.

83. Wagner, *An Mathilde Wesendonk,* 285. In this letter to Mathilde from Paris in August 1860, the composer wrote: "Nur die tiefsinnige Annahme der Seelenwanderung konnte mir den trostreichen Punkt zeigen, auf welchen endlich alles zur gleichen Höhe der Erlösung zusammenläuft . . . Nach der schönen buddhistischen Annahme wird die fleckenlose Reinheit des Lohengrin einfach daraus erklärlich, dass er die Fortsetzung Parsifals—der die Reinheit sich erst erkämpfte—ist. Ebenso würde Elsa in ihrer Wiedergeburt bis zu Lohengrin hinanreichen. Somit erschien mir der Plan zu meinen 'Siegern' als die abschliessende Fortsetzung von 'Lohengrin.' Hier erreicht 'Sawitri' (Elsa) den 'Ananda' vollständig."

84. Wagner, *Sämtliche Schriften und Dichtungen,* 10:330:

Ja, eine Verwünschte mag sie sein
hier lebt sie heut'
vielleicht erneu't,
zu büssen Schuld aus früher'm Leben,
die dorten ihr noch nicht vergeben.

85. Ibid., 10:345–46: "Herauf! Hieher! zu mir! Dein Meister ruft dich Namenlose: Urteufelin! Höllenrose! Herodias war'st du, und was noch? Gundryggia dort, Kundry hier: Hieher! Hieher denn, Kundry! Zu deinem Meister, herauf!"

86. In this regard, see also the *Prosa-Entwurf* of 1865 (Wagner, *Sämtliche Schriften,* 11:404), where we learn that Kundry lives "ein unermessliches Leben unter stets wechselnden Wiedergeburten."

87. Wagner, *Sämtliche Schriften und Dichtungen,* 10:360:

Kenntest du den Fluch,
der mich durch Schlaf und Wachen,
durch Tod und Leben,
Pein und Lachen
zu neuem Leiden neu gestrählt,
endlos durch das Dasein quält?

See also 10:345–46: ". . . seit Ewigkeiten—harre ich deiner, des Heilands, ach! so spät, den einst ich kühn verschmaht, Oh!" Cited in Suneson, *Richard Wagner,* 107, where Suneson draws the parallel between Prakriti and Kundry.

88. Ibid., 10:361. This parallel is suggested by Suneson, *Richard Wagner*, 107.

89. Wagner was well aware of the *bodhisattva* ideal. In a letter to Liszt (Wagner and Lizst, *Briefwechsel zwischen Wagner und Liszt,* 2:83), he wrote: "Ein solcher Heiliger war jener Buddha; nach seiner Lehre von der Seelenwanderung wird jeder Lebende in der Gestalt desjenigen Wesens wiedergeboren, dem der, auch bei sonst reinstem Lebenswandel irgend einen Schmerz zufügte, damit er selbst diesen Schmerz kennen lerne, und nicht eher hört diese leidenvolle Wanderung für ihn auf, nicht eher wird er somit nicht wiedergeboren, als bis er nach einer Wiedergeburt in einem Lebenslaufe keinem Wesen ein Leid mehr zufügte, sondern im Mitgefühl mit ihnen sich, seinen eigenen Lebenswillen, vollkommen verneinte." Suneson (*Richard Wagner,* 108) draws this analogy.

90. Wagner, *Sämtliche Schriften und Dichtungen,* 10:369:

Und ich—ich bin's,
der all' diess Elend schuf!
Ha! Welcher Sünden,
welcher Frevel Schuld
muss dieses Toren-Haupt
seit Ewigkeit belasten.

91. Ibid., 10:361:

Auch dir bin ich zum Heil gesandt,
bleib'st du dem Sehnen abgewandt.
Die Labung, die dein Leiden endet,

beut nicht der Quell aus dem es fliesst:
das Heil wird nimmer dir gespendet,
Wenn jener Quell sich dir nicht schliesst.

92. Wagner, *An Mathilde Wesendonk,* 110: "Mein Kind, wohl hatte der herrliche Buddha recht, als er streng die Kunst ausschloss. Wer fühlt es deutlicher als ich, dass diese unselige Kunst es ist, die mich ewig der Qual des Lebens und allen Widersprüchen des Daseins zurückgibt? Wäre diese wunderbare Gabe, dieses so starke Vorherrschen der bildnerischen Phantasie nicht in mir, so könnte ich der hellen Erkenntnis nach, dem Drange des Herzens folgend—Heiliger werden . . . Dann wären wir frei: Ananda und Sawitri!—Aber so ist's nicht. Denn sieh'! auch dies, dieses Wissen, diese deutliche Einsicht—Sie macht mich nur immer wieder zum Dichter, zum Künstler. Sie steht, im Augenblicke da ich sie gewinne, als Bild vor mir . . . ich muss es . . . aufzeichnen, es ausführen, als eine eigene Schöpfung es beleben."

93. Wagner, *Sämtliche Schriften und Dichtungen,* 1:148: "Das, was die Musik, ausspricht, ist ewig, unendlich und ideal; sie spricht nicht Leidenschaft, die Liebe, die Sehnsucht dieses oder jenes Individuums in dieser oder jener Lage aus, sondern die Leidenschaft, die Liebe, die Sehnsucht selbst, und zwar in den unendlich mannigfaltigen Motivierungen, die in der ausschliesslichen Eigentümlichkeit der Musik begründet liegen, jeder andern Sprache aber fremd und unausdrückbar sind." Cited in Suneson, *Richard Wagner,* 51.

94. Schopenhauer, *World as Will and Representation,* 1:321, cited in Suneson, *Richard Wagner,* 52.

95. In *Die Sieger,* the woman's redemption was to act as the catalyst for the Buddha's final *nirvāṇa,* a state of transcendence that Wagner hoped to express primarily in the musical score. See Wagner, *An Mathilde Wesendonk,* 109: "Hiermit gewann ich etwas ungemein Wichtiges. Ohne allen Zwang erhält mein Plan eine grosse mächtige Erweiterung. Das Schwierige war hier, diesen vollkommen befreiten, aller Leidenschaft enthobenen Menschen, den Buddha selbst, für die dramatische und namentlich musikalische Darstellung geeignet zu machen . . ."

96. Wagner, *Mein Leben,* 542: "Ausser der tiefsinnigen Schönheit des einfachen Stoffes bestimmte mich zu seiner Wahl alsbald ein eigentümliches Verhältnis desselben zu dem in mir seitdem ausgebildeten

musikalischen Verfahren. Vor dem Geiste des Buddha liegt nämlich das vergangene Leben in früheren Geburten jedes ihm begegnenden Wesens offen, wie die Gegenwart selbst, da. Die einfache Geschichte erhielt nun ihre Bedeutung dadurch, dass dieses vergangene Leben der leidenden Hauptfiguren als unmittelbare Gegenwart in die neue Lebensphase hineinspielte. Wie nur der stets gegenwärtig miterklingenden musikalischen Reminiszenz dieses Doppellebens vollkommen dem Gefühle vorzuführen möglich werden durfte, erkannte ich sogleich, und dies bestimmte mich, die Aufgabe der Ausführung dieser Dichtung mit besonderer Liebe mir vorzubehalten." Cited in Suneson, *Richard Wagner,* 52.

97. C. Wagner, *Die Tagebücher,* 1:226: "Nur die Musik vermag das wiederzugeben, das Geheimnis der Wiedergeburten." Cited in Suneson, *Richard Wagner,* 52.

98. R. Wagner, *The Diary of Richard Wagner 1854–1882: The Brown Book,* annot. Joachim Bergfeld, trans. Georg Bird (Cambridge: Cambridge University Press, 1980), 148. For an analysis of this schema, see Suneson, *Richard Wagner,* 53.

99. Nietzsche counted several noted Indologists among his friends. In fact, he first encountered Wagner in the house of H. Brockhaus. This historic meeting had been arranged by another Indologist who had studied with Nietzshe at Schulpforta, E. Windisch. Nietzsche, furthermore, maintained a long friendship with the translator of the *Vedānta Sūtras,* Paul Deussen.

100. Most of Nietzsche's information concerning Buddhism came from Deussen and Windisch. Mistry (*Nietzsche and Buddhism,* 16) notes that Nietzsche's library contained the following books on Indian philosophy: Deussen's *Die Elemente der Metaphysik* (Aachen, 1877), *Das System des Vedānta* (Leipzig, 1883), *Die Sūtras des Vedānta aus dem Sanskrit übersetzt* (Leipzig, 1887); O. Böhtlingk's, *Indische Sprüche* (Saint Petersburg, 1870/73); Max Müller's *Essays* (Leipzig, 1869); Jakob Wackernagel's *Über den Ursprung des Brahmanismus* (Basel, 1877); and Hermann Oldenberg's *Buddha, Sein Leben, seine Lehre, seine Gemeinde* (Berlin, 1881). Lou Andreas Salomé maintained that Deussen's *Das System des Vedānta* was one of the last scholarly works that Nietzsche studied thoroughly. See L. Andreas-Salomé, *Friedrich Nietzsche in seinen Werken* (Vienna: C. Konegan, 1911), 242.

101. Friedrich Nietzsche, *Joyful Wisdom,* § 99.

102. Friedrich Nietzsche, *Sämtliche Werke,* Grossoktav ed., 2d ed., 19 vols. (Leipzig: A. Körner, 1901–03), Nachschrift 1.

103. Nietzsche, *The Genealogy of Morals,* sec. 3.3. This is not to say that he did not think that music could aspire to the state of *nirvāṇa*. Von Bülow wrote a composition entitled "Nirvana." Nietzsche called it "terrible" and contrasted von Bülow with Liszt, who, he says, captured in some church compositions "the character of that Indian nirvana excellently . . . above all in his 'Bliss beati sunt que.' " See also the letters of 24 November and 1 December 1875 to Gersdorff. Cited Mistry, 182.

104. Nietzsche, *The Will to Power,* § 580.

105. Nietzsche, *The Birth of Tragedy,* § 3.

106. Nietzsche, *Schopenhauer as Educator,* § 3.

107. Ibid., § 5. In *The Genealogy of Morals,* § 3.17, Nietzsche wrote: "The Buddhist considers both good and evil to be fetters: the Awakened one must master both. The Vedantist, likewise, confirms of the sage that what is done and undone do not hurt him; he shakes off from him what is good and evil . . . his kingdom suffers no longer from any act; he goes beyond good and evil."

108. Nietzsche, *The Will to Power,* § 458. I have relied on Walter Kaufmann's translation.

109. Ibid., § 155.

110. Nietzsche, *Kritische Gesamtausgabe,* edited by G. Colli and M. Montinari (Berlin: De Gruyter, 1967ff), 7,1; 7 (42), 264.

111. Nietzsche, *The Antichrist,* § 22; *Joyful Wisdom,* § 134.

112. Nietzsche, *The Geneology of Morals,* § 3.17.

113. Paul Deussen, *Das System des Vedānta* (Leipzig: F. A. Brockhaus, 1883), chaps. 12, 27, 31, 35, esp. §§ 2–4.

114. Nietzsche's letter to Deussen dated August 1886 in Deussen's *Erinnerungen an Friedrich Nietzsche* (Leipzig: F. A. Brockhaus, 1901), 91. See also Nietzsche, *The Antichrist,* § 32.

115. Nietzsche, *Joyful Wisdom,* § 285.

116. Nietzsche, *Zarathustra,* § 2.2: "Upon the Blessed Isles."

117. Nietzsche *The Will to Power,* §§ 852–53.

118. Nietzsche, *Beyond Good and Evil,* § 56; I have relied on Walter Kaufmann's translation; see also *The Will to Power,* § 91.

119. Nietzsche, *The Antichrist,* §§ 20, 22; *Dawn,* § 136. Thankfully, in contrast to Christianity, Buddhism did not seek to construct concepts such as sin, God, or devil to explain earthly torment.

120. Köppen, *Die Religion des Buddha,* 476, cited Mistry, 113–14.

121. Ibid., 478–80: "The ethics of the Buddha is negative; it is, as has frequently been emphasized, a morality of renunciation and self-abnegation, not a striving and creating; it teaches suffering and endurance, not action and work . . . it can . . . only relax and exhaust, lame and weaken in the final instance. In particular—and this is perhaps its worst aspect—it is politically enslaving . . . Furthermore, it is also essentially negative because it is otherworldly and transcendent and because the real world, the earth with what it bears, is of no value to it."

122. Oldenberg, *Buddha. Sein Leben, seine Lehre, seine Gemeinde* (Berlin: W. Hertz, 1881), 233, 235. For a realistic view of the role of pain in Buddhism, see T. Stcherbatsky's *The Conception of Buddhist Nirvāṇa* (The Hague: Mouton, 1965), 55–56. Of the 121 classes of consciousness, 63 are associated with joy, 3 with pain, and 55 with indifference.

123. Nietzsche, *The Will to Power,* § 366. Nietzsche viewed "Buddhist pity" as the most characteristic aspect of Schopenhauer's philosophy.

124. Nietzsche, *The Genealogy of Morals,* preface, § 5: "The beginning of the end, the most sinister symptom of our modern European civilization . . . The route along which that civilization slid on its way to a new Buddhism?—to a European species of Buddhism?—to Nihilism?"

125. Nietzsche, *The Antichrist,* § 7. R. J. Hollingdale's translation.

126. Schopenhauer, *World as Will and Representation,* 1:68.

127. Nietzsche, *The Birth of Tragedy,* §§ 9, 25; *The Will to Power,* § 853 (ii).

128. Nietzsche, *The Birth of Tragedy,* § 21.

129. Nietzsche, *Thus spoke Zarathustra,* "The Drunken Song," § 4.19.12: "Deep is the pain (of the world)/Joy, deeper still that joy of the heart/Pain says 'Die off'/But all joy wants eternity."

130. Nietzsche, *The Will to Power,* § 853 (i–iv).

131. Köppen, *Die Religion des Buddha,* 306: "Nirvana is . . . first and foremost the total extinction of the soul, the extinction in nothingness, plain destruction, or according to the . . . theory of metempsychosis, the final, definitive extinction of the sequence of succession of souls . . . Nirvana is the blessed Nothingness; Buddhism is the gospel of annihilation." See also p. 216: "All ragamuffins . . . are brothers, for misery makes soft and equal. So also the Buddhist nothingness, emptiness, insubstantiality, which is the essence of all things."

132. Ibid., 56, 481, cited Mistry, 180.

133. Oldenberg, *Buddha,* 238–39: "Nirvana is incumbant upon joyful striving: 'He strives towards nirvana with the same joy of victory with which the Christian envisions his aim, the eternal life.' "

134. Nietzsche, *The Antichrist,* § 18.

135. Ibid., § 7.

136. Nietzsche, *The Geneology of Morals,* § 2.21. Walter Kaufmann's translation.

137. Nietzsche, *Joyful Wisdom,* preface to 2d edition.

138. Nietzsche, *Kritische Gesamtausgabe,* 7,1; 21 (6), 637.

139. Walter Kaufmann, *Nietzsche: Philosopher, Psychologist, Antichrist,* 3d ed. (Princeton: Princeton University Press, 1968), 277.

140. Ibid., 179.

141. Köppen, *Die Religion des Buddha,* 479: "The ethic of the Buddha . . . a morality of renunciation and self-abnegation, not of striving and creating; it teaches suffering and endurance, not action and work." Oldenberg (*Buddha,* 309–10) separates the creative man from the monk: "The true saintly life [in Buddhism] is the life of the monk; the worldly life is imperfect, necessarily dissatisfying one. The basic requirement for the monk is not—to live in this world and create it in such a way that it is worthy of living—but, rather to detach himself from this world."

142. Carl Bleibtreu, *Der Heilskönig* (Berlin and Leipzig: Fr. Lienhardt, 1903), 125: "Aber was heisst Euch Vaterland? Euer eigner Vorteil! Darum habt Ihr Euch den König gesetzt zum Götzen, in ihm betet Ihr Euch selber an, Euer Vorrecht und Vorurteil. Der angestammte Herr vor dem Ihr Knie beugt, ist Euer eigne angestammte Kaste. Ich aber sage Euch: Das wahre Land und Reich, das ist das Volk. Das Volk, von dem Ich selber nur ein Teil, so wie auch Ich, der König."

143. *Die Kritik,* 15 October 1898, 47.

144. *Bhagavad Gita—Der Gesang der Erhabenen,* trans. Theodor Springmann (Hamburg: n.p., 1920), 15.

145. Ibid., 9.

146. Ibid., 11.

147. Ibid., 12.

Chapter 6. Néantisme

1. Giuseppe Tomasi di Lampedusa, *Opera: II gattopardo* (Milan: Feltrinelli, 1958), 284–5: "La nostra sensualità è desiderio di oblio, le schioppettate e le coltellate nostre, desiderio di morte, desiderio di immobilità voluttuosa, cioè ancora di morte, la nostra pigrizia, i nostri sorbetti di scorsonera o di cannella; il nostro aspetto meditativo è quello del nulla che volesse scrutare . . . gli enigmi del nirvana . . . le novità ci attraggono soltanto quando sono defunte, incapaci di dar luogo ai correnti vitali; da ciò l'incredibile fenomeno della formazione attuale di miti che sarebbero venerabili se fossero antichi sul serio, ma che non sono al-

tro che sinistri tentativi di rituffarsi in un passato che ci attrae soltanto perché è morto."

2. Silvestre de Sacy, "Discours sur l'utilité de la langue arabe," in *Journal asiatique* (8 June 1826): 1826: 321–40.

3. Gautier, *L'Orient,* 1:3. See also his *Fortunio* (1849) and *Caprices et zigzags* (1845).

4. For example, the following description of the ascetic in T. Gautier, *La partie carrée* (Paris: E. Tasquelle, 1857), 193: "Je me suis voué, pendant trente ans, aux plus effroyables austérités . . . J'ai voulu détruire cette chair infirme pour que l'âme dégagée pût remonter à la source des choses et lire dans la pensée des dieux . . . la pluie a fait ruisseler ses torrents glacés et le soleil ses torrents de feu sur mon corps immobile dans la position la plus gênante. Mes ongles ont, en poussant, persé mes mains fermées . . . hideux, souillé de poussière . . . des termites bâtissaient leur cité à côté de moi; les oiseaux du ciel faisaient leur nid dans mes cheveux hérissés en brousaille."

5. Gautier, *Caprices et zigzags,* 260: "L'art y (en Inde) vaut encore plus que la matière, le goût le plus pur, le plus fin, le plus inventif. Nos langues du Nord sont trop froides, trop pauvres, trop mesquines pour décrire toutes les somptuosités."

6. Gautier sets other works in India, such as *Avatar* (1854) and the ballet *Sacountala* (1858).

7. Gautier, *Egypte et Nubie,* préface: "L'inquiétude qui nous dévore depuis un siècle nous pousse, malgré nous souvent, à la recherche des vérités éparses parmi les peuples qui couvrent la terre. En face de chaque civilisation éteinte ou vivace nous nous arrêtons; nous interrogeons ses morales, ses religions, ses traditions, ses efforts . . . puis nous reprenons notre course, contents d'emporter au-dedans de nous-mêmes un peu de cette Vérité vers laquelle nous tendons sans cesse . . . mais Elle dort dans son puits, la grande Déesse, en attendant que les temps soient révolus, et nous ne la saisissons jamais et nous rentrons tristes, découragés."

8. Paul Bourget, *Essais de psychologie contemporaine* (Paris: Plon, 1899), 6.

9. Charles Baudelaire, *Oeuvres complètes,* ed. Claude Pichois (Paris: Bibliothèque de la Pléiade, 1973), 2:140, 201.

10. See also the poem "Squellette laboureur," where Baudelaire writes: "Qu'envers nous le Néant est traître."

11. I have coined the term *néantisme* to delimit the larger thematic cluster of exotic pessimism dealing with issues of ethical retribution (*karma*), the illusory nature of the world (*māyā*), and the destruction of individual consciousness (*nirvāṇa*).

12. In reference to the "Oriental" Île de la Réunion, Baudelaire spoke of: "le monde stupéfié [qui] s'affaisse lâchement et fait la sieste, une sieste qui est une espèce de mort savoureuse où le dormeur, à demi éveillé, goûte les voluptés de son anéantissement."

13. François Bernier, "Mémoire sur le quiétisme des Indes," in *Histoire des savants,* 1688. Bernier's article was the source material for Leibniz's *Discours de la conformité de la foi avec la raison,* § 10, "Quiétisme de Foë" in the *Essais de théodicée* (1710).

14. Under the rubric "Brachmanes," note K

15. Denis Diderot, *Encyclopédie,* under the rubric "Indiens, philosophie des." Diderot notes: "Ils assurent que le monde n'est qu'une illusion, un songe, un prestige, et que les corps pour exister véritablement doivent cesser d'être en eux-mêmes, et se confondre avec le néant qui par sa simplicité fait la perfection de tous les êtres. Ils font consister la saintété à ne rien vouloir à ne rien penser à ne rien sentir . . . Cet état ressemble si fort au sommeil, qu'il paraît que quelques grains d'opium sanctifieraient un brahme bien plus sûrement ques tous ses efforts."

16. Abbé Jean Baptiste Gabriel Alexandre Grosier, *Description générale de la Chine,* 7 vols. (Paris: Pillet, 1818–20), 2:202–30.

17. Eugène Burnouf, *Le lotus de la bonne loi, traduit du sanskrit, accompagné d'un commentaire et de vingt et un mémoires rélatifs au bouddhisme* (Paris: Imprimerie Nationale, 1852).

18. Antoine Fréderic Ozanam, *Mélanges,* in *Oeuvres complètes,* 11 vols. (Paris: J. Lecoffre, 1859), 8:219–51 ("Essais sur le bouddhisme").

19. Edgar Quinet, *Le génie des religions,* in *Oeuvres complètes,* 11 vols. (Paris: Pagnerre, 1857), 1:209: "Si la société indienne a vécu, c'est qu'elle a eu la conscience profonde de l'Être, même après avoir traversé le scepticisme. Mais cette idée, toute grande qu'elle est ne suffit pas à l'homme. Individualité, morale, conscience, où les trouvons-nous? Ce n'est pas dans le génie indien, puisque selon le brahmanisme comme selon le bouddhisme, l'inaction, le sommeil éternel au sein de l'éternelle substance, voilà le bien, la porte de salut! Il faut que le monde échappe à ce prodigieux enchantement."

20. Henri de Lubac, *Le rencontre du bouddhisme et de l'occident* (Paris: Aubier, 1952), 154.

21. Hippolyte Adolphe Taine, *Nouveaux essais de critique et d'histoire* (Paris: Hachette, 1884), 376–77. He bases his judgments of Buddhism on the Buddha's image, about which he sees nothing virile: "C'est un corps amolli, gras, dont la poitrine et le ventre ressemblent à ceux d'une femme, avec une expression de repos inerte et d'indifférence bienveillante qui va jusqu'au demi-sourire terne."

22. Charles Renouvier, *Science de la morale* (Paris: Ladrange, 1869), 324.

23. André Lefèvre, *Essais de critique générale: Religions et mythologies comparées,* 2d ed. (Paris: n.p., 1878), 271–90.

24. Joseph Ernest Renan, *Nouvelles études d'histoire religieuse* (Paris: Calmann Lévy, 1874), préface: "Il n'est pas possible qu'il y ait des gens aussi bêtes que ça . . ."

25. Joseph Ernest Renan, *Dialogues et fragments philosophiques* (Paris: Calmann Lévy, 1876), 52: "Je vois clairement avec Schopenhauer qu'il y a un grand égoïste qui nous trompe, mais à la différence de Schopenhauer, je me résigne. J'accepte, je me soumets aux fins de l'Être Suprême. La morale se réduit ainsi à la soumission. L'immortalité, c'est la révolte contre un état de choses dont on voit la duperie."

26. He rejected *nirvāṇa* as "a monstrous conception which is repugnant to all the instincts of human nature" and "revolts reason." See Jules Barthélemy Saint-Hilaire, *Le Bouddha et sa religion* (Paris: Didier, 1862), 177.

27. Jules Barthélemy Saint-Hilaire, *Du Bouddhisme* (Paris: B. Duprat, 1855), vii: "Espérance du néant, devenue une religion . . . l'adoration du néant."

28. In a letter to Mme. Amiel (31 December 1873), Sully-Prudhomme noted: "Sans même faire appel aux succession et aux prolongements vertigineux de la vie sidérale, mais en contemplant seulement le fourmillement lointain de l'histoire humaine, j'arrive à un état qui doit être celui des rêveurs indiens. Je me compte alors pour rien . . . Quand je me prends au sérieux, c'est que je m'oublie." See René-François-Armand Sully-Prudhomme, *Journal intime* (Paris: Lemerre, 1922).

29. Henri Frédéric Amiel, *Fragments du journal intime* (Paris: n.p., 1882), 3 June 1870: "C'est que la vie individuelle est un néant qui s'ignore."

30. He notes that his instinct is "in harmony with the pessimism of Buddha and Schopenhauer"; he is "encompassed and overshadowed" by the "black melancholy of Buddhism." See *Amiel's Journal,* trans. Mrs. Humphry Ward (New York: Macmillan, 1928), 34, 216, 218, 385.

31. Ibid., 80, 95, 301–2.

32. Amiel, *Fragments du journal intime,* 18 March 1869: "De regret en désenchantement, j'ai dérivé jusqu'au Bouddhisme, jusqu'à la lassitude universelle."

33. Louis Ménard, "Prométhée delivré," "Nirvana," "La sirène," "Le rishi." Ménard was also the author of *Histoire des anciens peuples de l'orient* and the *Rêveries d'un païen mystique.*

34. Ménard, "Nirvana":

L'universel désir guette comme une proie
Le troupeau des vivants, tous viennent tour à tour
À la flamme brûler leurs ailes, comme autour
D'une lampe, l'essaim des phalènes tournoie.

35. Ibid.:

Néant divin, je suis plein du dégoût des choses;
Las de l'illusion et des métempsychoses,
J'implore ton sommeil sans rêve, absorbe-moi,

Lieu des trois mondes, source et fin des existences,
Seul vrai, seul immobile au sein des apparences,
Tout est dans toi, tout sort de toi, tout rentre en toi.

36. Ibid.:

Heureux qui, sans regrets, sans espoir, sans amour,
Tranquille et connaissant le fond de toute joie,
Marche en paix dans la droite et véritable voie,
Dédaigneux de la vie et des plaisirs d'un jour.

37. Laforgue writes: "Vie on Néant! Choisir." One must avoid the false perception of reality ("Mais, fausse soeur, fausse humaine, fausse mortelle, / Nous t'écartèlerons des hontes sensuelles"). See also his *Mélanges posthumes, pensées et paradoxes* (Paris: Mercure de France, 1903), 14–15: "En fait de religion, de vie organisée, systématique, il n'y a de choix qu'entre deux: ou bien vous voulez le néant, la voie est toute tracée—nirvana—opium de la marmotte—suicide, Platon Karataieff. Si votre religion est la vie, elle doit avant tout prendre son centre, sa clef, sa lumière dans ce qui est l'essence de la vie, de sa continuation, etc., l'amour des sexes. Aimez et laissez faire le reste . . . La création humaine a beau se montrer le cou, elle est organisée pour le bonheur, d'autres disent l'Illusion.

Quoi qu'il en soit,
O Maïa
Tout est pour toi
Alléluia."

38. Jules Laforgue, "La lune est stérile":

Mais l'être impur paraît! ce frêle révolté
De la sainte Maïa déchire les beaux voiles
Et le sanglot des temps jaillit vers les étoiles . . .
Mais dors, c'est bien fini, dors pour l'éternité.

39. Alfred de Vigny, *Journal inédit,* cited in Georges Bonnefoy, *La pensée religieuse et morale d'Alfred de Vigny* (Paris: Hachette, 1944), 316: "L'absorption est le système entier de la nature pour les Indiens."

40. Alfred de Vigny, *Journal inédit,* cited in Vera Summer, *L'orientalisme d'Alfred de Vigny* (Paris: Honoré Champion, 1930), 185: "Ne crains point l'absorption indienne. Ton âme perfectionnée ne saurait périr, ne saurait être privée de ce qu'elle a conquis de vertu et de savoir."

41. Christians, he maintained, were selfish in cultivating hopes for the resurrection of man's "vilain petit corps." He reproached Christianity for its egotism and praised Buddhism for its disinterest. Alfred de Vigny, *Journal,* ed. F. Baldensperger (London: Scholartis, 1928), 144 (29 August 1859): "La perfection du Bouddha est plus belle que celle du Christianisme, parce qu'elle est plus désintéressé . . . [le Bouddha] enseignait l'espoir seulement d'arriver par la vertu et la science à mériter l'anéantissement, le Nirvana."

42. Vigny, *Journal inédit* (19 June 1859), cited in Summer, *Vigny,* 188. In this regard, he was very much influenced by Barthélemy Saint-Hilaire, his *confrère* at the Institute. In fact, Vigny's understanding of Buddhist doctrine is often a mere paraphrase of that of Barthélemy Saint-Hilaire whom he found to be more interesting than Burnouf and more polemical against Buddhism. See Barthélemy Saint-Hilaire, *Le Bouddha et sa religion,* 158. Vigny rejected, however, Barthélemy Saint-Hilaire's interpretation of *nirvāṇa* as expressed in *Le Bouddha et sa religion* 177: "Le Nirvana, ou le néant, est une conception monstrueuse qui répugne à tous les instincts de la nature humaine, qui révolte la raison, et qui implique l'athéisme." In the *Journal inédit* (19 June 1859), cited in Summer, *Vigny,* 188, Vigny writes: "La vie n'est qu'un long tissu de douleurs et de misères. Le salut consiste à n'y jamais rentrer. Chaque être à vécu des multitudes de vies avant son existence, il faut qu'il s'applique par la science à se perfectionner afin de mériter le néant."

43. Alfred de Vigny, *Daphné,* appendix in *Oeuvres posthumes,* ed. Fernand Gregh (Paris: Delagrave, 1913), 228–29.

44. Vigny, *Journal,* 258.

45. Vigny, *Journal inédit* (29 August 1959), cited in Summer, *Vigny,* 189.

46. Ibid. (4 March 1863): "Ne parle jamais, n'écris jamais sur Dieu. La divinité une ou triple est inconnue, invisible et muette." In this regard, the final quatrain of "Le Mont des Oliviers" is particularly instructive: "Le silence de Dieu. Faites comme Bouddah [*sic*], silence sur celui qui ne parle jamais;" see *Les destinées*, cited in Edmond Estève, *Alfred de Vigny: Les destinées, poèmes philosophiques* (Paris: Hachette, 1924), 125.

47. Vigny, *Journal inédit*, cited in Summer, *Vigny*, 193: "Bouddha lui seul n'a point parlé des récompenses célestes . . . Il console l'Orient en détruisant l'idée d'une éternelle métempsychose et des incarnations successives de Brahma et il dit: Soyez charitables, donnez tout et vous aurez enfin le repos dans le Nirvana. Est-ce l'union à Dieu ou le néant? Là est la question."

48. Ibid. (September 1859), 190: "Toute la doctrine de Brahma est là . . . Elle pense sans fin et cherche à se dégager de l'action du mal et du bien pour arriver pour la contemplation à la splendeur divine en remplissant tous les devoirs de l'inaction."

49. Vigny, *Journal inédit* (20 February 1861), in a note for the *Daphné* dossier, cited in Bonnefoy, *Vigny*, 394. Vigny reproaches Brahmanism for its renunciation of actions and works; that is why Julian ultimately turns to Christ.

50. Vigny, *Journal inédit,* cited in Summer, *Vigny,* 194.

51. Henri Cazalis, a physician by profession, took the *nom de plume,* "Jean Lahor."

52. Henri Cazalis [pseud. Jean Lahor], *La gloire du néant* (Paris: Lemerre, 1896), 131: "Sachez que cet enfant, longtemps même avant sa conception, vous le portez en vous et qu'il devra hériter de vos vertus comme aussi de vos folies et de vos vices. C'est l'idée du bouddhisme." See also pp. 201, 203. The combination of Buddhist and Darwinian influences inform a number of Lahor's poems, such as "Jeux d'atomes," "Le tourbillon," "La pitié du Bouddha," "Le sage," "La mort du soleil," and "Réminiscences."

53. See specifically, *La gloire du néant,* 137. Lahor adapted Indian philosophy to contemporary scientific notions such as the monism

taught by Häckel and Büchner of the German Materialist School. In monism, Lahor discovered the scientific confirmation of Buddhist metaphysics and drew analogies between the scientific pessimism of Darwin and the Buddhist idea of individual irreality.

54. Jean Lahor, "Réminiscences":

Et que j'ai transmigré dans des formes sans nombre,
Et que mon âme était, sous tous ces corps divers,
La conscience et l'âme aussi, splendide ou sombre
Qui rêve et se tourmente au fond de l'univers!

Lahor's pantheistic vision is most clearly seen in "Karman," "Matinée de printemps," "Timour," "Étoile lointaine," "Atavisme," "Crimes d'amour."

55. "Enterrement d'une marionnette," "Quatrains d'Al Ghazali," "La méditation du Bouddha," "Le nuage," "Sur la plage," "Nox," "Le silence des morts," "Le couvercle du mort," "Nada," "Entre deux gouffres," "L'éveil en songe," "Entre deux néants," "Le cap nord," "L'ineffable baiser," "Théâtre des marionnettes," "Le sphinx," "Requium aeternam," "Jour des morts," "Notre Dame de la mort," and "Le génie du repos éternel."

56. Lahor asserts that *māyā* is found not only in Hinduism and Buddhism, but in Sufism and Islam. See "Le muezzin," "Allah parle au poète," "L'epervier d'Allah," "Les trésors d'Allah," and "La caravane du monde."

57. Jean Lahor, *La gloire du néant,* 177:

Maya, déesse de l'illusion, je reviens à ton culte oublié et je voudrais, mère des choses que ce livre, moins obscurément, reflétât ton visage. Oui, tout est destiné à périr, tout n'est qu'apparences et visions. Je suis un rêve échappé de tes rêves, un fantôme parmi les fantômes. J'ai tremblé, d'abord, voyant le néant qui était en moi et dans les pensées et les oeuvres des hommes. Je rêve tranquille aujourd'hui, ne te demandant plus que de radieux mensonges, des illusions nouvelles de beauté, d'amour et de foi.

58. Jean Lahor, "Brahma":

Je suis la large et vague et profonde substance
Ces mondes infinis que mon rêve a fait naître
Néant qui prend pour nous l'apparence de l'être
Sont lueur passagère et vision qui fuit,
Les fulgurations dont s'éclaire ma nuit.

"Allah parle au poète":

Quand tu redescendras, o poète inspiré
Chante mes passions et mon néant sacré . . .
L'illusoire splendeur de l'éternel néant.

"La passion de Śiva":

J'étais au temps passé, l'âme de l'univers,
J'étais le jour, j'étais la nuit, j'étais l'aurore,
J'étais le printemps clair, les étés, les hivers
L'immense vie ardente, et l'amour qui dévore.

See also "À Śiva" and "L'éternité de Śiva," both inspired by E. Lamairesse's *Chansons populaires du sud de l'Inde* (Paris: Lacroix, 1869).

59. "Brahma" and "Identité."

60. Jean Lahor, *La gloire du néant,* 241.

61. It was crowned by the Academy in 1892. Added to the definitive edition of *La gloire du néant,* this poem marked the end of Lahor's poetic creation.

62. Hindu mythology has it that Kāma interrupted Śiva's penitence and was incinerated by his anger.

63. Jean Lahor, "L'enchantement de Śiva":

Te violà donc, objet des délices du monde!
L'illusion voulant me troubler t'envoya,
Fantôme cher à ceux qu'égare la Maya.

64. Ibid.:

O Nature, dont luit splendide la surface,
Aux yeux que j'ai fermé tout ton néant s'efface.
Danseuse aux voiles d'or, dont le corps radieux
Tourbillonne devant les hommes et les Dieux,
Et dont la vanité dans la leur se reflète,
Sous tes gloires je vois se dresser ton squelette . . .
Mais ta vraie et durable image, la voilà,
Néant que le Désir à mon esprit voila!

65. Ibid.:

Et gisant sous ses pieds, au lieu de cette femme,
Coulait et s'étalait, infect et repoussant
Tout un putride amas de chair, d'os et de sang.

66. Noteworthy in this regard are the descriptions found in Dumas's *La dame aux camélias,* Zola's *Nana,* and Baudelaire's "Le charogne," to cite a few examples. For a recent study of sexual images of decay in French literature and art, see Bernheimer, *Figures of Ill-Repute.*

67. Such realism is true to its Buddhist inspiration. Indeed, in the *Lalita Vistara* (*Développement des jeux—contenant l'histoire de Bouddha Çakya Mouni depuis sa naissance jusqu'à sa prédication,* ed. and trans. Ph. Ed. Foucaux [Paris: E. Leroux, 1884–92], chaps. 15, 103, 104), the Buddha denounces the illusion of female beauty: "Produit du champ des oeuvres, né de l'eau du désir, donnant l'idée d'un amas de ruines, déformés par les larmes, la transpiration, l'humidité, l'urine, et plein de gouttes de sang, rempli des ordures du ventre, de moelle, de sang et des liquides du cerveau et laissant toujours couler des impuretés, tout rempli de choses impures et de mauvaises odeurs diverses, déformé par les eaux, les dents, les cheveux et les poils des pores."

68. See also Jean Lahor, "À Kali."

69. Jean Lahor, "L'enchantement de Śiva":

Quand pour eux Prakriti se dresse sous ses voiles . . .
Ils voient, à la clarté d'un éternel printemps
Dans leur rêve fleurir l'illusion des choses.

70. Jean Lahor, *Revue bleue,* 25 February 1893: "Ce néant, que je trouvais en moi, je le trouvais, en toute vie, et du Néant de toutes ses parties je concluais au néant de Tout, et ainsi au néant de ce Dieu, de cet Infini, dont nous sommes l'image."

71. Jean Lahor, "Le sage":

Il savait qu'eux aussi les Dieux devaient périr,
Que tous étaient encore plus que nous ne sommes,
Et qu'un mot suffirait pour faire évanouir
Ces fantômes crées par le songe des hommes.

72. Stéphane Mallarmé, *Correspondence 1862–71,* ed. Henri Mondor (Paris: Gallimard, 1959), 207:

Tu sais que tes idées sur le néant sont fort belles,
mais qu'elles sont comme certaines femmes fort belles
qui sont plus bêtes que leurs pieds.

73. See Jean Biès, *Littérature française et pensée hindoue, des origines à 1950* (1974); Jean-Marie Carré, *Voyageurs et écrivains français en Egypt* (1932); Marie-Louise Dufrenoy, *L'Orient romanesque en France* (1947); Hassan El'Nouty, *Le Proche Orient dans la littérature française de Nerval à Barres* (1958); Wilhelm Halbfass, *India and Europe* (1988); Pierre Jourda, *L'exotisme dans la littérature française depuis Chateaubriand* (1938); Rana Kabbani, *Europe's Myths of the Orient* (1986); Pierre Martino, *L'Orient dans la littérature française au XVIIe siècle* (1906); Edward Said, *Orientalism* (1978); Raymond Schwab, *La renaissance orientale* (1950).

74. The Indian poems, equal in number to the Scandinavian poems, are only outnumbered by the Greek collection. However, the poet's sympathy with Hindu doctrines remained with him throughout his entire life, beginning in 1852 and ending with his death, surviving his Scandinavian and Greek periods.

75. Jean Dornis dismissed Leconte de Lisle's Indian poems as comprising a stage by which the poet sought to escape God and Beauty. See Jean Dornis [Mme. Guillaume Beer], *Essai sur Leconte de Lisle* (Paris: P. Ollendorff, 1909), 308. Similar judgments were voiced by Jules Lemaître (*Les contemporains,* 2d series [Paris: Boivin, 1897], 27), and René Canat

(*Une forme de mal de siècle, du sentiment de la solitude morale chez les romantiques et les parnassiens* [Paris: Hachette, 1904], 252). Leconte de Lisle's colleagues themselves were skeptical of his involvement with Indian thought. Alphonse Daudet termed his Hindu venture a "mystification" to amuse the imagination rather than conviction. (Daudet, *Le petit chose: Histoire d'un enfant* [Paris: Charpentier, 1913], 223–24).

76. Leconte de Lisle wrote to Flaubert in a letter cited by Charles Clerc, *Le génie du paganisme* (Paris: Payot, 1926), 55: "Ce génie singulier, propre à notre siècle . . . reconstruit pièce à pièce les époques passées par leurs côtés puissants et idéalement vrais."

77. These can be broken down into two categories. Those dating prior to his involvement with Indian themes describe human life as transitory and the world as illusory. See "La dernière vision," "Spectres," "Secret de la vie," "Midi," and "Le dernier souvenir." Similarly, those poems written with knowledge of Hinduism, such as "Dies Irae" (1852), conclude with a vision of death as total annihilation. In "L'illusion," the poet pits the materialistic concept of life against the tragedy of death.

> Mais quand il s'en ira dans le muet mystère
> Où tout ce qui vécut demeure enseveli,
> Qui saura que ton âme a fleuri sur la terre,
> O doux rêve, promis à l'infaillible oubli.

78. Barbey d'Aurevilly recognized Leconte de Lisle's innovation in addressing and justifying his own innate pessimism by means of exotic and distorted religious dogma. See Jules Amédée Barbey d'Aurevilly, *Les oeuvres et les poètes,* pt. 3, "Les poètes" (Paris: Amyot, 1862), 227–38: "La Métaphysique indienne retient Monsieur Leconte de Lisle par son vide même, ce nihiliste naturel." He also thought that it was calculated to attract a reading public.

79. Before turning his attention toward India, Leconte de Lisle had temporarily assuaged his spiritual crisis by involvement with Fourier's thought. The doctrine of Fourier presented an ardent critique of society, a condemnation of the bourgeoisie and its dishonest business practices. Fourier believed that instincts should not be repressed (a theory common among other thinkers of the time—to wit, Louis Blanc, La Mennais, Auguste Comte, and the Saint-Simonists) but, rather, satisfied in a common

life community (*le phalanstère*). When he subsequently became disenchanted with his fellow man due to his experiences with war and the Commune, Leconte de Lisle sought consolation in the bonds of unity between human and animal established by the evolutionary theories of Darwin. French translations of the *Origin of the Species* appeared in 1862—three years after its first publication.

80. Of the poet, Baudelaire noted: "La part qu'il a faite aux religions asiatiques est énorme, et c'est là qu'il a versé à flots majestueux son dégoût naturel pour les choses transitoires, pour le badinage de la vie, et son amour infini pour l'immuable, pour l'éternel, pour le divin Néant." See Baudelaire, "Leconte de Lisle," in *L'art romantique* (Genève: Skira, 1964), 365.

81. Leconte de Lisle, *Poèmes antiques,* preface. Elsewhere, he noted that the necessary brute material for poetry was to be found in philosophy or science. See Leconte de Lisle, *Discours de réception, séance de l'Academie Française de 31 Mars. 1887* (Paris: Perrin, 1887); and Leconte de Lisle, *Poèmes antiques,* preface.

82. Prior to his reading of Burnouf, Leconte de Lisle composed the story *Princesse Yaso'da* (November 7, 1847, *Démocratie pacifique*), a sumptuous and barbarous decor piece ostensibly taken from Jayadeva.

83. He retains only the description of Narada, his mother's death, and the circumstances of his entreaty. He alters the original to the extent that, instead of the mother's death making Narada happy because it has freed her from *saṃsāra,* the French Narada offers a long and profound lamentation. Furthermore, Leconte de Lisle's Narada is discouraged by his meditation, not because, as in the original, he still has not attained God, but because he has not been able to alleviate the source of his tears and gain deliverance from his grief.

84. The characters' names were all inspired by the *Bhāgavata Purāṇa*.

85. Gladys Falshaw (*Leconte de Lisle et l'Inde* [Paris: Arthez, 1923], 94–95) maintains that these three characters represent the three sources of pain in the poet's own life, the thwarted love described in "La Manchy," his loss of faith, and his rupture with his family.

86. Leconte de Lisle, "Bhagavat":

Le principe et la fin, erreur et vérité
Abîme de Néant et de réalité.

87. The *Bhāgavata Purāṇa* sings the praises of Viṣṇu-Hari and his avataras and reminds the devotee that they do not really exist as illusions of illusions. Viṣṇu is to be adored, with the end of penetrating His nature and recognizing it to be one's own. Leconte de Lisle's poems cut across this process of salvation by ignoring the spiritual effort of purification: "Quand . . . ces formes que l'ignorance crée au sein de l'esprit ont été niées par la science, qui reconnaît ce qu'elles sont, c'est alors que l'on voit Brahman." By declaring forms to be illusory, the Hindu and Buddhist do not seek to deny their reality. In fact, an adoration of forms was admitted to have preparatory merit as the first stage of salvation (*Bhāgavata Purāṇa* 1.1.3.30, 33; Burnouf's translation, 1:25–27).

88. G. Falshaw (*Leconte de Lisle et l'Inde,* 79–115) amply documents Leconte de Lisle's specific references to material found in the *Bhāgavata Purāṇa*. In the twenty-five pages of the Sanskrit source material encapsulated by Leconte de Lisle, there is not one mention of a metaphysical void.

89. Although Leconte de Lisle makes no mention of the term *nirvāṇa,* this concept lies at the heart of much of his poetry. Catulle Mendès describes Leconte de Lisle's poetry as "un nirvana furibond." See Catulle Mendès, *Rapport à M. le Ministre de l'instruction publique et des beaux arts sur le mouvement poétique français de 1867–1900* (Paris: Imprimerie Nationale, 1902).

90. Leconte de Lisle, "La Maya":

Maya, qui dans ton sein invisible et béant
Contient l'homme et les dieux, la vie et le Néant.

91. See Leconte de Lisle, "Vision de Brahma":

Toute chose depuis fermente, vit, et s'achève;
Mais rien n'a de substance et de réalité . . .
O Brahma! Toute chose est le rêve d'un rêve.
La maya dans mon sein bouillonne en fusion

Dans son prisme changeant je vois tout apparaître
Car ma seule Inértie est la source de l'Être
La Matrice du Monde est mon Illusion.

92. Leconte de Lisle, "La Maya":

Mais qu'est-ce que le coeur des hommes éphémères:
O Maya! sinon toi, le mirage immortel.

93. The absence of an escape mechanism is most clearly seen in "La joie de Śiva," where the *néant* is personified. Deliverance necessitates the abolition of impatience, anger, hatred, and the expression of compassion. Leconte de Lisle's soteriology does violence not only to humans but also to gods. "La joie de Śiva" describes, with clear and pitiless brutality, the cosmic dissolution in the abyss (*Revue des deux mondes,* 15 October 1888). The source material for this poem relates how Śiva, the great destroyer, ranks superior to all and lasts longer than the gods and the earth. Leconte de Lisle's version presents a "marche vers le néant," with religion being the first to fall. With the destruction of the gods, humankind and nature quickly follow suit.

94. In "La paix des dieux," Leconte de Lisle wrote:

Et l'homme se souvient des heures de sa jeunesse,
Des heures de sa joie et des tourments soufferts,
Saisi d'horreur, tremblant que le passé renaisse.

95. This poem first appeared in the *Nouvelle Revue,* 1 December 1880.

96. See "Çunacepa" (1855), "Prière védique pour les morts" (1866), "Surya" (1852), and "La mort de Valmiki" (1881).

97. Vālmīki, *Rāmāyaṇa,* trans. Hippolyte Fauche, 9 vols. (Paris: A. Frank, 1854), 1:343.

98. Leconte de Lisle, "Çunacepa":

Tu vas sortir, sacré par l'expiation
Du monde obscur des sens et de la passion,
Et franchir, jeune encore, la porte de lumière
Par où tu plongeras dans l'essence première . . .

La Maya te séduit, mais si ton coeur est ferme,
Tu verras s'envoler comme un peu de vapeur
La colère, l'amour, le désir et la peur;
Et le monde illusoire aux formes innombrables
S'écroulera sous toi comme un monceau de sable.

99. *Mahābhārata,* trans. Hippolyte Fauche, 10. vols. (Paris: A. Durand & B. Duprat, 1863–70), 3:525.

100. Leconte de Lisle, "La mort de Valmiki":

Toujours, des millions [de fourmis] encore,
qui sans trêve,
Vont à l'assaut de l'homme absorbé dans son rêve,
Debout contre le trône du vieil arbre moussu,
Et qui s'anéantit dans ce qu'il a conçu,
L'esprit ne sait plus rien des sens ni de soi-même.

101. See also Leconte de Lisle, "Bhagavat."

102. Leconte de Lisle, "L'illusion suprême":

Soit! la poussière humaine, en proie au temps rapide,
Ses voluptés, ses pleurs, ses combats, ses remords,
Les Dieux qu'elle a conçus et l'univers stupide
Ne valent pas la paix impassible des morts.

103. For a discussion of the aims of art, see J. L. Masson and M. V. Patwardhan, *Aesthetic Rapture: The Rasādhyāya of the Nāṭyaśāstra,* 2 vols. (Poona: Deccan College, 1970), vol. 1, introduction.

Chapter 7. Indian Thought and the Formation of Aryan Ideology

1. Harald Arjuna Grävell van Jostenoode, "Das Ariertum und seine Feinde," *Ostara,* 25 (July 1908):4. "Aryavarta, wo alles Nähere mitgeteilt ist, wo Treue ist, Reinheit, Wahrhaftigkeit, Pflichtgefühl, Grossmut, Ehrenhaftigkeit, Ehrlichkeit—da ist Aryavarta. Wo Lug und Betrug herrscht, Untreue, Unkeuschheit; Egoismus, sich ausleben wollen, da beginnt Klingsors Reich, das Reich des Negativen."

2. Of particular use in this regard are the works of George Mosse: *The Crisis of German Ideology: Intellectual Origins of the Third Reich* (New

York: Grosset & Dunlap, 1964); *Nazi Culture: Intellectual, Cultural, and Social Life in the Third Reich* (New York: Howard Fertig, 1966); *The Nationalization of the Masses: Political Symbolism and Mass Movements in Germany from the Napoleonic Wars through the Third Reich* (New York: Howard Fertig, 1980); *Masses and Men: Nationalist and Fascist Perceptions of Reality* (New York: Howard Fertig, 1980); and *Toward a Final Solution: A History of European Racism* (New York: Harper & Row, 1978). Also important in this context are the works of Léon Poliakov: *Harvest of Hate: The Nazi Program for the Destruction of the Jews of Europe,* foreword by Reinhold Niebuhr (New York: Holocaust Library, 1979); *The Aryan Myth: A History of Racist and Nationalist Ideas in Europe,* trans. Edmund Howard (London: Heinemann, 1971); and *The History of Anti-Semitism,* trans. Miriam Kochan (New York: Vanguard, 1968). Also, Léon Poliakov and Josef Wulf, *Das Dritte Reich und seine Diener, Documente,* 2d. ed. (Berlin: Grunewald Verlag, 1956).

3. Léon Poliakov, *Le mythe aryen: Essai sur les sources du racisme et des nationalismes* (Paris: Calmann Lévy, 1971), 214, 384.

4. Léon Poliakov, *Le mythe aryen,* 217.

5. Raymond Schwab, *The Oriental Renaissance,* trans. Gene Patterson-Black and Victor Reinking, foreword by Edward Said (New York: Columbia University Press, 1984).

6. Amaury de Riencourt, *The Soul of India* (London: Jonathan Cape, 1960), 268: "The oriental Renaissance was bearing bitter fruits, and it is still an open question whether all this could have happened without the discovery of Aryan India in the 19th century." Cited in Jürgen Lütt, "Indische Wurzeln des Nationalsozialismus?" *Zeitschrift für Kulturaustausch* 3 (1987): 468. I am indebted to Lütt's discussion of this critical trend with reference to Poliakov, Schwab and de Riencourt.

7. Louis Pauwels and Jacques Bergier, *The Morning of the Magicians,* trans. R. Myers (New York: Avon, 1963); and J. H. Brennan, *The Occult Reich* (New York: New American Library, 1974). See also R. Alleau, *Hitler et les sociétés secrètes* (Paris: Grasset, 1969); T. Ravenscroft, *The Spear of Destiny* (New York: Bantam, 1973); J. M. Angebert, *The Occult and the Third Reich* (New York: Macmillan, 1974).

8. Lütt, "Indische Wurzeln," 468–79.

9. Clarence C. Brinton, "The National Socialists' Use of Nietzsche," *Journal of the History of Ideas* 1 (April 1940): 131-50; and Fritz Stern, *The Politics of Cultural Despair: A Study in the Rise of Germanic Ideology* (Berkeley: University of California Press, 1981).

10. Mosse, *The Crisis of German Ideology,* 1–10.

11. For the discussion of the use of the term *Aryan,* I have relied upon the studies of Jürgen Lütt, Rolf Peter Sieferle, and Hans Siegert.

12. A. F. Pott, "Indogermanisches Sprachstudium," *Allgemeine Encyclopädie der Wissenschaften und Künste,* ed. Johann Samuel Ersch and Johann Gottfried Gruber, 84 vols. (Leipzig: J. F. Gleditsch, 1840), 18.2.1. Cited in Rolf Peter Seiferle, "Indien und die Arier in der Rassentheorie," *Zeitschrift für Kulturaustausch* 3 (1987): 460; 466n 112.

13. Schlegel, *Kritische-Friedrich-Schlegel-Ausgabe,* 14:18ff.

14. Schlegel, *Über den Anfang unserer Geschichte und die letzte Revolution der Erde 1819,* in *Kritische-Friedrich-Schlegel-Ausgabe,* 8:520: "Unsre germanischen Vorfahren, während sie noch in Asien waren." Cited in Sieferle, "Indien und die Arier," 460

15. Schlegel, *Kritische-Friedrich-Schlegel-Ausgabe,* 8:520.

16. Ibid., 14:279: "War es irgendein wunderbarer Begriff von der hohen Würden und Herrlichkeit des Nordens, wie wir ihn in den indischen Sagen überall verbreitet finden?" Schelegel answered, "Der erste bestimmte Abfall von Gott."

17. Hans Siegert, "Zur Geschichte der Begriffe *Arier* und *arisch,*" *Wörter und Sachen: Zeitschrift für Indogermanische Sprachwissenschaft, Volksforschung und Kulturgeschichte* vol. 22, no. 4, (1941–42): 73–99.

18. Christian Lassen, *Indische Alterthumskunde* (Leipzig: L. A. Kittler, 1847–61), 1:404ff., 414, 478.

19. Gobineau depended heavily upon the research of Lassen.

20. Joseph Arthur de Gobineau, *Versuch über die Ungleichheit der*

Menschenrassen, trans. Ludwig Schemann, 4 vols. (Stuttgart: F. Frommann, 1939–40), 2:208.

21. W. D. Whitney, *Oriental and Linguistic Studies,* 2 vols. (Delhi: Sri Satguru, 1987), 1:45.

22. R. von Roth, "On the Morality of the Veda," trans. W. O. Whitney, *Journal of the American Oriental Society,* 3 (1853): 347.

23. F. Max Müller, *India: What Can It Teach Us?* (New York: Funk & Wagnalls, 1883), 6.

24. F. Max Müller, *Auld Lang Syne* (New York: Charles Scribner's Sons, 1901), 282.

25. F. Max Müller, "Lectures on the Origin and Growth of Religion as Illustrated by the Religions of India," *The Hibbert Lectures,* April–June 1878 (London: Longmans, Green, 1878), 148–49.

26. F. Max Müller, *Chips from a German Workshop,* 5 vols. (New York: Charles Scribner's Sons, 1895), 1:67.

27. Müller, *India,* 97.

28. Ibid., 15.

29. For the history of the concept of *Arier,* see Ruth Römer, *Sprachwissenschaft und Rassenideologie in Deutschland* (Munich: Wilhelm Fink, 1985), 65–66.

30. Müller, *Chips from a German Workshop,* 1:63.

31. Ibid., 1:63–64.

32. Ibid., 1:4.

33. Ibid., 4:210.

34. W. D. Whitney, *Oriental and Linguistic Studies,* 1:95–96.

35. F. Max Müller, *Ṛg Veda Saṃhitā: The Sacred Hymns of the Brahmins,* 6 vols. (London: William H. Allen, 1849–74), 3:xliii.

36. Müller, *Auld Lang Syne,* 188.

37. Ibid., 212.

38. Müller, *Chips from a German Workshop,*1:67: "We can watch in the Veda ideas and their names growing, which in Persia, Greece and Rome we meet with only as full-grown or fast decaying. We get one step nearer to that distant source of religious thought and language which has fed the different national streams of Persia, Greece, Rome and Germany."

39. Ibid., 2:12; 5:90.

40. Ibid., 1:65.

41. F. Max Müller, *The Science of Language,* 2 vols. (New York: Charles Scribner's Sons, 1891), 1:343.

42. F. Max Müller, *A History of Ancient Sanskirt Literature* (London: Williams & Norgate, 1860), 558.

43. Ibid., 526.

44. Ibid., 498.

45. Müller, *Chips from a German Workshop,* 1:5.

46. Ibid., 1:17.

47. Müller, *History of Ancient Sanskrit Literature,* 3.

48. Müller, *Essays,* 4:103–27.

49. See Müller, *Über die Resultate der Sprachwissenschaft: Vorlesungen gehalten in der kaiserlichen Universität zu Strassburg am xxiii, mai MDCCCLXXII* (Strasbourg: K. J. Trübner, 1872), 17. For a discussion of Müller's position, see Lütt, "Indische Wurzeln," 471.

50. Müller, *India,* 116.

51. For a discussion of these thinkers, see Sieferle, "Indien und die Arier," 451.

52. Theodor Poesche, *Die Arier: Ein Beitrag zur historischen Anthropologie* (Jena: H. Costenoble, 1878), 150: "Neger und Mulatten, die sich die herrliche Sprache einiger Vorfahren väterlicherseits zu erhalten wussten. Subtropische Natur hat in Indien leiblich und geistig die arische Art überwuchert und in Ihrer Fülle erstickt." Cited in Sieferle "Indien und die Arier," 452.

53. Enrico de Michaelis, *L'Origine degli Indo-Europei* (Turin: Biblioteca di Scienze moderne, 1903), cited in Sieferle, "Indien und die Arier," 452–3.

54. "Der Arier (auch Indogermanen, Japhetiten) sind einer der drei Zweige der kaukasischen (weissen) Rasse; sie zerfallen in die westlichen (europäischen) d.h. die oestlichen (asiatischen) Arier, d.h. die Inder (Hindus) und Iranier (Perser, Afganen, Armenier, Georgier, Kurden). Nichtarier sind daher: 1. die Angehörigen der beiden anderen Zweige der kaukasischen Rasse, nämlich die Semiten (Juden, Araber) und Hamiten (Berber). Die Finnen und Ungarn gehören zur mongolischen Rasse; es ist aber kaum die Absicht des Gesetzes, sie als Nichtarier zu behandeln." Cited in Sieferle, "Indien und die Arier," 461–62. By this law, all Jews who were not civil servants before World War I or could not show proof of front-line duty were excluded from the civil service.

55. Alfred Rosenberg, *Völkischer Beobachter,* 7 October 1926: "Der Staat ist nicht Selbstzweck, sondern Mittel zum Rassenschutz." Adolf Hitler, *Mein Kampf* (Munich: Zentral Verlag der NSDAP, 1934), 438–39: "Heute wissen wir, dass eine restlose Durcheinandermischung der Bestandteile unseres Volkskörpers uns infolge der dadurch entstandenen Einheit vielleicht zwar die äussere Macht geschenkt hätte, dass jedoch das höchste Ziel der Menschheit unerreichbar gewesen wäre, das der einzige Träger den das Schicksal ersichtlich zu dieser Vollendung ausersehen hat, im allgemeinen Rassenbrei untergegangen wäre."

56. Alfred Rosenberg, *Völkischer Beobachter,* 24 April 1920, 3: "Denn das gleiche Schicksal wollte, dass die Blutsfremden in unserer

Mitte mit ihrem anders gearteten Denken unser gesundes Fühlen auf Irrwege lockten."

57. Hitler, *Mein Kampf,* 420–21: "Erkennt die völkische Weltanschauung die Bedeutung der Menschheit in deren rassischen Urelementen. Sie sieht im Staat prinzipiell nur ein Mittel zum Zweck und fasst als seinen Zweck die Erhaltung des rassischen Daseins der Menschen auf. Sie glaubt somit keineswegs an eine Gleichheit der Rassen, sondern erkennt mit ihrer Verschiedenheit auch ihren höheren oder minderen Wert und fühlt sich durch diese Erkenntnis verpflichtet, gemäss dem ewigen Wollen, das dieses Universum beherrscht, den Sieg des Besseren, Stärkeren zu fördern, die Unterordnung des Schlechteren und Schwächeren zu verlangen . . . sie kann auch einer ethischen Idee das Existenzrecht nicht zubilligen, sofern diese Idee eine Gefahr für das rassische Leben der Träger einer höheren Ethik darstellt; denn in einer verbastierten und vernegerten Welt wären auch alle Begriffe des menschlich Schönheit und Erhabenen sowie alle Vorstellungen einer idealisierten Zukunft unseres Menschentums für immer verloren. Menschliche Kultur und Zivilisation sind auf diesem Erdteil unzertrennlich gebunden an das Vorhandensein des Ariers."

58. Helena Petrovna Blavatsky, *Die Geheimlehre, die Vereinigung von Wissenschaft,* 4 vols. (Vienna: Donau Verlag, 1955), 1:332: "Sie können ebensogut die vertriebene Chandalas des alten Indiens die von Veda-Vyasa und Manu erwähnten 'Ziegelmauer' sein . . . die semitische Sprachen sind die Bastardabkömmlinge der ersten Korruptionen der ältesten Kinder des frühen Sanskrit . . . Die Semiten, insbesondere die Araber, sind spätere Arier—entartet in Geistigkeit und Vervollkommenheit in Stofflichkeit. Zu diesen gehören alle Juden und Araber. Die ersteren sind ein Stamm, der von den Chandalas Indiens entstammt." Cited in Lütt, "Indische Wurzeln," 474.

59. F. Nietzsche, *Werke in drei Bänden,* ed. Karl Schlechta, 3 vols. (Munich: Hanser, 1954–56), 3:770.

60. Ibid., 2:649.

61. Ibid., 3:712.

62. Ibid., 3:701.

63. Ibid., 2:980–82: "Hier ist die Aufgabe gestellt, nicht weniger als vier Rassen auf einmal zu züchten: eine priesterliche, eine kriegerische, eine händler- und ackerbauerische, endlich eine Dienstbotenrasse, die Sudras . . . Aber auch diese Organisation hatte es nötig, furchtbar zu sein—nicht diesmal im Kampf mit einer Bestie, sondern mit ihrem Gegansatz-Begriff, dem Zucht-Menschen, dem Mischmasch-Menschen, dem Tschandala."

64. Nietzsche, *The Antichrist,* § 56.

65. This reference appears not in the Schlechta edition, but in Nietzsche, *Kritische Gesamtausgabe,* 13:378: "Der offizielle Begriff des Tschandala ist genau der eines Auswurfs und Excrements der vornehmen Classen."

66. Nietzsche, *Werke in drei Bände;* 2:981–82: "Diese Verfügungen sind sehr gleich genug: in ihnen haben wir einmal die *arische* Humanität, ganz rein, ganz ursprünglich—wir lernen, dass der Begriff 'reines Blut' der Gegensatz eines harmlosen Begriffs ist. Andrerseits wird klar, in *welchem* Volk sich der Hass, der Tschandala-Hass gegen diese 'Humanität' verewigt hat, wo er Religion, wo er Genie geworden ist . . . Unter diesem Gesichtspunkte sind die Evangelien eine Urkunde erstens Ranges, noch mehr das Buch Henoch.—Das Christentum, aus jüdischer Wurzel und nur verständlich als Gewächs dieses Bodens, stellt die *Gegenbewegung* gegen jede Moral der Züchtung, der Rasse, des Privilegiums dar—es ist die *antiarische* Religion *par excellence:* das Christentum die Unwertung aller arischen Werte, der Sieg der Tschandala—Werte, das Evangelium den Armen, den Niedrigen gepredigt, der Gesamt-Aufstand alles Niedergetretenen, Elenden, Missratenen, Schlechtweggekommenen gegen die 'Rasse'—die unsterbliche Tschandala-Rache als *Religion der Liebe . . .* "

67. According to *Manu,* even among outcastes, the *caṇḍāla* were the lowest like swine or dog and excluded from the village.

68. A popular theme for this lunatic fringe consisted in speculating a descendance through *śūdra* men and brahmin women. I borrow the term "lunatic fringe" from Sieferle "Indien und die Arier," 455) to refer to race theoreticians of the nineteenth century.

69. Lütt, "Indische Wurzeln," 473.

70. The population of Vienna tripled between 1870 and 1890.

71. In *Mein Kampf,* p. 135, Hitler wrote ". . . widerwärtig war mir das Rassenkonglomerat, das die Reichshauptstadt zeigte . . . Mir erscheint die Riesenstadt (Wien) als die Verkörperung der Blutschande."

72. "Wer ist der Starke von Oben?" in Johannes Balzli, *Guido von List: Der Wiederentdecker uralter arischer Weisheit* (Leipzig und Vienna: Guido von List Gesellschaft, 1917), 125–33.

73. Social Darwinists published from the 1890s through 1910. Ernst Häckel, the eminent zoologist who warned against the mixing of races, founded the Monist League in 1906 to popularize a racist version of social Darwinism among Germans.

74. Later racial theorists, such as Vacher de Lapouge (1854–1936) and Houston Stewart Chamberlain (1855–1927) based their theories on skull measurements and other physical characteristics such as hair color and eye color. The earlier racial theorists, such as Gobineau, relied on linguistics as the standard of racial distinction.

75. To draw these distinctions, heraldic devices, in which the Aryans supposedly had recorded the *karma* of their families, were studied. See Jörg Lanz von Liebenfels, "Grundriss der ariosophischen Geheimlehre," *Zeitschrift für Menschenkenntnis und Menschenschicksal* 1 (1925–26): 4–11.

76. Jörg Lanz von Liebenfels, *Theozoologie oder die Kunde von den Sodoms-Aefflingen und dem Götter-Elektron* (Vienna: Moderner Verlag, 1905), 147–52.

77. Jörg Lanz von Liebenfels, *Ostara* 1, second series (1912) [*Die Ostara und das Reich der Blonden,* special issue]. See also *Ostara* 36 (1910) [*Blond und Dunklen,* special issue].

78. Jeffrey A. Goldstein, "On Racism and Anti-Seminism in Occultism and Nazism," *Yad Vashem Studies* 13 (1979): 64; see also Mosse, *Nationalization of the Masses,* 197.

79. An anti-Semitic mayor of Vienna in the first decade of the twentieth century.

80. Jörg Lanz von Liebenfels, *Ostara* 28, 29 (April–May 1908) [*Das Gesetz des Manu und die Rassenpflege bei den alten Indo-Ariern,* special issue]: 22–23.

81. Ibid., 11.

82. Ibid., 3.

83. Note that Sir William Jones's translation of the *Laws of Manu* (1794) had been translated into German by Johann Christoph Hüttner under the title *Hindu-Gesetzbuch* (Weimar: Industrie Comptoirs, 1797) and had been examined in racist sense by a F. Gernandt, "Aus dem Hindu-Gesetzbuch des Manu," *Politisch-Anthropologische Revue* 3 (1904): 264–68. Nicholas Goodrick-Clarke, *The Occult Roots of Nazism: The Ariosophists of Austria and Germany 1890–1935* (Wellingborough, Northamptonshire: Aquarian Press, 1985), 242, suggests that this might have been Lanz's source.

84. See Wilfried Daim, *Der Mann, der Hitler die Ideen gab: Die sektierischen Grundlagen des Nationalsozialismus* (Vienna/Cologne/Graz: Böhlau, 1985), 146: "Die Juden als ein von allen historischen und vorhistorischen Rassen und aus den Schlacken aller untergeganenen Kulturvölker zusammengemischtes Tschandalenvolk." Cited in Lütt, "Indische Wurzeln," 475.

85. Lanz von Liebenfels, "Das Gesetz des Manu," 6, 16.

86. Ibid., 6.

87. Ibid., 8.

88. Ibid., 7.

89. Ibid., 16.

90. Ibid., 21.

91. Ibid., 25.

92. Ibid., 22.

93. Ibid., 23.

94. Ibid., 29–30: "Nun war aber die herrschende Kaste keine asiatische Kaste mehr, die schöne Schale des altarischen Rassentums war geblieben, aber ihr innerster Kern war von Tschandala-Würmen angefressen worden. Und so bietet das heutige Indien rassenhaft ein Bild, dass zu Manu's Gesetzbuch nicht mehr stimmt."

95. Hitler, *Mein Kampf,* 394–98.

96. The one exception to this rule was Karl Maria Wiligut (pseud. Weisthor), whom Goodrick-Clarke refers to as the "private magus" of Himmler (Goodrick-Clarke, *Occult Roots of Nazism,* 177). Wiligut was head of the Department of Race and Early History within the Race and Settlement main office of the SS; one of the duties of his department was to produce German *mantras*.

97. Lütt, "Indische Wurzeln," 477.

98. For an account of proto-Nazi history, see Rudolf von Sebottendorf, *Bevor Hitler kam: Urkundliches aus der Frühzeit der Nationalsozialistischen Bewegung* (Munich: Grassinger, 1934).

99. The Germanen Orden's official newsletter had the swastika on its cover, as well as on various pieces of organization jewelry. Although the swastika was current among various *völkisch* organizations, it was through the Germanen Orden and the Thule Society, its successor organization in postwar Munich, that this device came to be adopted by the Nazis. In a party speech (Munich, 13 August 1920), Hitler explained the origin of the swastika: "Sie finden dieses Kreuz als Hakenkreuz nicht nur sondern genauso in Indien und Japan in den Tempelpfosten eingemeisselt. Es ist das Hakenkreuz der einst von arischer Kultur gegründeten Gemeinwesen." See A. Hitler, *Sämtliche Aufzeichnungen 1905–24,* ed. Eberhard Jäckel and Axel Kuhn (Stuttgart: Deutsche Verlags-Anstalt, 1980), 186.

100. Lütt, "Indische Wurzeln," 476.

101. Lütt, "Indische Wurzeln," 478. For the contrary position, see Elizabeth de Fontenay, "Fuir l'histoire? La pitié dangereuse," in *Présences de Schopenhauer* ed. Roger-Pol Droit (Paris: Grasset, 1989), 84–85. Ac-

cording to Fontenay, Schopenhauer, Herder, Schelling, and F. Schlegel investigated India for no other purpose than to uproot Christianity from its Hebraic roots.

102. Oswald Spengler, *Neubau des deutschen Reiches* (Munich: C. H. Bec, 1924), 14. Cited in Sieferle, "Indien und die Arier," 457.

103. "Die Sozialisten verlassen die NSDAP, Das Gründungsmanifest der Schwarzen Front" (1930), in Otto Strasser, *Aufbau des Deutschen Sozialismus* (Prague: Heinrich Grunov, 1936), 138: "Für uns war und ist die Zustimmung zum Kampf des indischen Volkes um seine Freiheit von englischer Herrschaft und kapitalistischer Ausbeutung eine Notwendigkeit, die sich ebenso sehr aus der Tatsache ergibt, dass für eine deutsche Befreiungspolitik jede Schwächung einer Vertragsmacht von Versailles günstig ist, wie aus der gefühlsmässigen Zustimmung zu jedem Kampf, den unterdrückte Völker gegen ausbeutende Usurpatoren führen, da es eine zwingende Folge unserer Idee des Nationalismus ist, dass das Recht der Erfüllung völkischer Eigenart, das wir für uns in Anspruch nehmen, auch anderen Völkern und Nationen zusteht." Cited in Sieferle "Indien und die Arier," 457.

104. Otto Strasser, "Hitler, Gandhi, und das junge Deutschland," *Die Kommenden,* 8 August 1930, 376: "Bund der unterdrückten Nationen ist ein dummes Schlagwort . . . Wenn heute der Inder unter der Herrschaft Englandes lebt . . . oder der Schwarze unter der Herrschaft irgend eines europäischen Volkes, so ist dies in deren Inferiorität begründet . . . Der Freiheitskampf der Schwarzen, Inder, usw. ist der Versuch der Durchbrechung einer natürlichen Rangorden . . . Die Bewunderung von Gandhi ist in meinen Augen eine rassische Perversität." Cited in Sieferle, "Indien und die Arier," 457.

105. See Strasser, "Hitler, Gandhi, und das junge Deutschland," 377. Cited in Sieferle, "Indien und die Arier," 457.

106. Alfred Rosenberg, *Der Mythus des 20. Jahrhunderts* (Munich: Hoheneichen, 1943), 149: "Der alter Inder—und der war es, der Indien erschuf—sein Leben liess nicht um der Liebe, sondern um der Pflicht und Ehre willen. Ein ungetreuer wurde auch im arischen Indien verdammt, nicht weil er lieblos, sondern weil er ehrlos geworden war. 'Besser das Leben aufzugeben, als die Ehre zu verlieren: die Hingabe des Lebens fühlt man nur einen Augenblick, den Verlust der Ehre aber Tag für Tag' (O. Böthlingk, *Indische Sprüche*)."

107. Ibid., 28: "Nach dieser Scheidung zwischen Blut und Blut gestalteten die Arier sich ein Bild der Welt, das an Tiefe und Weiträumigkeit auch heute von keiner Philosophie überboten werden kann."

108. Ibid., 30.

109. Ibid., 31: ". . . nach langdauernden Auseinandersetzungen mit den immer wieder eindringenden Vorstellungen der niederrassigen Eingeborenen." Rosenberg was also influenced by Hans F. K. Günther, who described the process of Aryan racial degeneration in *Die nordische Rasse bei den Indogermanen Asiens* (Munich: J. F. Lehmann, 1934), 41: "Die Kastengesetzgebung wurde als Rassenschutz dadurch beeinträchtigt und schliesslich sinnlos, dass sie das Aufheiraten von Frauen aus der nächstniedrigen Kaste in die höhere zuliess . . . Auf solche Weise verdunkelte in zunehmendem Masse das arische Indertum sich selbst und entfremdete sich selbst dem Geiste seiner Vorväter. Durch Aufnahme nichtarischen Blutes wurde so im Lauf der Jahrhunderte aus dem Indertum das Hindutum, aus indischem Geiste der Hindugeist, der vom Indogermanentum schliesslich nur noch etwas Übertragbares, die Sprache bewahrte." Cited in Sieferle, "Indien und die Arier," 459. This process of degeneration corresponded to a gradual darkening of the Aryan, even in the highest caste. Through the crossing of races, the mixture of castes, and the environment, the Aryan race of India met its downfall. The "lastende feuchte Hitze Indiens," infant mortality, and higher sickness in general contributed to the spiritual *Widerstandswillen* of the Aryans. See Günther, *Die nordische Rasse,* 50: "Sie hat als eine immerwährende Qual immer von neuem dem ererbten Geiste mutiger arischer Lebensfrische entgegengewirkt, bis diesem mutigen, Lebensfrohen, dieseitigen, echt Indogermanischen Geiste beim Zusammenbruch wurde der Erbstämme des eingewanderten Indertums das Mark entzogen."

110. A. Hitler, "Der Zusammenbruch der Novemberrepublik und die Mission unserer Bewegung," in Eberhard Jäckel and Axel Kuhn, *Hitler: Sämtliche Aufzeichnungen, 1905–1924,* 1011: "Ja, ein Indien wollen sie aus Deutschland machen, ein traumendes Volk, das von der Wirklichkeit abkehrt."

111. Rosenberg, *Der Mythus des 20. Jahrhunderts,* 149–50: "Mit der auf das Erdenleben übertragenen Philosophie des Atman-Brahman verneinte—wie früher ausgeführt—der Arier seine Rasse, damit seine Persönlichkeit, damit aber auch die Idee der Ehre als seelisches Rückgrat seines Lebens."

112. Ibid., 30.

113. Ibid., 147: "Wir sprechen von Indien als von einer weichmütigen im All zerfliessenden, Menschenliebe und Mitleiden als Höchstes lehrenden Weltanschauung . . . Und doch ragen in diese liebe- und mitleidvollen Erzeugnisse der indischen Spätzeit ganz andere, ältere Anschauungen hinein, die nicht persönliches Glücksgefühl und Leidlosigkeit als einzig erstrebenswertes Ziel anerkennen, sondern Pflichterfüllung und Behauptung der Ehre."

114. Ibid., 342: "Und als eine solche Tragik wird Schopenhauer unserer Ehrfurcht stets gewiss sein, als das Beispiel eines heroischen—und in seiner Gewaltigkeit echt abendländischen—Kampfes um das Wesen der Welt; ein Mensch hat hier alles auf eine Karte gesetzt, und diese hat fehlgeschlagen. Die verzweifelten Aufraffungen zur Höhe enden immer mit einem zurückfallen ins Nichts. Aber auch der doch ganz unindische Schopenhauer bekannte, das Höchste, was ein Mensch erreichen könne sei ein 'heroischer Lebenslauf.' Das ist ein nordisches Bekenntnis, wie es schöner nicht gefunden werden kann und deshalb ist Arthur Schopenhauer—unser."

115. Ibid., 267: '[Der Inder] legt ein derart grosses Gewicht auf sie; dass er in letzter Konsequenz zu der auch ausgesprochenen Anschauung gelangt, die Tat als solche könne einem Wissenden, des Atman-Brahman Teilhaftigen, nichts anhaben. Er ist 'nicht durch das Werk befleckt, das Böse.' Alles Fleischliche sei sowieso nur Trug und Schein, was mit ihm geschehe, gleichgültig. Das ist die letzte Konsequenz Indiens."

116. Ibid., 660–61: "Jeder Europäer erblickt in Alt-Indien ein Land seiner Träume; inmitten einer Zeit technischer Bestialisierung tauchten nicht die Schlechtesten unter in die Gedanken Yajnavalkyas, Cankaras, entzückten sich an dem Helden Rama, dem Gotte Krischna, dem Dichter Kalidasa. Dies hatte zur Folge, dass diese Indiensucher Europas Erlösung durch Alt-Indien predigten und gar nicht bemerkten, dass dieses arische Indien einst gerade an den das Herz endlos erweiternden Gedanken der späten Upanishads zugrunde gegangen war."

117. Ibid., 622. See also pp. 661–62: "Wir sehen hier offen ein europäisches Lebensgefühl eingreifen, das allerdings sofort wieder durch die Bemerkungen abgeschwächt wird, dass weder Hautfarbe noch Ahnen den Brahmanen machten, sondern Charakter. Hier offenbart sich die

ganze Tragik selbst des über die 300 Millionen seiner Volksgenossen hinausragenden Inders. Denn, wollte er die Entfaltung der Arier schildern, so musste er bekennen, dass der Arier bis auf ganz geringe Spuren untergegangen ist. Hinterlassen hat et Heldengesänge, eine tiefe, grosse Philosophie, die, später ins Extreme, Uferlose, Dschungelartige getrieben, das Rassenchaos förderte."

118. Ibid., 36; see also p. 662: "Durch ein zu weites Atemholen sind diese Blutadern des Rassenkörpers gesprengt, arisch-indisches Blut fliesst aus . . . Die Zuchtkraft arisch-indischer Denk- und Lebensformen als Ergebnis von nordischer Rasse und indischer Natur ist zwar ungeheuer, aber die rassische Substanz, aus deren Seele einst die Gedanken und Staaten entstiegen, ist bis auf geringe Überreste verschwunden. Deshalb zeugte Indien auch nur den müden Gandhi mit seinem Pazifismus, nicht einen einer Neuschöpfung ermöglichenden Feldherrn."

119. In this regard, Rosenberg admitted his indebtedness to Houston Stewart Chamberlain, who was Richard Wagner's English-born son-in-law and a political philosopher who developed racial themes on Aryan superiority.

120. Rosenberg, *Der Mythus des 20. Jahrhunderts,* 82.

121. Ibid., 104.

122. A. Hitler, "Warum sind wir Anti-Semiten?" cited in Jäckel and Kuhn, *Hitler: Sämtliche Aufzeichnungen,* 195: "Erst muss eine Rasse entnationalisiert werden. Erst muss sie verlernen, dass ihre Kraft in ihrem Blut liegt, und wenn sie das erreicht hat, keinen Stolz mehr besitzt, so entsteht das Produkt, eine zweite Rasse, welche tiefer ist als die vorhergegangene, und diese tiefere braucht er, denn was der Jude nötig hat, um seine definitive Weltherrschaft zu organisieren, aufzubauen und erhalten zu können, ist die Senkung des Rassenniveaus der übrigen Völker, dass er als einziger rassenrein befähigt ist, über alle anderen letzten Endes zu herrschen, das ist die Rassensenkung, deren Wirkungen wir an einer Reihe von Völkern dieser Erde heute noch sehen. Wir wissen, dass die Hindu in Indien ein Volk sind, gemischt aus den hochstehenden arischen Einwanderern und der dunkelschwarzen Urbevölkerung, und dass dieses Volk heute Folgen trägt; denn es ist auch das Sklavenvolk einer Rasse, die uns in vielen Punkten nahezu als zweite Judenheit erscheinen mag."

123. Alfred Rosenberg, *Blut und Ehre: Ein Kampf für deutsche Wiedergeburt* (Munich: Franz Eher, 1939).

124. Rosenberg, *Der Mythus des 20. Jahrhunderts,* 201–3.

125. Günther, *Die nordische Rasse,* 51f: ". . . Zerfallserscheinung nordischen Rassengeistes in tropisch-indischer Umwelt." Cited in Sieferle, "Indien und die Arier," 459.

126. Rosenberg, *Der Mythus des 20. Jahrhunderts,* 36: ". . . eine Rassenschande, deren Erzeugnisse heute als armselige Bastarde in den Wassern des Ganges eine Heilung für ihr verkrüppeltes Dasein erflehen." Cited in Sierferle, "Indien und die Arier," 462.

Concluding Remarks

1. Gilman, *Decadence,* 154.

2. Cited in J. P. Stern, "Germans and the German Past," a review of Harold James's *German Identity, 1770–1990* (London: Weidenfeld, 1990) in the *London Review of Books,* 21 December 1989, 8. Cited also in J. P. Stern, *Hitler: The Führer and the People* (London: Fontana, 1975), 19.

3. Jules Michelet, *La Bible de l'humanité* (Paris: Chamerot, 1864), 485.

4. The European institutional rejection of Indian philosophy is viewed as the vengeance of frustrated desire (Droit, *L'oubli de l'Inde,* 145). In this regard, see also W. Halbfass, *India and Europe.*

5. See Said, *Orientalism;* S. Timpararo's introduction to F. Schlegel's *Über die Sprache und Weisheit der Inder;* Ronald Inden, "Orientalist Constructions of India"; Catherine Weinberger-Thomas, *L'Inde et l'imaginaire.*

6. Droit, *L'oubli de l'Inde,* 157.

7. Müller, *India,* 49. Similarly, in the introduction to his edition of the *Ṛg-Veda-Saṃhitā,* (3:ix), Müller notes: "We must . . . discover for

ourselves the real vestiges of these ancient poets; and if we follow them cautiously we shall find that with some effort we are still able to walk in their footsteps."

8. Hofmannsthal, *Das Tagesbuch,* 1:33: "Das christliche Herz, der Wille zum Leben, klammert sich an jedes teuere Erbe, jedes ehrwürdige Wort, will wollen, will hoffen, will glauben. Der heidnische Geist, die Erkenntnis, drängt zum Pessimismus, zum Quietismus, zum Nirwana. Sie ringen miteinander, und jede Kraft und Begabung, Schärfe des Blicks und Macht der Dialectik, deutsche Philosophie und universalische Bildung, wirken mit, diesen Kampf qualvoller zu gestalten. Hundertmal beginnt der Wille eine ohnmächtige Beweisführung, sich selbst zurückzuzwingen in die verlorene Naivetät, sich zum Vorurteil, zur Nation, zur Individualität zurückzuzwingen, hundertmal schlagen die Wogen eines alldurchschauenden, trostlosen Erkennens über dem wankenden Gebäude von erstorbenen Begriffen zusammen: 'Nada,' klingt es aus, 'Nirwana,' 'Nichts,' 'Leere.' Das Herz will Folgerungen aus Urteilen, aus 'Wahrheiten' ziehen, an die der Kopf nicht mehr glaubt: daraus kann nur Krankheit entstehen, wie aus einem körperlichen Missverhältnis."

9. Barthélemy Saint-Hilaire, *Le Buddha et sa religion,* 182.

10. Jules Barthélemy Saint-Hilaire, *L'Inde anglaise, son état actuel, son avenir* (Paris: Perrin, 1887), 320.

BIBLIOGRAPHY

Ahmad, Aijaz. *In Theory: Classes, Nations, Literatures.* Bombay: Oxford University Press, 1993.

———. "Jameson's Rhetoric of Otherness and the 'Natural Allegory,' " *Social Text* 5, no. 17 (1986): 7–12.

Alleau, R. *Hitler et les sociétés secrètes.* Paris: Grasset, 1969.

Amiel Henri Frédéric. *Amiel's Journal.* Translated by Mrs. Humphry Ward. New York: Macmillan, 1928.

———. *Fragments d'un journal intime.* Paris: n.p., 1882.

Andreas-Salomé, Lou. *Friedrich Nietzsche in seinen Werken.* Vienna: C. Konegan, 1911.

Angebert, J. M. *The Occult and the Third Reich.* New York: Macmillan, 1974.

Baird, Jay W. *To Die for Germany: Heroes in the Nazi Pantheon.* Bloomington: Indiana University Press, 1990.

Balzli, Johannes. *Guido von List: Der Wiederentdecker uralter arischer Weisheit.* Leipzig and Vienna: Guido von List Gesellschaft, 1917.

Barbey d'Aurevilly, Jules Amédée. *Les oeuvres et les poètes.* Paris: Amyot, 1862.

Barbosa, Duarte. *A Description of the Coasts of East Africa and Malabar.* Translated by Henry E. J. Stanley. New York: Johnson, 1970.

Barthélemy Saint-Hilaire, Jules. *Le Bouddha et sa religion*. Paris: Didier, 1862.

———. *Du Bouddhisme*. Paris: B. Duprat, 1855.

———. *L'Inde anglaise, son état actuel, son avenir.* Paris: Perrin, 1887.

Baudelaire, Charles. *L'art romantique*. Geneva: Skira, 1964.

———. *Oeuvres complètes*. Edited by Claude Pichois. Paris: Bibliothèque de la Pléiade, 1973.

Beer, Michael. *Der Paria*. Leipzig: Reclam, n.d.

Bernal, Martin. *Black Athena: The Afroasiatic Roots of Classical Civilization*. Vol. 1. London: Free Association Books, 1987.

Bernheimer, Charles. *Figures of Ill-Repute*. Cambridge: Harvard University Press, 1989.

Bertuch, Friedrich Justin, and Johann Severin Vater. *Allegemeines Archiv für Ethnographie und Linguistik*. Weimar: Industrie-Comptoir, 1806.

Bhabha, Homi K. *Nation and Narration*. London: Routledge, 1990.

———. "The Other Question: Difference, Discrimination, and the Discourse of Colonialism." In *Out There: Marginalization and Contemporary Cultures,* edited by Russell Ferguson, et al. Cambridge: MIT Press, 1990, 71–87.

———. "Signs Taken for Wonders: Questions of Ambivalence and Authority under a Tree outside Delhi, May 1817." *Critical Inquiry* 12, no. 1 (Autumn 1985): 144–65.

———. "Sly Civility." *October* 34 (Fall 1985): 71–80.

Bhagavad Gita—Der Gesang der Erhabenen. Translated by Theodor Springmann. Hamburg: n.p., 1920.

Bhagavad Gita, Id est THESPESION MELOS sive Almi Chrishnae et Arjunae Colloquium de rebus divinis. Textum recensuit, Adnotationes criti-

cas et interpretationem Latinam adiecit. Translated by August Wilhelm Schlegel. Bonn: Eduard Weber in Academia Borusska Rhenana, 1823.

Bhāgavata Purāṇa ou, Histoire poétique de Kirchna. Translated by Eugène Burnouf. Paris: Imprimerie Royale, 1840.

Bhartṛhari. *The Epigrams Attributed to Bhartṛhari*. Edited by D. D. Kosambi. Cambridge: Harvard University Press, 1950.

———. *Die Sprache des Bhartṛhari*. Edited by Peter von Bohlen. Hamburg: A. Campe, 1835.

Blavatsky, Helena Petrovna. *Die Geheimlehre, die Vereinigung von Wissenschaft*. 4 vols. Vienna: Donau Verlag, 1955.

Bleibtreu, Carl. *Der Heilskönig*. Berlin and Leipzig: Fr. Lienhardt, 1903.

Bongie, Chris. *Exotic Memories: Literature, Colonialism, and the Fin de Siècle*. Stanford: Stanford University Press, 1991.

Bonnefoy, Georges. *La pensée religieuse et morale d'Alfred de Vigny*. Paris: Hachette, 1944

Bourget, Paul. *Essais de psychologie contemporaine*. Paris: Plon, 1899.

Bracciolini, Poggio, and Ludovico di Varthema. *Travelers in Disguise: Narratives of Eastern Travel*. Translated by J. W. Jones. Cambridge: Harvard University Press, 1963.

Brennan, J. H. *The Occult Reich*. New York: New American Library, 1974.

Brinton, Clarence C. "The National Socialists' Use of Nietzsche." *Journal of the History of Ideas*, 1 (April 1940): 131–150.

Burnouf, Eugène. *Introduction à l'histoire du bouddhisme indien*. Paris: Imprimerie Royale, 1844.

———. *Le lotus de la bonne loi, traduit du sanskrit, accompagné d'un commentaire et de vingt et un mémoires rélatifs au bouddhisme*. Paris: Imprimerie Nationale, 1852.

Butler, E. M. *The Tyranny of Greece over Germany*. Cambridge: Cambridge University Press, 1935.

Canat, René. *Une forme de mal de siècle, du sentiment de la solitude morale chez les romantiques et les parnassiens*. Paris: Hachette, 1904.

Carcassonne, Emile, "Leconte de Lisle et la philosophie indienne." *Revue de littérature comparée* 35 (1931): 618–46.

———. "Notes sur l'indianisme de Leconte de Lisle." *Revue d'histoire littéraire de la France* 38 (1932): 429–34.

Cardona, George. *Pāṇini: A Survey of Research*. The Hague: Mouton, 1976.

Caro, Emile, *Le pessimisme au XIXe siècle*. Paris: Hachette, 1889.

Challemel-Lacour, Paul. "Un bouddhiste contemporain en Allemagne." *Revue des deux mondes*. 15 March 1870.

———. *Études et réflexions d'un pessimiste*. Paris: Charpentier, 1901.

Chatterjee, Partha. "More on Modes of Power and the Peasantry." In *Selected Subaltern Studies,* edited by Ranajit Guha and Gayatri Chakravorty Spivak. New York: Oxford University Press, 1988.

———. *Nationalist Thought and the Colonial World—a Derivative Discourse?* Delhi: Oxford University Press, 1986.

Chézy, Helmina von. *Unvergessene Denkwürdigkeiten aus dem Leben von Helmina von Chézy*. Leipzig: F. A. Brockhaus, 1858.

Chinard, Gilbert. *Amérique et le rêve exotique dans la littérature française au XVIIe et au XVIIIe siècle*. Paris: Hachette, 1913.

Clerc, Charles, *Le génie du paganisme*. Paris: Payot, 1926.

Colebrooke, Henry Thomas. *Essays on the Religion and Philosophy of the Hindus*. London and Edinburgh: Williams & Norgate, 1858.

———. "On the Philosophy of the Hindus." Parts 1, 2. *Transactions of the Royal Asiatic Society* 1 (1824): 19–43, 93–118.

Condillac, E. B. de. *Essai sur l'origine des connaissances humaines*. Paris: Le Roy, 1947.

Cousin, Victor. *Cours de l'histoire de la philosophie*. Paris: Pichon & Didier, 1829.

Creuzer, Friedrich. *Symbolik und Mythologie der alten Völker, besonders der Griechen*. 3d ed. Leipzig and Darmstadt: C. W. Leske, 1837–42.

Daim, Wilfried. *Der Mann, der Hitler die Ideen gab: Die sektierischen Grundlagen des Nationalsozialismus*. Vienna/Cologne/Graz: Böhlau, 1985.

Daudet, Alphonse. *Le petit chose: Histoire d'un enfant*. Paris: Charpentier, 1913.

Dauer, Dorothea. *Schopenhauer as Transmitter of Buddhist Ideas*. Berne: Herbert Lang, 1969.

Descher, G. *Gobineau und Deutschland*. Ph.D. diss., University of Erlangen, 1967.

Deussen, Paul. *Erinnerungen an Friedrich Nietzsche*. Leipzig: F. A. Brockhaus, 1901.

———. *Das System des Vedānta*. Leipzig: F. A. Brockhaus, 1883.

Dornis, Jean [Mme. Guillaume Beer]. *Essai sur Leconte de Lisle*. Paris: P. Ollendorff, 1909.

Dorville, André Guillaume Dontant. *Histoire des differens peuples du monde, contenant les cérémonies religieuses, l'origine des religions, leurs sectes, leur superstitions, et les moeurs et usages de chaque nation*. 6 vols. Paris: n.p., 1770.

Drew, John. *India and the Romantic Imagination*. Delhi: Oxford University Press, 1987.

Droit, Roger-Pol, *L'oubli de l'Inde, une amnésie philosophique*. Paris: Presses Universitaires de France, 1989.

———. "Victor Cousin, la Bhagavad Gītā et l'ombre de Hegel." In *L'Inde et l'imaginaire*. Edited by Catherine Weinberger-Thomas. Paris: École des Hautes Études en Sciences Sociales, 1988.

Dubois, Jean Antoine. *Description of the Character, Manners, Customs of the People of India*. London: Longman, Hurst, Rees, Orme & Brown, 1817.

Esquiros, Alphonse. *Les vierges folles*. 2d ed. Paris: Auguste le Gallois, 1841.

Estève, Edmund. *Alfred de Vigny: Les destinées, poèmes philosophiques*. Paris: Hachette, 1924.

Falshaw, Gladys. *Leconte de Lisle et l'Inde*. Paris: Arthez, 1923.

Feyerabend, Paul. *Wissenschaft als Kunst*. Frankfurt: Suhrkamp, 1984.

Figueira, Dorothy M. *Translating the Orient*. Albany: State University of New York Press, 1991.

Flaubert, Gustave. *Correspondence*. Paris: Conard, 1926.

———. *Correspondence*. Edited by Jean Bruneau. 2 vols. Paris: Pléiade, 1973, 1980.

———. *Oeuvres complètes*. 2 vols. Paris: Seuil, 1964.

———. *Oeuvres complètes de Gustave Flaubert*. Paris: Conard, 1930.

Flottes, Pierre. *Leconte de Lisle, l'homme et l'oeuvre*. Paris: Hatier-Boivin, 1954.

———. *Le poète Leconte de Lisle. Documents inédits*. Paris: Perrin, 1929.

Fontenay, Elizabeth de. "Fuir l'histoire? La pitié dangereuse." In *Présences de Schopenhauer*. Edited by Roger-Pol Droit. Paris: Grasset, 1989.

Foucault, Michel. *Les mots et les choses*. Paris: Gallimard, 1966.

Gadamer, Hans-Georg. *The Relevance of the Beautiful and Other Essays*. Translated by Nicholas Walker and Robert Bernasconi. Cambridge: Cambridge University Press, 1986.

———. *Wahrheit und Methode*. Tübingen: J. C. B. Mohr, 1960.

Gates, Henry Louis, Jr. "Critical Fanonism." *Critical Inquiry* 17 (Spring 1991): 457–70.

Gautier, Théophile. *Caprices et zigzags*. Paris: Hachette, 1855.

———. *Histoire de l'art dramatique en France depuis vingt-cinq ans*. 6 vols. Paris: Edition Hetzel, 1858–59.

———. *La partie carrée*. Paris: E. Tasquelle, 1857.

———. *L'Orient*. 2 vols. Paris: Charpentier, 1877.

Gérard, René. *L'Orient et la pensée romantique allemande*. Paris: Didier, 1963.

Gestering, Johann Joachin. *German Pessimism and Indian Philosophy: A Hermeneutic Reading*. Delhi: Ajanta: 1986.

Gilman, Richard. *Decadence: The Strange Life of an Epithet*. New York: Farrar, Straus & Giroux, 1978.

Gipper, Helmut. "Understanding as a Process of Linguistic Approximation: The Discussion between August Wilhelm Schlegel, S. A. Langlois, Wilhelm von Humboldt, and G. W. F. Hegel on the Translation of the *Bhagavad Gītā* and the Concept of Yoga." In *Studies in the History of Western Linguistics in Honor of R. H. Robbins*. Edited by Theodora Bynam and F. R. Palmer. Cambridge: Cambridge University Press, 1986.

Gobineau, Joseph Arthur de. *Versuch über die Ungleichheit der Menschenrassen*. Translated by Ludwig Schemann. 4 vols. Stuttgart: F. Frommann, 1939–40.

Goethe, Johann Wolfgang. *Goethes Briefwechsel mit einem Kinde*. Edited by Jonas Fränkel. 2 vols. Jena: E. Diederichs, 1906.

Goldstein, Jeffrey A. "On Racism and Antisemitism in Occultism and Nazism." *Yad Vashen Studies* 13 (1979): 53–70.

Goodrick-Clarke, Nicholas. *The Occult Roots of Nazism: The Ariosophists of Austria and Germany 1890–1935*. Wellingborough, Northamptonshire: Aquarian Press, 1985.

Grosier, Abbé Jean Baptiste Gabriel Alexandre. *Description générale de la Chine*. 7 vols. Paris: Pillet, 1818–20.

Gubernatis, Angelo de. *Storia dei viaggiatori italiani nelle Indie orientali*. Livorno: F. Vigo, 1875.

Guha, Ranajit, ed. *Subaltern Studies, Writings on South Asian History and Society*. Vols. 1, 3, 5, 6. Delhi: Oxford University Press, 1982–89.

Guha, Ranajit, and Gayatri Chakravorty Spivak, eds. *Selected Subaltern Studies*. New York: Oxford University Press, 1988.

Günderrode, Karoline von. *Karoline von Günderrode und ihre Freunde*. Edited by Ludwig Geiger. Stuttgart: Deutscher Verlag, 1895.

———. *Der Schatten eines Traumes*. Edited by Christa Wolf. Berlin: Luchterhand, 1981.

Günther, Hans F. K. *Die nordische Rasse bei den Indogermanen Asiens*. Munich: J. F. Lehmann, 1934.

Habermas, Jürgen. *Der philosophische Diskurs der Moderne*. 3d ed. Frankfurt: Suhrkamp, 1986.

Halbfass, Wilhelm. *India and Europe*. Albany: State Univeristy of New York Press, 1988.

Hartmann, Karl Eduard von. *Philosophische Fragen der Gegenwart*. Leipzig: W. Friedrich, 1885.

Hasenclever, Walter. *Nirwana: Eine Kritik des Lebens*. Berlin: Moderner Verlag, 1909.

Hegel, G. W. F. *Briefe von und an Hegel*. Edited by J. Hoffmeister. 4 vols. Hamburg: F. Meiner, 1954.

———. *Phénoménologie de l'esprit*. Edited by Jean Hyppolite. Paris: Aubier, 1939–41.

———. *Sämtliche Werke, Neue kritische Ausgabe*. Edited by G. Lasson and J. Hoffmeister. 2d ed. Leipzig: F. Meiner, 1928.

———. *Vorlesungen über die Geschichte der Philosophie*. Edited by J. Hoffmeister. 2d ed. Leipzig: F. Meiner, 1944.

———. *Vorlesungen über die Philosophie der Religion*. Edited by G. Lasson. 2d ed. Hamburg: F. Meiner, 1966.

———. *Vorlesurgen über die Philosophie der Weltgeschichte*. In *Die Vernunft in der Geschichte,* edited by J. Hoffmeister, 5th ed., Hamburg: F. Meiner, 1955. II: *Die orientalische Welt,* edited by G. Lasson, 3d ed., Hamburg: F. Meiner, 1968.

———. *Berliner Schriften,* vol. 11, *Werke in zwanzig Bänden, Theorie Ausgabe*. Edited by E. Moldenhauer and K. M. Michel. Frankfurt: Suhrkamp, 1970.

Heine, Heinrich. *Sämtliche Werke*. Edited by Ernst Elster. 7 vols. Leipzig and Vienna: Bibliographisches Institut, 1893.

Herder, Johann Gottfried. *Sämtliche Werke*. Edited by B. Suphan. 33 vols. Berlin: Weidmannsche Buchhandlung, 1877–1913.

———. *Zerstreute Blätter.* Gotha: C. W. Ettinger, 1792.

Hitler, Adolf. *Mein Kampf.* Munich: Zentral Verlag der NSDAP, 1934.

———. *Sämtliche Aufzeichnungen, 1905–24*. Edited by Eberhard Jäckel, and Axel Kuhn. Stuttgart: Deutsche Verlags-Anstalt, 1980.

Hofmannsthal, Hugo von. *Das Tagesbuch eines Willenskranken: Prosa,* Edited by Herbert Steiner. 4 vols. Frankfurt: S. Fischer, 1956.

Hopfner, Gerhard. *Die indischen Studien Fr. Schlegels in Zusammenhang seines Denkens*. Ph. D. diss., University of Breslau, 1921.

Hulin, Michel. *Hegel et l'Orient*. Paris: Vrin, 1979.

Humboldt, Wilhelm von. *Gesammelte Werke*. 7 vols. Berlin: G. Reimer, 1841.

Inden, Ronald B. *Imagining India*. Oxford: Basil Blackwell, 1990.

———. "Orientalist Constructions of India." *Modern Asian Studies* 20, no. 3 (1986): 401–46.

Ingalls, D. H. H. Review *The Epigrams Attributed to Bhartṛhari*, by Bhartṛhari, edited by D. D. Kosambi. *Harvard Journal of Asiatic Studies* 13 (1950): 257–58.

James, Harold. *A German Identity, 1770–1940*. London: Weidenfeld, 1990.

Jameson, Fredric. "Third-World Literature in the Era of Multinational Capitalism." *Social Text* 5, no. 15 (1986): 66–88.

Jones, Sir William. "The Third Anniversary Discourse on the Hindus." Reprinted in *A Reader in Nineteenth-Century Historical Indo-European Linguistics*, edited by W. Lehmann. Austin: University of Texas Press, 1967.

Jostenoode, Harald Arjuna Grävell van. *Ostara* 25 (1908) [*Das Ariertum und seine Feinde*, special Issue].

Jourda, Pierre. *L'exotisme dans la littérature française depuis Chateaubriand*. Vol. 1, Paris: Boivin & Cie., 1938. Vol. 2, Paris: Presses Universitaires de France, 1956.

Kaufmann, Walter. *Nietzsche: Philosopher, Psychologist, Antichrist*. 3d ed. Princeton: Princeton University Press, 1968.

Köppen, Karl Friedrich. *Die Religion des Buddha und ihre Entstehung*. Berlin: Schneider, 1857–59.

Körner, Jakob. *Krisenjahre der Frühromantik, Briefe aus dem Schlegelkreis*. Berlin: R. M. Rohrer, 1936–58.

Kurth-Voigt, Liselotte E. "Existence after Death in Eighteenth-Century Literature," *South Atlantic Review* 52, no. 2 (1987): 3–14.

Lacan, Jacques. *The Four Fundamental Concepts of Psychoanalysis*. Translated by Alan Sheridan. New York: Norton, 1978.

Laforgue, Jules. *Mélanges posthumes, pensées et paradoxes*. Paris: Mercure de France, 1903.

Lahor, Jean [Henri Cazalis]. *La gloire du néant*. Paris: Lemerre, 1896.

Lalita Vistara: Développement des jeux—contenant l'histoire du Bouddha Çakya Mouni depuis sa naissance jusqu'à sa prédication. Edited and translated by Ph. Ed. Foucaux. Paris: E. Leroux, 1884–92.

Lamairesse, E. *Chansons populaires du sud de l'Inde*. Paris: Lacroix, 1869.

La Mennais, Abbé François de. *Essai sur l'indifférence en matière de religion*. Paris: Meguignon Fils ainé et Bointe Père, 1823.

La Motte Fouqué, Friedrich de. *Etwas über den deutschen Adel*. Hamburg: Perthes & Besser, 1819.

Lampedusa, Giuseppe Tomasi di. *Opera: Il gattopardo*. Milan: Feltrinelli, 1958.

Lanz von Liebenfels, Jörg. *Ostara* 28, 29 (1908) [*Das Gesetz des Manu und die Rassenpflege bei den alten Indo-Ariern,* special issue].

———. *Ostara* 35 (1910) [*Blond und Dunkeln,* special issue].

———. *Ostara* 1, second series (1912) [*Die Ostara und das Reich der Blonden,* special issue].

———. "Grundriss der ariosophischen Geheimlehre." *Zeitschrift für Menschenkenntnis und Menschenschicksal* 1 (1925–26): 4–11.

———. *Theozoologie oder Die Kinde von Sodoms Aefflingen und dem Götter-Elektron*. Vienna: Moderner Verlag, 1905.

Lassen, Christian. *Indische Alterthumskunde.* Leipzig: L. A. Kittler, 1847–61.

Leconte de Lisle, Charles Marie René. *Discours de réception, séance de l'Academie française du 31 Mars, 1887.* Paris: Perrin, 1887.

———. *Oeuvres.* Edited by Edgar Pich. 4 vols. Paris: Les Belles Lettres, 1978.

Lefèvre, André. *Essais de critique générale: Religions et mythologies comparées.* Paris: n.p., 1878.

Leibniz, Georg Wilhelm. *Nouveaux essais sur l'entendement humain.* Amsterdam and Leipzig: Raspe, 1765.

Lamaître, Jules. *Les contemporains.* 2d series. Paris: Boivin, 1897.

Leslie, Julia I. *The Perfect Wife.* Delhi: Oxford Universeity Press, 1989.

Lowen, Sharon, "An American Sanskrit Scholar." *Span* 31, no. 4 (1990): 16–18, 33.

Lubac, Henri de. *Le rencontre du bouddhisme et de l'occident.* Paris: Aubier, 1952.

Lütt, Jürgen. "Indische Wurzeln des Nationalsozialismus?" *Zeitschrift für Kulturaustausch* 3 (1987): 468–79.

Mahābhārata. Translated by Hippolyte Fauche. 10 vols. Paris: A. Durand & B. Duprat, 1863–70.

Mainländer, Philipp [Philipp Batz]. *Die Philosophie der Erlösung.* Berlin: T. Grieben, 1876.

Major, R. H., ed. *India in the Fifteenth Century.* New York: Burt Franklin, 1957.

Mallarmé, Stéphane. *Correspondence 1862–71.* Edited by Henri Mondor. Paris: Gallimard, 1959.

Mani, Lata. "Contentious Traditions: The Debate on Sati in Colonial India." In *Recasting Women: Essays in Colonial History,* edited by K. Sangari and S. Vaid. New Delhi: Kali for Women, 1988, 88–126.

Manu. *Hindu Gesetzbuch*. Translated by Johann Christoph Hüttner. Weimar: Industrie Compagnie, 1797.

Martino, Pierre. *L'Orient dans la littérature française aux XVIIe siècle.* Paris: Hachette, 1906.

Masson, J. L. and M. V. Patwardhan. *Aesthetic Rapture: The Rasādhyāya of the Nāṭyaśāstra*. 2 vols. Poona: Deccan College, 1970.

Mendès, Catulle. *Rapport à M. Ministre de l'Instruction publique et des beaux arts sur le mouvement poétique français de 1867–1900*. Paris: Imprimerie Nationale, 1902.

Méry, Joseph. *Héva*. Paris: Calmann-Lévy, 1860.

Michelis, Enrico de. *L'Origine degli Indo-Europei*. Turin: Biblioteca di Scienze Moderne, 1903.

Michelis, Johann David. *De l'influence des opinions sur le langage*. Bremen: G. L. Forstieri, 1762.

Michelet, Jules. *La Bible de l'humanité*. Paris: Camerot. 1864

Mistry, Freny. *Nietzsche and Buddhism*. Berlin: De Gruyter, 1981.

Moeller van den Bruck, Arthur. *Das Recht der jungen Völker.* Munich: R. Piper, 1919.

Mosse, George. *The Crisis of German Ideology: Intellectual Origins of the Third Reich*. New York: Grosset Dunlap, 1964.

———. *Masses and Men: Nationalist and Fascist Perceptions of Reality*. New York: Howard Fertig, 1980.

———. *The Nationalization of the Masses: Political Symbolism and Mass Movements in Germany from the Napoleonic Wars through the Third Reich*. New York: Howard Fertig, 1980.

———. *Nazi Culture: Intellectual, Cultural, and Social Life in the Third Reich.* New York: Howard Fertig, 1966.

———. *Toward the Final Solution: A History of European Racism.* New York: Harper & Row, 1978.

Müller, Friedrich Max. *Auld Lang Syne.* New York: Charles Scribner's Sons, 1901.

———. *Chips from a German Workshop.* 5 vols. New York: Charles Scribner's Sons, 1895.

———. *Essays.* 4 vols. Leipzig: W. Englemann, 1869–76.

———. *A History of Ancient Sanskrit Literature.* London: Williams & Norgate, 1860.

———. *India: What Can It Teach Us?* New York: Funk & Wagnalls, 1883.

———. "Lectures on the Origin and Growth of Religion as Illustrated by the Religions of India." *The Hibbert Lectures, April–June 1878.* London: Longmans, Green, 1878.

———. *Ṛg Veda Saṃhitā: The Sacred Hymns of the Brahmins.* 6 vols. London: William H. Allen, 1849–74.

———. *The Sacred Books of the East.* Vol. 1. Oxford: Clarendon Press, 1879.

———. *The Science of Language.* 2 vols. New York: Charles Scribner's Sons, 1891.

———. *Über die Resultate der Sprachwissenschaft: Vorlesungen gehalten in der kaiserlichen Universität zu Strassburg am xxiii. mai MDCCCLXXII.* Strasbourg: K. J. Trübner, 1872.

Naipaul, V. S. *India: A Million Mutinies Now.* London: Minerva, 1991.

Nandy, Ashis. *The Intimate Enemy: Loss and Recovery of Self under Colonialism.* Delhi: Oxford University Press, 1983.

Nerval, Gérard de. *Oeuvres complémentaires de Gérard de Nerval: La vie des lettres*. Edited by Jean Richard. Paris: M. J. Minard, 1959.

———. *Oeuvres complémentaires de Gérard de Nerval: La vie du théâtre*. Edited by Jean Richard. Paris: M. J. Minard, 1959.

Nietzsche, Friedrich. *Beyond Good and Evil: Prelude to a Philosophy of the Future*. Translated by Walter Kaufmann. New York: Random House, 1966.

———. *Der Fall Wagner: Schriften und Aufzeichnungen über Richard Wagner.* Edited by D. Borchmeyer. Frankfurt: Insel, 1983.

———. *Kritische Gesamtausgabe*. Edited by G. Colli and M. Montinari. Berlin: De Gruyter, 1967ff.

———. *On the Genealogy of Morals, with Ecce Homo*. Translated by Walter Kaufmann. New York: Random House, 1967.

———. *Sämtliche Werke*. Grossoktav ed, 2d ed., 19 vols. Leipzig: A. Körner, 1901–3.

———. *Twilight of the Idols and the Anti-Christ*. Translated by R. J. Hollingdale. New York: Penguin, 1969.

———. *Werke in drei Bände*. Edited by Karl Schlechta. Munich: C. Hanser, 1954–56.

———. *The Will to Power.* Translated by Walter Kaufmann and R. J. Hollingdale, and edited by Walter Kaufmann. New York: Random House, 1968.

Novalis [Friedrich Freiherr von Hardenberg]. *Schriften*. Edited by Paul Kluckhohn. 4 vols. Leipzig: Bibliographisches Institut, 1929.

Oldenberg, Hermann. *Buddha. Sein Leben, seine Lehre, seine Gemeinde*. Berlin: W. Hertz, 1881.

Olearius, Adam. *The Voyages and Travels of the Ambassadors*. Translated by John Davies. 3 vols. London: Thomas Dring & John Starkey, 1662.

Olender, Maurice. *The Languages of Paradise: Race, Religion, and Philology in the Nineteenth Century*. Translated by Arthur Goldhammer. Cambridge: Harvard University Press, 1992.

Oppenberg, Ursula. *Quellenstudien zu Friedrich Schlegels Übersetzungen aus dem Sanskrit*. Marburg: N. G. Elwerk, 1965.

Osthoff, Wolfgang, "Richard Wagners Buddha-Projekt *Die Sieger*, seine Ideen und strukturellen Spuren im *Ring und Parsifal*." *Archiv für Musikwissenschaft* 40, no. 3 (1983): 188–211.

Ozanam, Antoine Frédéric. *Oeuvres complètes*. 11 vols. Paris: J. Lecoffre, 1859.

Parry, Benita. "Problems in Current Theories of Colonial Discourse." *Oxford Literary Review* 9, 1–2 (1987): 27–58.

Pauwels, Louis, and Jacques Bergier. *The Morning of the Magicians*. Translated by R. Myers. New York: Avon, 1963.

Pires, Tomé. *The Suma Oriental*. Liechtenstein: Kraus, 1967.

Poesche, Theodor. *Die Arier: Ein Beitrag zur historischen Anthropologie*. Jena: H. Costenoble, 1878.

Poliakov, Léon. *The Aryan Myth: A History of Racist and Nationalist Ideas in Europe*. Translated by Edmund Howard. London: Heinemann, 1971.

———. *Harvest of Hate: The Nazi Program for the Destruction of the Jews of Europe*. Foreword by Reinhold Niebuhr. New York: Holocaust Library, 1979.

———. *The History of Anti-Semitism*. Translated by Miriam Kochan. New York: Vanguard, 1968.

———. *Le mythe aryen: Essai sur les sources du racisme et des nationalismes*. Paris: Calmann-Lévy, 1971.

Poliakov, Leon, and Josef Wulf. *Das Dritte Reich und seine Diener: Dokumente*. 2d ed. Berlin: Grunewald Verlag, 1956.

Pott, A. F. "Indogermanisches Sprachstudium." In *Allgemeine Encyclopädie der Wissenschaften und Künste,* edited by Johann Samuel Ersch and Johann Gottfried Gruber, 84 vols. Leipzig: J. F. Gleditsch, 1840.

Preisedanz, Karl. *Die Liebe der Günderrode.* Munich: K. Piper, 1912.

Putter, Irving. *The Pessimism of Leconte de Lisle.* Berkeley: University of California Press, 1954.

Quinet, Edgar. *Oeuvres complètes.* 11 vols. Paris: Pagnerre, 1857.

Ravenscroft, T. *The Spear of Destiny.* New York: Bantam, 1973.

Remak, Henry H. H. "Exoticism in Romanticism." *Comparative Literature Studies* 15, no. 1 (1978): 53–65.

Renan, Joseph Ernest. *Dialogues et fragments philosophiques.* Paris: Calmann-Lévy, 1876.

———. *Nouvelles études d'histoire religieuse.* Paris: Calmann-Lévy, 1874.

Renouvier, Charles. *Science de la morale.* Paris: Ladrange, 1869.

Richer, Jean. *Études et recherches sur Théophile Gautier, prosateur.* Paris: A. G. Nizet, 1981.

Ricoeur, Paul. *Le conflit des interprétations: Essais herméneutiques.* Paris: Seuil, 1969.

———. *Du texte à l'action: Essais d'herméneutique.* Vol. 2. Paris: Seuil, 1986.

Riencourt, Amaury de. *The Soul of India.* London: Jonathan Cape, 1961.

Rogerius, Abraham. *Offne Thür zu dem verborgenen Heydenthum.* Nuremberg: J. Schipper, 1663.

———. *Le théâtre de l'idolatrie ou la porte ouverte.* Translated by Thomas La Grue. Amsterdam: J. Schipper, 1670.

Rogers, T. *Buddhaghoṣa's Parables*. London: Trübner, 1870.

Rosenberg, Alfred. *Blut und Ehre: Ein Kampf für deutsche Wiedergeburt*. Munich: Franz Eher, 1939.

———. *Der Mythus des 20 Jahrhunderts*. Munich: Hoheneichen, 1943.

Sacy, Silvestre de. "Discours sur l'utilité de l'étude de la langue arabe." *Journal asiatique* 8 (June 1826): 321–40.

Said, Edward W. "Kim, the Pleasures of Imperialism." *Raritan* 7, no. 2 (1987): 27–64.

———. *Orientalism*. New York: Pantheon, 1978.

———. *The World, the Text, and the Critic*. Cambridge: Harvard University Press, 1983.

Sassetti, Filippo. *Lettere edite e inedite*. Edited by Ettore Marcucci. Florence: F. le Monnier, 1855.

Schelling, F. W. von. *Sämtliche Werke*. Edited by K. F. A. Schelling. 6 vols. Stuttgart and Augsburg: J. G. Cotta, 1856–61.

Schlegel, Friedrich. *Friedrich Schlegels Briefe an dem Bruder August Wilhelm*. Edited by O. Walzel. Berlin: Speyer & Peters, 1890.

———. *Kritische-Friedrich-Schlegel-Ausgabe*. Edited by Ernst Behler. 24 vols. Munich: Ferdinand Schöningh, 1966.

———. *Philosophische Vorlesungen aus den Jahren 1804–1806*. 2 vols. Bonn: Edward Weber, 1836–37.

———. *Sämtliche Werke*. 15 vols. Vienna: I. Klang, 1846.

———. *Seine prosaischen Jugendschriften, 1792–1802*. Edited by Jakob Minor. 2d ed., 2 vols. Vienna: C. Konegan, 1906.

———. *Über die Sprache und Weisheit der Indier*. Edited by S. Timpanaro. Amsterdam Studies in the Theory and History of Linguistic Science. Amsterdam: Benjamins, 1977.

Schmitt, Anke. *Der Exotismus in der deutschen Oper zwischen Mozart und Spohr.* Hamburg: Karl Dieter Wagner, 1988.

Schopenhauer, Arthur. *Fragments sur l'histoire de la philosophie.* Paris: Alcan, 1912.

———. *Gesammelte Briefe.* Edited by Arthur Hübscher. Bonn: Bouvier Verlag Herbert Grundmann, 1978.

———. *Gespräche und Selbstgespräche.* Edited by E. Grisebach. Berlin: E. Hofmann, 1902.

———. *Handschriftlicher Nachlass.* Edited by E. Grisebach. 4 vols. Leipzig: Reclam, n.d.

———. *Parerga und Paralipomena: Kleine philosophische Schriften.* 2 vols. Leipzig: F. A. Brockhaus, 1877.

———. *The World as Will and Representation.* Translated by E. F. Payne. 2 vols. New York: Dover, 1969.

Schwab, Raymond. *The Oriental Renaissance: Europe's Rediscovery of India and the East, 1680–1880.* Translated by Gene Patterson-Black and Victor Reinking. Foreword by Edward W. Said. New York: Columbia University Press, 1984.

Sebottendorff, Rudolf. *Bevor Hitler kam: Urkundliches aus der Frühzeit der Nationalsozialisten Bewegung.* Munich: Grassinger, 1934.

Sieferle, Rolf Peter. "Indien und die Arier in der Rassentheorie." *Zeitschrift für Kulturaustausch* 37, no. 3 (1987): 444–67.

Siegert, Hans. "Zur Geschichte der Begriffe *Arier* und *arische.*" *Wörter und Sachen: Zeitschrift für Indogermanische Sprachwissenschaft, Volksforschung und Kulturgeschichte* 22, no. 4 (1941–42): 73–99.

Silverman, Kaja. *Male Subjectivity at the Margins.* New York: Routledge, 1992.

Sonnerat, Pierre. *Reise nach Ostindien und China.* Frankfurt: A. G.: Schneider, 1784.

———. *Voyage aux Indes orientales et la Chine,* 2 vols. Paris: n.p., 1782.

Sosnoski, James J. *Token Professionals and Master Critics: A Critique of Orthodoxy in Literary Studies.* Albany: State University of New York Press, 1994.

Spengler, Oswald. *Neubau des deutschen Reiches.* Munich: C. H. Bec, 1924.

Spivak, Gayatri Chakravorty. *In Other Worlds: Essays in Cultural Politics.* New York: Routledge, 1987.

———. "The Rani of Sirmur." In *Europe and Its Others,* vol. 1, *Proceedings of the Essex Conference on the Sociology of Literature, July 1984,* edited by Francis Barker et al. Colchester: University of Essex, 1985.

———. "Three Women's Texts and a Critique of Imperialism." *Critical Inquiry* 12, no. 1 (Autumn 1985): 243–61.

Spoelberch de Lovenjoul, Victor Maximilien Albert Vicomte de. *Histoire des oeuvres de Théophile Gautier.* 2 vols. Paris: Charpentier, 1887.

Stambaugh, Joan. *Nietzsche's Thought of the Eternal Return.* Baltimore: Johns Hopkins University Press, 1972.

Stcherbatsky, T. *The Conception of Buddhist Nirvāṇa.* The Hague: Mouton, 1965.

Stern, Fritz. *The Politics of Cultural Despair: A Study in the Rise of Germanic Ideology.* Berkeley: University of California Press, 1981.

Stern, J. P. "Germans and the German Past." *London Review of Books,* 21 December 1989, 7–9.

Strasser, Otto. *Aufbau des deutschen Sozialismus.* Prague: Heinrich Grunov, 1936.

———. "Hitler, Gandhi und das junge Deutschland." *Die Kommenden,* 8 August 1930.

Strenski, Ivan. *Four Theories of Myth in the Twentieth Century*. Iowa City: University of Iowa Press, 1987.

Sully-Prudhomme, René-François-Armand. *Journal intime*. Paris: Lemerre, 1922.

Summer, Vera A. *L'orientalisme d'Alfred de Vigny*. Paris: Honoré Champion, 1930.

Suneson, Carl. *Richard Wagner und die indische Geisteswelt*. Leiden: E. J. Brill, 1989.

Taine, Hippolyte Adolphe. *Nouveaux essais de critique et d'histoire*. Paris: Hachette, 1884.

Thielicke, Helmut. *Nihilism*. New York: Harper & Brothers, 1961.

Tull, Herman W. "F. Max Müller and A. B. Keith: Twaddle, the Stupid Myth, and the Disease of Indology." *Numen: International Review for the History of Religions* 38, no. 1 (June 1991): 27–58.

Vacher de Lapouge, Georges. *L'aryen, son rôle social*. Paris: A. Fontemoing, 1899.

de la Vallée-Poussin, L. *The Way To Nirvana*. Cambridge: Cambridge University Press, 1917.

Vālmīki. *Rāmāyaṇa*. Translated by Hippolyte Fauche. 9 vols. Paris: A. Frank, 1854.

Van Tieghem, Paul. *Le romantisme dans la littérature européenne*. Paris: Michel, 1969.

Varthema, Ludovico di. *The Travels of Ludovico di Varthema*. Translated by J. W. Jones. New York: Burt Franklin, 1963.

Vianey, Jean. *Les sources de Leconte de Lisle*. Montpellier: Coulet et Fils, 1907.

———. *Journal*. Edited by F. Baldensperger. London: Scholartis, 1928.

———. *Oeuvres posthumes*. Edited by Fernand Gregh. Paris: Delagrave, 1913.

The Viṣṇu Purāṇa. Translated by H. H. Wilson. London: John Murray, 1840.

Viswanathan, Gauri. *Masks of Conquest: Literary Study and British Rule in India*. New York: Columbia University Press, 1989.

Viyagappa, Ignatius. *G. W. F. Hegel's Concept of Indian Philosophy*. Rome: Università Gregoriana, 1980.

Wagner, Cosima. *Die Tagebücher, 1878–1883*. 2 vols. Edited by M. Gregor-Dellin and D. Mack. Munich and Zurich: Piper, 1977.

Wagner, Richard. *Briefe: Richard Wagners an Otto Wesendonck*. Edited by Albert Heintz. Charlottenburg: Verlag der Allgemeinen Musik-Zeitung O. Lessmann, 1898.

———. *Briefe: Die Sammlung*. Edited by Burrel, and with commentary by J. N. Burk. Frankfurt: S. Fischer, 1953.

———. *The Diary of Richard Wagner, 1854–1882; The Brown Book,* Annotated by Joachim Bergfeld, and translated by Georg Bird. Cambridge: Cambridge University Press, 1980.

———. *Dichtungen und Schriften: Jubiläumsausgabe in zehn Bänden*. Edited by Dieter Borchmeyer. Frankfurt: Insel, 1983.

———. *Gesammelte Schriften*. Edited by Julius Kapp. 14 vols. Leipzig: Hesse & Becker, 1914.

———. *Gesammelte Schriften und Dichtungen,* Edited by W. Golther. 10 vols. Berlin, Vienna, and Stuttgart: Deutsches Verlags Bong, 1913.

———. *Mein Leben*. Edited by M. Gregor-Dellin. 2 vols. Munich: List, 1967.

———. *An Mathilide und Otto von Wesendonk: Tagebuchblätter und Briefe*. Edited by J. Kapp. Leipzig: Hess & Becker, 1915.

———. *Richard Wagner an Mathilde Wesendonk: Tagebuchblätter und Briefe 1853–1871*. Edited W. Golther. Leipzig: Breitkopf & Härtel, 1914.

———. *Sämtliche Schriften und Dichtungen*. Edited by H. von Wolzogen and R. Sternfeld. Leipzig: Breitkopf & Härtel, 1914.

———. *Wagner on Music and Drama*. Edited by Albert Goldman and Evert Sprinchorn. New York: E. P. Dutton, 1964.

Wagner, Richard, and Franz Liszt. *Briefwechsel zwischen Wagner und Liszt*. 2 vols. Leipzig: Breitkopf & Härtel, 1887.

Weinberger-Thomas, Catherine. *L'Inde et l'imaginaire*. Paris: Editions de l'École des Hautes Études en Sciences Sociales, 1989.

Weinsheimer, Joel C. *Gadamer's Hermeneutics: A Reading of Truth and Method*. New Haven: Yale University Press, 1985.

Weisstein, Ulrich. "The Little Word *und:* Tristan und Isolde as Verbal Construct." In *Wagner in Retrospect: A Centenial Reappraisal,* edited by Leroy R. Shaw, Nancy R. Cirillo, and Marion S. Miller. Amsterdam: Rodopi, 1987.

Welbon, Guy Richard. *The Buddhist Nirvāṇa and Its Western Intepreters*. Chicago: University of Chicago Press, 1968.

White, Hayden. *Tropics of Discourse*. Baltimore: Johns Hopkins University Press, 1978.

Whitney, W. D. *Oriental and Linguistic Studies*. 2 vols. Delhi: Sri Satguru, 1987.

Wilhelm, Richard, *Die Günderrode, Dichtung und Schicksal*. 2 vols. Frankfurt: Societäts Verlag, 1938.

Willson, A. Leslie. *A Mythical Image: The Ideal of Indian German Romanticism*. Durham: Duke University Press, 1964.

Wilson, H. H. *Chefs d'oeuvres du théâtre indien*. Translated by Simon Alexandre Langlois. 2 vols. Paris: Dondey-Dupré, 1828.

Windisch, Ernst. *Geschichte der Sanskrit-Philologie und indischen Alterthumskunde*. 2 vols. Strasbourg: K. J. Trübner, 1917–20.

INDEX